VICTOR OF CIRCUMSTANCES

VICTOR OF CIRCUMSTANCES

Highlight the day-to-day struggle that the underprivileged undergo to find love and security.

CALVIN RILEY

AuthorHouse™ LLC
1663 Liberty Drive
Bloomington, IN 47403
www.authorhouse.com
Phone: 1-800-839-8640

Published by AuthorHouse 08/09/2013

ISBN: 978-1-4567-9045-5 (sc)
ISBN: 978-1-4567-9046-2 (e)

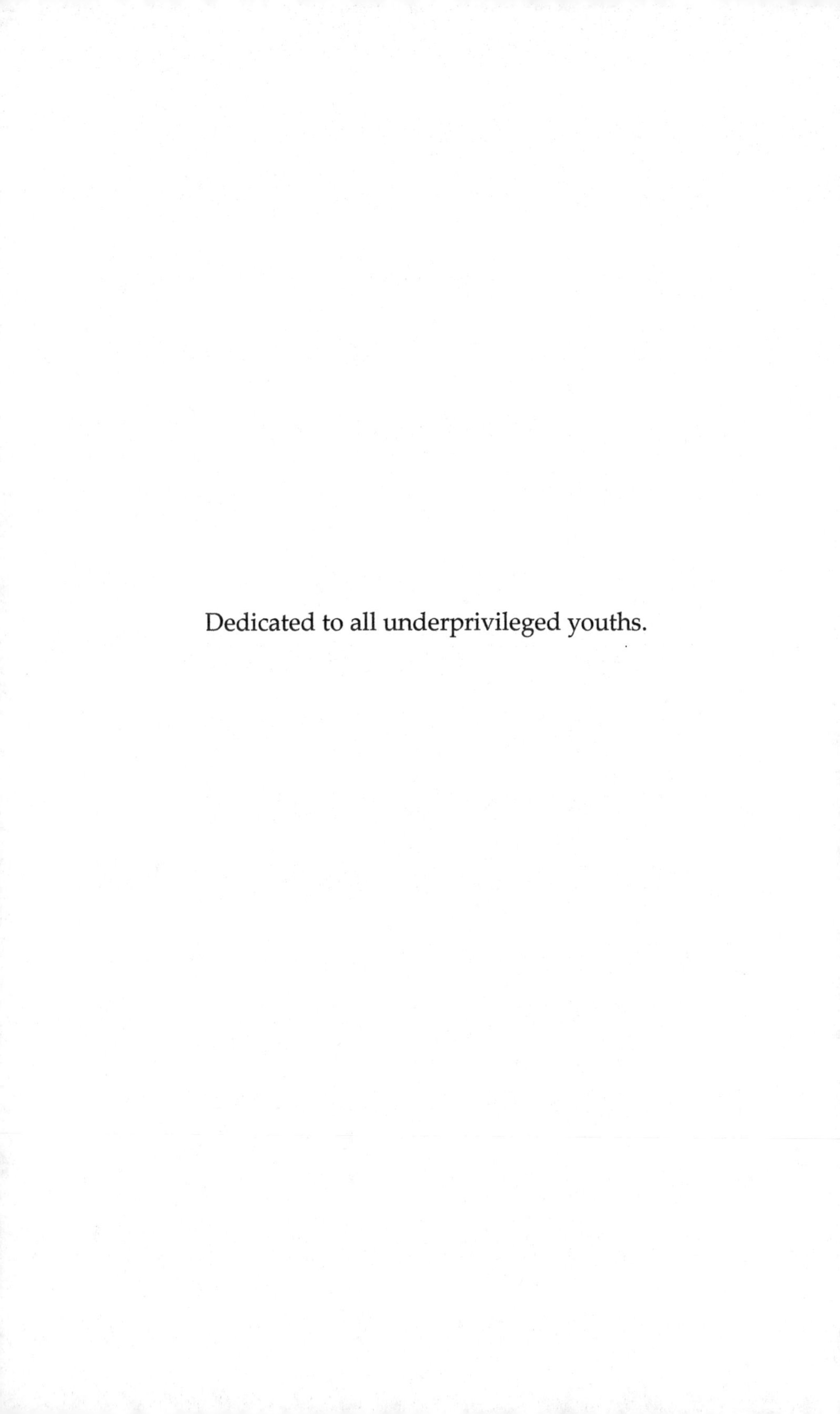

Dedicated to all underprivileged youths.

CONTENTS

ACKNOWLEDGEMENTS

Many thanks to the following people for their encouragement and support from the day I decided to put my life's story on paper and continuing throughout the process of writing this book.

Claudette Harris, the manual typewriter that you bought me was one of my best gifts. Thank you also for your undiluted love and support throughout the years. Stephen Harris (aka Wonder), thank you for giving me the opportunity to explore another world, and thank you also for being a good friend.

Sue Hayton, I could never forget you. I remember when you used to put your job on the line in order to help me just a little bit more. Thank you for having the patience to teach me how to put words into the right context and also for your belief in me.

Cyrlene Braithwaite (Passionate), I never stop! Thank you for showing me the way to true love and for holding me up when my world was turned upside down. I couldn't have cleared that final hurdle so comfortably if you hadn't been there as my rock.

Catherine Mooney, I was likened to a wild, fruitless tree when I met you, but your encouragement and direction changed everything.

Nicki, you came into my life and changed it. Thank you for believing in my dreams and aspirations and for giving me the chance to pursue them.

Thank you, Jim and Brett Knight, for opening the door of opportunity when I was in the process of transition.

Dr Cedric Rodrigues, my respect for you is huge. You are an inspiration, and I'm proud to identify you as my role model. Penelope Rodrigues (Penny), I always relished the conversations that we had. Your profound knowledge is like food to my brain. A very good woman you are. Melanie Rodrigues, although you weren't conscious of it, nonetheless, you've given me so much motivation, and your encouragement and tips were always appreciated. Last but not least, Chris Smith, without your technical help I couldn't have moved forward.

This is a message to Zweli, my son, and my daughter, Amia. I wouldn't want you to experience life the way I have.

Blessed is the man/woman
Who walks not in the counsel of the ungodly,
Nor stands in the path of sinners,
Nor sits in the seat of the scornful;
But his/her delight is in the law of God
And in their God they meditate day and night.
They shall be like a tree
Planted by the rivers of water
That brings forth its fruits in its season,
Whose leaf also shall not wither
And whatever they do shall prosper.
—Psalm 1:1–3, paraphrased after NKJV

PROLOGUE

It was 10:00 a.m. on Monday, the sixth of May, 1968, in a little district called Anchovy, eight miles outside of the renowned city of Montego Bay (Mobay) in Jamaica. Ruby Riley had just given birth, and the pain that she was experiencing was excruciating, but as the nurse handed her the child, wrapped in a white cotton blanket, the agonising pain suddenly started to fade away.

Affectionately Ruby admired her little brown-skinned son, smiled, and then silently took an oath that under no circumstances would she get pregnant again.

"It's an eight-pound, two-ounce bouncing boy baby," the nurse proudly told her. "Have you got a name for him already?"

"His name is Calvin Riley," Ruby replied happily, smiling from ear to ear, as she continued to look at her son with pride and joy.

"Eight children should be enough now, Ruby, what do you have to say about that? The nurse asked, with both urgency and sympathy in her tone.

"This is the last one, nurse," Ruby replied boldly, in her strong native accent (patois).

The nurse mumbled a few words to herself, while she completed her task. After a while shook her head sadly and sighed. Then she picked up her bag, said good luck to Ruby, and walked away. She was fully expecting Ruby to call her out again, within the next year or two, to receive another child, because each time she gave birth, she always said, "Nurse, it's the last one."

As soon as the nurse made her exit, Ruby began to curse Percy Riley in her native language. "That man is nothing but a waste of space," she began, and as she continued to curse Percy in his absence, her mixed grief and pain was evident in the raw resonance of the patois slang.

"Wonder if him coming home today, dear God?" she eventually grumbled to herself, while she lay on her back in bed, staring at a damp patch on the ceiling of the small bedroom.

After all was said and done, it was Monday, and Percy Riley hadn't come home since he left the yard on Saturday afternoon. "Me soon come" were the last spoken words Ruby had heard from him.

"Your father is nothing but a no-good man," Ruby whispered to her baby, who yawned in response. "Him have a heart of stone," she continued in patois. "Him know the condition that I was in, yet him leave me all on my own with the rest of children, and all now he hasn't returned," she concluded.

Ruby was fed up with Percy's worthless, inconsiderate ways, but there was nothing she could do about it at this point in her sad life, because she was tired of running from one man to the other. Suddenly she felt lonely, sad, and hopeless, as tears began to flow from her tired eyes and roll into her ears. Like a leaf on a branch, her weary body quivered as she choked back the tears and gently stroked her baby's head.

Meanwhile, a mile or so away, Percy was busy shouting for number seven, as the two bone dice rolled onto the ground behind the furniture shop.

I should've gone home when Ruby sent me the message earlier, he thought to himself. *At least I would still have 'half of my money in my pocket now.* His thoughts were cut short as the two bone dice came to a sudden halt, but they hadn't stopped on number seven.

Disappointed, Percy got up off his knees, shook his head from side to side despondently, and then walked away silently from the group of men and the stale cloud of alcohol and tobacco breath.

A few of the men from the group laughed spitefully as he turned the corner of the building, but it was nothing new; they did it every time they won his money.

As he walked along the dusty road towards his home, with his shoulders slouched and head drooping, he took an oath that he would never gamble again, but the words were like an old, broken record, because he repeated them each time they won his money.

Back at the house, Marika and Devon, two of Ruby's and Percy's younger children, were playing in the yard, while Ruby was in bed thinking about her first love and her shattered dreams.

She'd been only thirteen years old when she got pregnant for the first time. She'd looked and acted quite mature from the tender age of twelve. On the whole, she wasn't looking for love at that stage in her life, but Mr James came along and captured her young heart. She couldn't resist him, even if she'd tried, because he looked so much like the type of man that she'd spent her young life dreaming about.

Mr James was dark and handsome and, most of all, well dressed. He was a little on the short side, but his height was compensated by the amount of money in his pocket. Although Ruby was much younger than he was, it didn't matter; he swept her off her feet by promising her the world.

She for her part believed every word he said, because she thought he was the man of her dreams, who was going to put her on a pedestal – but once she got pregnant, everything changed. For instance, Mr James became obsessed with controlling her, and didn't want her to go anywhere without him. But who could blame him? After all, Ruby turned heads everywhere she went, unlike most girls her age, and even the older women in the community grew jealous of all the attention that she was getting from everybody, especially their husbands.

On the whole, Ruby hadn't had much education, but she was blessed with five feet, of plump ripeness' for her tender age. Above all, she had a mixed race complexion, which usually drove men on the island nuts. Mr James thought he was a winner when he met her, but eventually Dick, Tom, and Harry began to compete with him for Ruby's heart.

After she'd given birth to a son that she named Salomon, the relationship began to fall apart, until eventually Ruby, only fourteen years old, walked out, leaving her son behind with Mr James.

There were lots of men waiting for the chance to be with Ruby. She on the other hand loved the attention, and so she decided to play the field with Dick, Tom and Harry. Almost before anybody could say, "Who is that?" she was moving in with Mr Beckford, who'd also promised her the world. Consequently, less than a year later she got pregnant again, and nine months later she was giving birth to a daughter that she named Janet. Again, though, things began to get from bad to worse in the relationship, and Ruby decided to do a runner.

Covertly, Ruby started to plan her next move. She waited and waited until one day, while Mr Beckford was at work, she packed her things and left, leaving Janet asleep in her father's bed, never to return to the house.

Before long she met Mr Bent and later moved into his parent's home, where he was living. Not long after that she was pregnant again with her third child, but before the child was born, the relationship was on the verge of breaking up. Months after the birth of Van, her second son, and the relationship reached the breaking point, and Ruby walked out, leaving Van behind with Mr Bent and his family, but Mr Watson was waiting patiently to take her in.

While she was living with Mr Watson, her relationship with Mr Bent rekindled. During that time, she had never stopped playing the field with Dick, Tom, and Harry either. However, she got pregnant again and later gave birth to a beautiful daughter, whom she named Barbara Watson (Babs).

Like the other men before, Mr Watson didn't have what it took to control Ruby. Once again, she was on the move in search of Mr Right.

As always, another man was waiting patiently around the corner for his chance of a lifetime with Ruby. The lucky man this time was Percy Riley.

What she felt for Percy was completely different from what she'd felt for the other men. It was sheer love at first sight. She was captivated by the way he dressed and his kind and humorous attitude. He didn't have a lot of money, but he was tall, dark, slim, and cute, and that was a big bonus.

The night they met, Percy was buying drinks for everybody in the rum bar, and he treated her like a lady – unlike other men, who were only waiting for the chance to take off her clothes. She was shocked when Percy told her that his surname was also Riley, but she thought it was cool, because people would think they were really married.

Not long after they met, Ruby got pregnant again. She named Percy as the father, and together they moved into an old rented board house.

After the birth of Ruby's fifth child and Percy's first, a daughter they named Marika, she eventually ended the undercover relationship with Mr Bent and the other men. One year later, Ruby broke her own record by allowing Percy to get her pregnant for the second time. This time, it was another son, and they named him Devon. Two years later they were naming another son Freddy.

Two miserable years later, Ruby was on her own in bed, beside Percy's fourth child, and he wasn't there to see the birth of his baby, because he'd rather to be at the gambling house instead.

Suddenly Calvin started to cry, and it brought her back to reality.

Ruby turned on her side, guided one of her nipples into Calvin's mouth, and looked on her son tenderly as he struggled to suck the milk. "If my seventh child hadn't died, you wouldn't be here today," she whispered softly to Calvin, "but you are going to be a star when you grow up; you just wait and see." She stroked her baby's cheek with one finger as he struggled to keep the nipple between his lips.

A few months later, Percy, Ruby, Marika, Devon, and Calvin moved two miles away to live in Carey Village, an adjoining district, where Percy started to build a board house on a half-acre of family land.

Although the village was dull and bleak, the land was rich with many kinds of fruit.

The house had the foundation laid out for two bedrooms, one bathroom, living room, dining room, and veranda, but only one bedroom was completed, which the five of them had to share.

It was meant to be a new start, but Percy and Ruby didn't have any immediate plans for the future.

CHAPTER ONE

The Foundation

Life is a laborious journey that everybody has to travel, and destiny is a mystery.

Some families stick together and strive to achieve their goals. Many other people struggle single-handedly to make a place of their own in society. Then there are the disgruntled and dispirited, who get isolated in destitution, and pushed against a wall with no prospect of escaping hopeless poverty. At length the underprivileged youths get restless and decide to hit the streets in search of a better way of living, and some will stop at nothing to achieve their goals.

Calvin Riley was one of those underprivileged youths, who eventually became ill-fated and disorderly on the rugged streets of Jamaica, where most youths either spend their lives in detention or find an early, permanent residence six feet under the ground.

As he reminisced about his journey through life, Calvin vividly told the story of how his colourless, disenchanted and aimless life had been from his third birthday.

*

"It was a bright and sunny Sunday morning, on the sixth of May, 1971," he began. "The dew was glistening on the green leaves of the logwood trees that stretched across the hillside above our house, and clumps of fog were still lingering beneath the ridges of the faraway mountains, but even then the sky was blue, a fresh, cool breeze was also blowing, and birds were singing in the trees."

As he spoke, the expression in his eyes changed with the magnitude of each passion that his memories conjured up. He went on, "I can still distinctly smell the burning firewood, the aroma from the steamed calalloo" – a vegetable similar to spinach – "the roast breadfruit, the boiled green bananas, and pig's liver that the other neighbours were cooking. Unfortunately, everybody that was present seemed to be happy except Mama and me."

Mass Percy, as most people, including his children used to call him, wasn't present that morning, because he was still at the gambling house where he had been since Friday, after work. Calvin didn't know the reason for his dad's absence until he grew older and witnessed the recurrence of his father's thoughtless behaviour – which he himself later carried on.

Ruby was in a bad mood, because she didn't have any money to buy food for her children's Sunday dinner. (In Jamaica, Sunday dinner is considered very special.) Calvin also was sad, because he hadn't got anything for his birthday, even though Mass Percy had promised to bring something home for him, but he was still at work (as Calvin had been told).

Also present was a Rastafarian man who went by the name of John. He was there to pull down the old board house of Calvin's great grandmother, Miss Fan.

John was the first Rasta man Calvin had ever known. He died many years ago. (Rest in peace, John.)

John was tall, with a dark complexion and slim build, with long dreadlocks cascading down his back. He was also respectable, a man of moral values and profound principle. He and Mass Percy were good friends. They were old-school rude boys, but other than that, everybody loved and respected them.

Whenever John saw Calvin, he always gave him a sweet or a fruit. On the whole, he treated him like his own son. Nonetheless, on this bright Sunday morning he was provoking Calvin, which was a habit for everybody, and when they did that, he would always cry and curse. The latter usually gave him problems, because he would stammer, but this morning he gave everybody a surprise, including himself.

In the first place, Calvin was annoyed at John's tickling him and aping his stutter while tickling him, besides being irked that he had not got any birthday present. As a result, he reacted defiantly and shouted a Jamaican swear word: "Wah de bumboclaat yuh nuh lef' mi alone?" (Why don't you leave me alone?)

His sudden, despicable outburst was his first mistake and it won for him the prize of a harsh beating from Ruby, despite it being one of the few times he'd managed to speak without stammering.

Apart from the licks he got from his mama, he also got some nice dinner from his neighbour, Cherry Campbell.

Cherry was everybody's darling in the community. She had the most beautiful voice in the choir of the Mount Carey Baptist Church, where she was a member. She was close to twenty years old, of light brown complexion and less than five feet tall.

She loved Calvin genuinely from the day that she met him as a baby, and later she was to become one of his elementary schoolteachers, whose disciplinary duty extended beyond the school compound.

The dinner Calvin got from Cherry that day consisted of rice and peas, cooked with dry coconut milk; a fried chicken leg with some lovely gravy; a cup of carrot juice laced with vanilla essence and nutmeg and sweetened with condensed milk, and for dessert a bowl of ice cream. As for Mass Percy, he didn't return home until the following day.

**

Carey Village was one of many small, scarcely populated, post-slavery districts, westward from the small town of Mount Carey, and although most of the land was shaped into steep hills and deep gullies, it was fertile and laden with a variety of fruits.

The quality of life was low for most of the settlers in the district, but it didn't bother them, because they were accustomed to it. On the whole, most people with children worked hard to provide them with the best education, which they hoped would elevate them out of poverty. They couldn't afford to buy lots of clothes, toys, and gifts or even throw parties for the kids on their birthdays. As for Calvin, the only toy he ever got was a water gun that Mass Percy gave him for Christmas, when he was six or seven years old. As for clothes, the only time he would get a new suit was at Christmas, or sometimes for Independence Day (sixth of August each year).

Mount Carey was the local town for Carey Village and neighbouring districts, such as York Bush, Eden, Flower Hill, Margony, and Mount Pelier, but Anchovy was the central town for all the districts, including Mount Carey, Ruhamton, Lethe, Catherine Mount, and Comfort Hall.

The local police station, library, post office, railway station, barkey, large grocery shops, social clubs, secondary and primary schools were located at Anchovy.

Percy Riley's house was situated just over a mile from Mount Carey and two and a half miles from Anchovy. It was also one of the houses closest to the jungle.

The house faced eastward, catching the first rays of the sun, as it ascended over the green trees every morning.

There was a rough footpath, used by the neighbours and farmers, lay about three yards from the front of the house. Some thirty yards beyond it lived Mr Bee (Berres Riley), one of Percy's older relatives, in a two-bedroom concrete house with his girlfriend, Miss Cassie.

About forty yards to the right of Percy's house lay the remains of Calvin's great grandmother's old house and her partly broken-down outside lavatory, which Percy and his family usually used.

Forty yards or so below the remains of Miss Fan's house lived Cherry Campbell, her two younger sisters, Audrey and Maxine, her grandmother Aunty Beck and her grandfather Mass Arthur, in a two-bedroom post-slavery board house. About fifty yards farther below lived Pappa Seta and his dad, in another two-bedroom board house

Seventy yards farther right, on top of a slope, lived another of Percy's cousins, who went by the name of Man-man. He was living on his own in one of the post-slavery board houses. Man-man was considered partly insane, and frequently a lot of people, including Calvin and his siblings, teased him by calling him 'Bull in a mi coco', which would make him curse and chase his provoker with a machete and stones.

Thirty yards to the right of Man-man's house, on top of the same slope, lived Mr Shaw (Barber) and his family, in a three-bedroom concrete house, and eighty yards to the left, down another slope and upon a hill lived Sitta and Bauloo, with their grandchildren, Precious, Dimples, Paul Rose, and Carl Scott, in a two-bedroom board house.

Mother Mira, the local bush doctor, occupied the near two acres of semi-level prime land, some five yards above Sitta's and Bauloo's house. She had a church in her yard, and she was living in the biggest concrete house in the whole community. She also had four other small houses on her property, where some of her children and workers were living.

Forty yards behind Sitta's and Bauloo's house, and a few yards from Mother Mira, lived Money Man (another of Percy's relatives) and his family, and about thirty-five yards farther west from him lived his wife's mother, Miss Ivy, with her husband, Bad Son.

Money Man and his wife, Miss Jeneita, had twelve children, of which the last two were twins. The eldest daughter and son moved away, leaving the remaining ten children to share the two-bedroom board house with their mother and father.

Continuing seventy yards to the right from Mr Shaw's house, down another slope, lived Mass Johnny (another of Percy's relatives) in a four-bedroom concrete house with his family. Eighty yards below Mass Johnny lived Miss Dinie, with her husband and grandchildren, in a two-bedroom semi-concrete house.

The footpath led from Percy's house to Mr Shaw's house, where it turned into an unpaved single-lane road. This road ran past Mass Johnny's and continued towards Miss Dinie's house. There it joined with the main road of the village, which was bad in most places and worse in others.

Going right from Miss Dinie's house, where most of the villagers lived, the district's main road, which was mainly unpaved, went through a high embankment and then down and over a number of rough, steep, hills for about a mile before turning into a steep, rocky footpath that led to the districts of Eden and York Bush.

Miss Maude, another of Percy's relatives, was living in a two-bedroom board house with a veranda at the front, on the opposite side of the embankment where Miss Dinie lived.

Going left from Miss Dinie's gate, after thirty yards the road went up twenty yards of rough unpaved hill. On top of the hill, a single-lane road veered to the left, into Mother Mira's yard. She was one of the first people to own a motorcar in the village and one of few homes that had access for cars to drive into the yard.

From Mother Mira's gate, a level unpaved road continued for a few hundred yards, before rising to the top of a steep hill, which is called Pan Bottom Hill.

From the level road, you could also see people walking on the road in York Bush, which was in a valley, and at Margony, which was farther out on top of another hillside.

There were two turning points on the left-hand side, along the rough, unpaved road. The one that was closest to Mother Mira was Miss Ivy and Money Man's gate, and the other track was used by everybody who was living on that side of the village.

Half way down the five hundred yards of Pan Bottom Hill, the road ran between two high embankments. The one on the right was overgrown with shrubs, and Mr Smith and Miss Heffy, an elderly white couple, were living on the left-hand side in a two-bedroom board house. They also owned nearly two acres of prime land. Miss Heffy regularly visited her relatives in America, but Mr Smith never left the island.

**

There was no fence around Percy's house, therefore the neighbours and the farmers who used the footpath could see all that went on in and around his house.

No water or electricity was attached to most of the houses, and people like Mother Mira, who had a gas stove, would have to buy gas by the cylinder.

Percy's house was no exception: they didn't have the luxuries of water and electric utilities; nor did they have a gas stove.

When it didn't rain for a while, like the rest of residents, Percy and his family would make trips back and forth, up and down steep, rough terrain, to fetch water from the public standpipe, or at a nearby spring.

To reduce the number of trips to the standpipe or the spring, many of the women from the village did their laundry at the standpipe or the spring.

At night, when the moon was shining elsewhere, those who couldn't afford a torch (flashlight) would make one with a glass bottle and kerosene oil to see in the dark. There was also a special type of flying insects (peenie wallie) that came out at night, with bright, blue, gleaming eyes. Frequently Calvin and his siblings would catch the insects, put them in a glass bottle or jar, and place it in one corner of the room to illuminate the darkness.

In one corner of the house (bedroom) there was a brown Singer sewing machine, which Ruby used to make clothes on. Stood in another corner, was a brown wooden and glass cabinet. On top of it sat the only glass kerosene lamp, and all around the lampshade the words "Home Sweet Home" were inscribed. At nights, Calvin would lie awake in bed squinting his eyes at the flame of the lamp, to create sparks, until he fell asleep. As he got older he would read the inscribed words on the lampshade and count the letters over and over.

In the cabinet Ruby stored food, the few chalk plates, glasses, and cups and saucers that they had.

There was also a white centre table in the middle of the room with an old China vase perched on top, with water and some wild creeper flowers. Calvin would often count every single leaf of the creeper.

The best furniture in the room was Ruby's and Mass Percy's bed, dressing table, and chest of drawers.

Calvin used to sleep in the same bed with Mass Percy and Ruby, while Marika and Devon shared an old, double-panel bed, and whenever the other siblings visited, they would sleep on the old panel bed too.

As the years went by, the mattress on the old panel bed started to degenerate, because of the amount of urine that was shed on it, mainly by Marika and Calvin (after he was later transferred to that bed). However, the mattress never got replaced whilst the urinating continued; thus as time went by, the tired, worn-out springs began to fall apart. The children's only escape from the disturbance of the broken springs was to cushion the mattress with whatever old clothes they could find. Gradually, the old panel bed got invaded by a posse of bugs, which they used to called chink. The scent that came from the chinks when they killed them was sickening, to put it mildly.

Marika and Devon often cut leaves from a cedar tree and placed them in the bed. At those times the vicious bites from the bugs would be minimal, but sleep would be impossible, because of the strong smell of the cedar leaves.

It was a luxury back then for the poorer class to own kerosene stoves. Percy and his family were fortunate, being able to cook on a two-burner kerosene stove, but during dry season, they would make a wood fire to cook on, which saved them from buying oil.

Whenever any cooking was in process, Calvin was always present, because he enjoyed inhaling the scent of the kerosene and watching the blue flames underneath the pot. It was even better when they were cooking dumplings, because whoever was cooking would always give him a piece of the dumpling dough, which he used to make his own little dumpling, place it on a stick, and then set it at the edge of the fire until it was roasted.

At mealtimes they sat either on the beds, on the floor, in the doorway, or on one of the big stones in the yard to eat.

The only source of information they had was an old transistor radio, which they would turn on in the mornings at about half past six, but the main attraction was the BBC world news at 8 a.m. In the evenings, at seven o'clock, everybody would converge in the bedroom to listen to a Jamaican story that they called "Dulcemina, Her Life in Town".

It was many years later before Calvin saw a newspaper. At that time, the only reading materials available for him to read were an ABC book, the slate that he used to write on, and some cowboy magazines. Mass Percy did have about six books in the house, but Calvin wasn't allowed to touch them. However, in later years, he and Marika and Devon played a game with the books that they called "find me the word". In time the children started to use the pages of the books for kindling, until the books disappeared.

Nor did Calvin behold a television for many more years. Miss G-G, one of his relatives, who lived close to Pan Bottom Hill, was one of the first people in the community to own a black-and-white television.

A lot of people would converge in Miss G-G's yard to watch her television. Those who couldn't fit in her front room would sit on her veranda to watch it. Some people – like Calvin at times – got to see only a little part of the television screen, but the beauty of it was amazing.

Calvin started to attend elementary school at the age of four, and his first school was at the home of Miss Winter, one of the senior members in the community. Miss Winter was living at the foot of Pan Bottom Hill, on a hillside above the road.

In those days, community spirit was strong on the island, and people who possessed a bit of education used to set up basic schools at their homes, and men would sometimes get together and built a small school out of bamboo in the community to house the children.

Every child used to get accepted in school – even those with physical impairment and those who were suffering from a disorder of any kind. Some people reacted by laughing when they came across someone with a physical impairment or a disorder. Cruelly they would heckle that person to despair, but as for Calvin, he was of a different breed. Those who knew him well thought twice before they laughed at him when he was struggling to speak, because by then he was quite frustrated and he was developing a bad temper. In a way, his anger was only a kind of self-defence. Gone were the days when he cried when people laughed and mocked him as he struggled to speak. At that point, he was getting tougher each day and he wasn't afraid to defend himself verbally or physically.

He was learning how to cope with his stammering, sometimes by speaking very quickly or, when he was sitting down, by bouncing his buttocks up and down to force the words out. If he was standing, he stamped vigorously on the ground while holding his head erect and clenching his fists. At such times, if anybody should laugh, that person would feel the vigour of his wrath. On the whole, to release his anger he would bite, scratch, or assault his provoker with whatever object he could reach. When he couldn't get close, he would swear and threw stones at them.

Despite the fact that the stuttering syndrome was turning Calvin into a little monster, his learning ability was exceptionally good. Unlike many other kids his age, it was his greatest delight to be in school, but due to his persistent, uncontrollable temper, he wasn't allowed to settle in class, because he couldn't make it through a week without getting into trouble with the teacher or one of the other kids. Frequently Miss Winter sent him home until finally she told him not to return.

Not long after Miss Winter last sent Calvin home, Ruby got him enrolled in a bamboo school at Mount Carey (which the locals called "down de ole"), but a similar clash occurred a few months later. This time he bit another little boy for laughing at him while he was stuttering.

There was another bamboo school at Mount Carey, near Rasta John's house. They thought Calvin would do well there, because John was living next door, but he proved them wrong a few weeks later after he got into another brawl, and they told him not to return.

He was at home for a while until Ruby got a space for him in the Margony Basic School.

The Margony Basic School was one of the best schools around. It was built out of concrete, and the children had to wear proper uniforms, but before the first week ended they summoned Ruby to collect Calvin, because he had thrown a stone at a teacher for shouting at him while he was trying to speak.

By then Ruby was getting frustrated, and she felt alone, because Percy didn't care whether the kids went to school or not. However, during that same period, Miss Maude decided to open a basic school on her veranda, and Calvin was one of the first pupils to enrol. In the end, Miss Maude was the only school that could tolerate his intolerable behaviour.

Miss Maude and Cherry Campbell were the only teachers at the school, and Aunt Maude (as everybody called her) was very strict; everybody in and around the little community respected her. She could bring Calvin and other unruly children under control when they got into a bad mood.

Later in life, as Calvin grew older, he recognised some of the reasons why he used to behave in such an unscrupulous manner. He acknowledged that on the whole he was very frustrated because of his stammering, but on the other hand, he was only acting out some of what he'd seen at home; which was the boisterous and ignorant behaviour from his parents, their way of always fighting verbally and physically with each other, and the way they cursed and beat Devon and Marika for the simplest things. On the contrary, he did not blame his parents outright for their behaviour, because he believed they were living their lives the only way that they knew, on account of poverty and the mental slavery that they had inherited along the way.

As parents, Ruby and Percy were lacking in every way what it took to be good role models. They were more concerned about maintaining their lifestyle than about the well-being of their children.

As Calvin described his parents, the bitter memories were evident, and he didn't try to conceal it.

Mass Percy would always dress up smartly and act as if he was "the man", but behind his smooth appearance lived a man who was very lazy in certain respects.

Calvin claimed that most of the men around the little neighbourhood had a farm,(garden) where they grow plenty of food each year to feed their families, but his mother had to buy their food from the local market (when she could afford to do so) because Mass Percy couldn't be bothered to cultivate any food for his family.

"Only twice do I remember my dad cultivating food, and he sold most of it when the crop came in and gambled with the money," Calvin stated with some anger.

"As a child," he continued, "I often felt sorry for Mama, especially when she didn't have any food to offer us. As for Mass Percy, he certainly did not care whether his children had a meal to eat before they went to bed at night."

Percy was an expert painter (decorator) but unfortunately he was a very poor man, and not because he couldn't get any jobs, but because he'd chosen to gamble, drink, and smoke cigarettes and ganja. Whenever he worked and got paid, he went straight to the gambling house, and oftentimes he lost everything, but when he did win, food was on the table for a while.

By then it was getting more painful for Calvin to speak as he gave an account of his parents' lifestyle, but he continued nonetheless.

As for Ruby, her life was messed up from when she had her first child, at the tender age of fourteen. She certainly did not get the chance to grow up, and she lived her life acting like a young girl, even when she was getting grandchildren from all sides.

In an astute way, Ruby used to represent what they called fashion in those days, and sometimes she would put herself first, in order to keep up with the trends, even when there wasn't enough food in her children's bellies. All her life she worked as a domestic helper, and she was very good at it too, but unfortunately she never stayed at one place for too long. On the whole, she was a woman with a lot of pride in certain respects, and for that reason she wouldn't take any "fuckries" (as she often bragged) from any of her employers. Therefore, when they treated her improperly, she would curse them and walk off the job.

"A lot of tears were frequently shed in our home," Calvin declared, "but more of sorrows than of joy, and life was like a roller coaster for me and my family. Sometimes everything seemed to be all right, but other times nothing seemed right and one thing for sure: it never got better."

Oftentimes Ruby would get drunk and quarrel with the neighbours, but it never took them long to get over their differences. On the whole, the neighbours were aware of her drinking addiction, so she was usually forgiven by the time she got sober.

Mass Percy and Ruby didn't seem to be bothered by what anybody had to say about their behaviour. In actual fact, if anybody was to say anything about Ruby's or Mass Percy's conduct, Ruby would start to curse, and she often used the foulest language.

The hurt Calvin experienced then was overpowering to say the least, and there was always that feeling of embarrassment, especially when all eyes and ears from the neighbours were focusing on their house.

"From that early stage in my life, I used to observe how my parents would always get drunk and argue and fight physically with each other, and sometimes I wished it would just stop. As the years went by, I learnt how to tolerate their sadistic behaviour, but the hurt I felt when Mass Percy regularly locked Mama inside the house and beat her was beyond description. Those occasions would mainly occur when Mass Percy came home from one of his drinking sprees, or when he'd lost all his money at the gambling house. He would start by accusing Mama of something that she knew nothing about, just to find a reason to beat her. While Mass Percy was beating Mama, Marika and I always cried until he was satisfied with his whipping and walked out of the yard, leaving Mama inside the house crying. At times she would end up in the Cornwall Regional Hospital in Mobay, and other times when she escaped the beating she would go to some of her relatives to seek refuge.

"Sometimes Mass Percy would go to the relative's house and manage to persuade Mama to return with him. Sometimes he gave her a good beating on their return, but on one of those occasions Mama used a scissors to stab him in one leg.

"If Devon used to feel any emotion when our dad was beating Mama, nobody will ever know, but again, maybe he didn't give a damn about whatever they wanted to do to each other."

At one stage Devon got fed up with staying at home and he headed for the streets instead, which caused Mass Percy to get really furious and carry out an intense search. When Devon was found, Percy tied him up and then beat him very badly, but that couldn't deter him, because before long he ran away again. This time, when Percy found him, he hammered him so badly that he ended up in Cornwall Hospital half paralyzed.

Everybody was shocked when Devon recovered and got released from the hospital. On the other hand, nobody did anything to deter Mass Percy's behaviour, so he continued.

Neither Ruby nor Mass Percy was religious, even though Ruby would often call upon God. On the whole, Calvin had never seen his parents go to church or pray, and they never taught the kids how to pray. He could remember only two or three times as a child when his parents sent him to Sunday school with his brother and sister at Mount Carey Baptist Church.

In many ways, the people around the community used to look on Calvin and his family as rejects. The lack of communication between Percy and Ruby, and the uneasiness that their conflicting lifestyles frequently inflicted on the kids, didn't do much good for them either, when it came to good upbringing.

As he got older, Calvin began to observe the way other families around the vicinity were conducting their lives, and even though he was only a child, he knew that his family was not living an ordinary lifestyle.

Eventually, he began to adopt his parents' rowdiness, by using some of the vile language to other people on the streets, like what he'd often heard them use to each other, the neighbours, and his brother and sister. At length he and his siblings started to fight with each other, and frequently they would fight with the kids from around the area, and as time went by they started to curse the other kids' parents too.

3 of Marika's younger children

Looking on the remains of Percy Riley's house from behind.

Marika with six of her eight children

Aunty Beck's extended house.

Viewing Percy's house from Berres Riley's house.

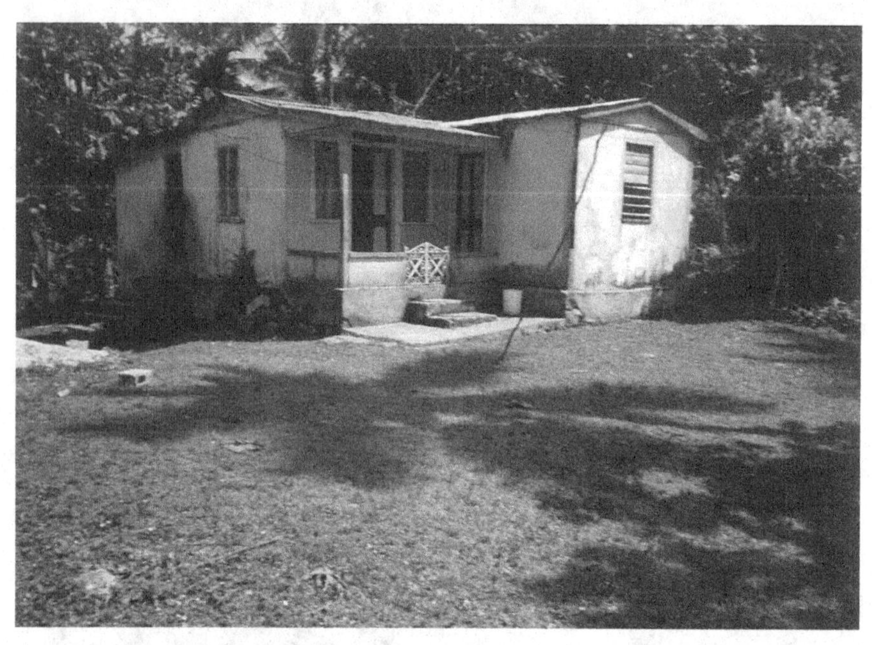

Looking on Berres Riley's house from Percy's house.

CHAPTER TWO

Finding the Way

On the whole, things had changed dramatically regarding Calvin's living conditions. He was six years old and still attending Miss Maude's school. His anger was subsiding a lot, and he was one of the brightest pupils.

Marika and Devon were attending the Anchovy Primary School, and they were also doing well in school.

For once, Percy and Ruby were moving in the right direction. Percy was getting a lot of jobs, and they'd decided to open a grocery shop in Mount Carey.

Ruby normally ran the shop and looked after the children, and Percy helped out in the shop most evenings.

They appeared to be a normal, coordinated family to the general public, but underneath the surface there were lots of huge cracks. Eventually, the truth began to come to light. For a start, Percy was getting jealous of the attention that Ruby was getting from various men, and as a result his ego was crushed. He allowed his foolish pride to take full control of him, and in the process it blighted his spirit. From there on, he would often get drunk and beat up Ruby, even in the shop, in front of customers. It continued like that for a while until one day they decided to close the shop down.

Calvin was very upset when he realised that the shop had closed, because he was having the time of his life. For him, just being in the shop alone was freedom itself. Moreover, he was always the centre of attention, especially when Mass Percy gave him the opportunity to put the records on the stereo turntable.

Not long after the shop closed, Ruby got herself a job doing domestic work with a family at Anchovy. She was a live-in helper, so she was away for up to four days a week. Some weekends when she went home, Percy would beat her up for the slightest pretext.

At that point, Percy wasn't around much, because he was either at work, in the rum bar, or at the gambling house.

During the week Marika and Devon were in charge of looking after themselves and Calvin. They would get Calvin ready and drop him off at Miss Maude's before they went to school. In the evenings Marika would get dinner ready (when there was food) while Devon picked up Calvin from school.

"It was always a pleasure to be in Devon's company, but for some reason he beat me up on a regular basis," Calvin explained with gleaming eyes as he recalled when Devon used to pick him up from Miss Maude's school. "Those were some of my best days," he declared proudly, "I would always look forward to those times when Devon was coming to pick me up at school, because that would mean spending some quality time with my brother."

In a special way Devon was his hero, because he didn't know of any other brothers at the time. It was only by chance he'd get to know about his other siblings one day.

It was an early autumn evening, and he was on his way to Anchovy with Marika and Devon to meet Percy. It was a regular occurrence. They'd started to do it when they didn't have any food to eat, because Percy would always buy a loaf of bread and a tin of corned beef for them after he got away from the gambling house or the rum bar.

That evening, while they were walking through the hills towards Anchovy, he overheard Marika telling Devon about Salomon. Curious, he stuttered and asked his sister, "Who is Salomon?"

Marika and Devon were alarmed by the sudden question, and they looked at each other dubiously, before they began to tell him about his other siblings.

From the outset, the whole concept of Calvin's intelligence was changed by the information that Marika and Devon divulged to him.

As they educated him, he started to ask stuttering questions about his other siblings' whereabouts, but they only told him to shut up and listen, because they themselves didn't know much. Nonetheless, they told him that Salomon was a rude boy and that he was living in Mobay. Van, his other brother, was living in Kingston, and he was also a rude boy; his other sister, Babs, was living in Mobay too.

Initially, he got very confused, because he was convinced that Marika was the eldest child and Devon the second eldest. He knew that he'd had another brother named Freddy (rest in peace) who was born after Devon, but he died; Ruby occasionally spoke about him. She always said that her best child died, but she never mentioned the others who were living away from the rest of the family.

Ultimately, even though Calvin was shocked by the revelation, he felt proud to know that he had two other brothers and a sister.

As time went by, he began to gather information about his other siblings, before he eventually met Salomon. Still, at the time he couldn't understand why his older brothers and sister were living away from him. He would often ask Ruby about them, but most times she ignored him, and when she did answer, he couldn't understand what she was saying to him.

At length he started to daydream about his other siblings. Most often he would sit and visualise his big brother's dad as being a rich man, who was living in a big house on top of a hill. Regrettably, he never got the privilege to meet Mr James or his relatives, and nobody told him anything about them.

Calvin was still attending Miss Maude's school when his big brother turned up out of the blue one day. He felt very proud when he went home from school and saw him, but he ran to his mum and hid behind her while he checked out Salomon covertly.

Salomon was resting his back against the house, with arms folded, as he smiled lovingly at his little brother.

Wow! Look how strong those arms are. He looks cool behind the sunglasses too, Calvin thought, while tugging on his mother's blouse.

Suddenly he whispered to Ruby, "Him have brown skin like me and Marika," but Ruby didn't reply. On the other hand, there was an unmistakable tension between her and Salomon, but

Calvin didn't care. The important thing was that his brother was there in the physical form, and that was all that mattered.

Eventually, he released his hold on Ruby's blouse and gingerly went over to meet his big brother.

On the whole, Salomon's presence changed the atmosphere at home and around the whole community.

Calvin didn't know exactly the reason for the tension between Ruby and his brother. Nor could he understand why most of the residents were wary of him, but it didn't matter to him what anybody thought of his big brother.

Although Ruby didn't care much about Salomon, whenever she cooked, she always gave him a meal. Nonetheless, many years passed before they spoke to each other properly.

The following morning, while Salomon was washing his face with a cup of water at one side of the house, Calvin noticed that he had only one eye. However, he didn't have the courage to ask him about it; instead, he went and asked Devon and Marika, who told him that Salomon, lost the eye in a gang war.

Calvin used to believe everything that his brother and sister told him. Therefore, even if it wasn't so, that's what he was made to believe.

During Salomon's stay, he would sometimes take his little brother to school or pick him up there, which was one of the happiest times for Calvin, because Salomon's presence was itself a message to all the potential troublemakers.

This is a well-known factor in many youths' upbringing: so long as they have a big, bad brother, an uncle who has been to jail, or a dad who's been arrested, they start to think they are untouchable. As a result, they too begin to behave in a disorderly way.

Now depending on crime and violence often causes people to think they are above the law, and when young people begin to believe that, there is little chance of telling them otherwise at a later date. At length, such children will start to practice what they have been taught. In contrast, some of the problems that Calvin would normally face on the streets with the other kids were diminished after Salomon came and went. Consequently, he began to show more signs of rebelliousness at school, on the streets, and at home. Unconsciously, his journey on the wrong side of the community was in process, because like what most youths believe, he too thought it was trendy and cool to be a rude boy.

Later in life when he gathered more information about Salomon, he found out that his big brother lived in Mobay for most of his life, except when he was behind bars in the St. Catherine District Prison. He also heard through the grapevine that Salomon had lived with Ruby at one stage, but they didn't have a good relationship, so he went to live with his dad's family. Ultimately, Salomon decided to go on his own quest to find his place in the underworld society, the community where the disillusioned, deprived, and underprivileged youths thrived.

Calvin was about seven years old when he met his second eldest brother Van, and he didn't act shy, as he had when he met Salomon. He only wondered why Van had a darker complexion.

Van was the same height as Salomon, but he didn't have a muscular body. He definitely wasn't the smiling type either, and there was also something unusual about his smooth conduct, something sinister. From what Calvin gathered, Van's dad was better off than the rest of Ruby's other baby fathers. Oftentimes she cursed all her children, except Calvin and Freddy, and she always said Mr Bent bought Van a fishing boat at one point, but he chose to be an outlaw instead. It was also rumoured that Van had killed a lot of people and had been in many shootouts with the police and other gangs, but neither of them could conquer him.

Calvin realised that the people around the vicinity were afraid of Van too, but they were more wary of him than Salomon. He thought it was cool for his rude boy brother to have such an impact on the community. On the other hand, Van was very fond of him and always hung out with him. As for Devon, he was on the verge of becoming a rude boy at that point; therefore, he was always rebelling against Percy and Ruby's rules, and he would often sleep in the bushes like a cowboy to prove he was tough.

"As a child, and just like what many other youths in my position would've probably done, I fed my brain with the negative information about my brothers, and oftentimes I considered becoming a rude boy when I got older too."

Calvin's second eldest sister Babs also grew up in Mobay. He'd just started to attend the Anchovy Primary School when he met her.

Babs turned up at the house unannounced one day, and Calvin was happy to meet her. On the whole, her presence had a different effect from that of Salomon and Van, because she would join in the games that they created, and it felt more like family, with less hatred and tension in the air.

Babs had a similar complexion to Marika, Salomon, and Calvin, and just like Marika, she was tall and beautiful.

Calvin met Babs's dad, Mr Watson, when he was about twelve years old.

CHAPTER THREE

LEARNING TO COPE

Calvin started to attend the Anchovy Primary School in September 1975, and he took his first exam the following spring – not knowing it would also be the last time that he took an exam in school. Although he was enthusiastic about school, because of financial difficulties, his parents were unable to send him regularly. On the contrary, whenever he did go to school, he would get twenty cents or sometimes twenty-five cents for his lunch money, which could only buy one small spice bun and a cherry malt drink, but he was grateful nonetheless.

At that point, Devon was completing his last year at the primary school, and Marika was attending the secondary school. The following year, Devon joined Marika at the secondary school, and Calvin was left on his own at the primary.

"Back then I had only two friends, who were attending the same school too, Cleveland Shaw (aka Monkey) and Carl Scott, and although the three of us were inseparable, I often felt lonely. In fact, I used to feel like an outsider, because most of the other pupils, including Monkey, had siblings who were attending the same school or had groups of friends to hang out with. As for Carl, even though he didn't have any siblings attending school, he was very popular, because he would swing from one group of pupils to the other."

Monkey was Mr Shaw's grandson and he lived with his family at his grandfather's house. Carl was living nearly next door to them with Sitta and Bauloo, his grandparents.

Unlike Monkey and Calvin, Carl didn't like school, so he was always absent from his classes and far behind in his lessons. For that, the teachers would delay his progress to get into a higher class.

Calvin, like most of the children, walked to and from school, which was fun, especially when various types of fruits were in season.

All the children had to be assembled in the school auditorium for the morning devotion, which started at eight o'clock, and anybody who missed the devotion would get rewarded with a hard beating from the principal's cane.

Most mornings when Calvin arrived at school, the little piece of bread or the piece of roast breadfruit and the cup of bush tea that he had for breakfast would have already disappeared out of his system.

The morning recess was at 10:30 a.m., but during that time Calvin wouldn't dare go near the shops, the vendors who were selling all kind of goodies outside the school gate, or for that matter anywhere near the other pupils when they were eating. On the whole, he was too embarrassed, and watching the others eat their meals would only increase his hunger.

Monkey was given more lunch money than Calvin and Carl, but he would spend some of it on his way to school, which put him in a similar predicament.

One morning, after Calvin moved into year two, he was walking on the train line to school with Monkey, who suddenly grabbed a vulnerable boy and took away his lunch, ate it, and even searched the boy's pocket before letting him go.

"I didn't tell Monkey that he was wrong to take away the boy's lunch; nor did I partake of it. But months later, when he suggested that we both do it, because none of us had any lunch money, I quickly said yes, without thinking of the consequences.

"Unconsciously we were taking a conspicuous step into crime, which was the result of living in poverty.

"We would get ready for school early in the mornings, position ourselves in numerous secluded areas, and stop the vulnerable kids when they were passing by. Those who had only lunch with them would lose it, and those who took money and lunch would lose everything. The ones who were rebellious would get threatened with a dose of nettle bush (scratch bush). This particular bush grows wild at the wayside, and it stings when it touches the body, but it is also used for many medicinal purposes on the island. In fact, the plant has been widely studied for its value in the treatment of arthritis and gout. This bush is also extremely rich in vital nutrients, including vitamin D, which is rare in any plant, as well as vitamins C and A, and minerals including iron, calcium, phosphorus and magnesium.

"We continued with our notoriety until the victims' parents or bigger brothers and sisters had to start escorting their siblings to school, and when we couldn't find anybody else to rob, we would go to the nearby bakery and beg disqualified bread.

Sometimes we were lucky to get a few pieces of stale bread; other times we were not."

Before Calvin completed his first year at the Anchovy Primary School, Ruby decided to walk out on Percy, but she also walked out on her children.

"It felt like I was in a dream when Mama decided to walk out on us," Calvin declared, "and everything seemed unreal for a while until I got accustomed to her absence."

Marika automatically took on the role of the housewife. She was just over thirteen years old, but she had the maturity of an adult. She was also one of the prettiest girls around the community. She was tall and slim with a very light brown complexion and a good head of hair.

Marika was Mass Percy's favourite child and Ruby's worst nightmare, because for some unknown reason Ruby didn't like the very ground that she walked on. She hated her with a passion. As for Calvin, Marika was like his second mother, and she was also his best family member, because he could always confide in her and rely on her.

After Ruby walked out of the family home she got herself a job in Westmoreland, a little district about thirty miles from where they were living. By the look of it things seemed to be all right, because Ruby would come home nearly every fortnight with groceries and a few pieces of clothes for the children, and before she returned to work the following Monday she would also leave money with Mass Percy, to help send the children to school. By then they were at least talking again.

A few months later, Ruby went back to Percy with a big suitcase of clothes. It always seemed inevitable that she would be back one day, so nobody was really surprised to see her.

Calvin on the other hand was happy to have his mother back, but eventually tension started to build up between Marika and Ruby.

By then, Marika was well conscious of the role that she was playing at home, and she'd grown used to her responsibilities, which automatically became her way of life. So she felt threatened after Ruby reappeared.

Ruby on the other hand was jealous, because Percy was showing his affection to Marika, and he didn't give a damn about her. Ultimately, bitter arguments started to develop between Marika and her mum.

Ruby would often curse Marika and accuse her of having an affair with Percy. Marika in turn would tell her father about her mother's conduct when he got home, and for that he would often beat up Ruby.

It continued for a little while until Ruby got herself another job, doing domestic work with a family at a place called Cotton Tree, about a mile and a half from Percy's house.

During that time, Van appeared out of the blue at Carey Village, and it was alleged that he had been placed on the police most-wanted list in Kingston.

By then everything was changing in Calvin's life, apart from his living conditions. At a fast pace his world was turning into a jungle, where one had to fight and struggle to survive. Quickly he was learning how to fend for himself, both physically and otherwise. On the whole, at that point in his life, he allowed only Ruby and Percy to reprimand him; when anyone else tried, he fought back. However, one day he was being mischievous while at home with Van, Marika, and Devon. Van decided to award him a few slaps for his mischief, which resulted in Calvin running for a knife to defend himself.

When Calvin returned with the knife, Van skilfully held his little brother down and tried to take the knife away, but in the process Calvin got a cut on his left thumb, and when he saw the blood he started to bawl. He didn't hesitate; he ran the mile and a half to where Ruby was working to plead his case.

Ruby got furious when she saw her baby's hand covered in blood, but what she did later wasn't what Calvin had expected.

She didn't bother to find out from Van what had happened, even though she, like everybody else, knew that Calvin was a little spoilt brat. Instead, she went straight to the police station to lodge her complaint.

It is clear that Ruby told the Anchovy police that the police in Kingston wanted Van dead or alive and that he was hiding at her house. The Anchovy police called Kingston and confirmed that Van was really on their most wanted list. They subsequently planned a surprise attack on him, but he was fortunate that Mass Percy heard about what was going to happen and forewarned him. It was said that Mass Percy also gave him some money and told him to keep on running.

After Van disappeared, Calvin asked many questions about his brother's whereabouts, but he got no answer. At length he learnt how to tolerate the lack of knowledge of his disillusioned family.

A few months later, Ruby walked off her new job, and her altercations with Marika started afresh, but at length Ruby couldn't take it anymore. One day she packed her suitcase and decided enough was enough.

This time it felt real to Calvin, and deep down he knew that his mother wasn't coming back – unlike Marika, who was happy to finally get her freedom.

It was 1976, the year Marika and Devon's school days ended. Devon wasn't quite twelve years old, and Marika was months away from her fourteenth birthday.

Occasionally Mass Percy would tug Devon along with him to work, which happened to be the best thing that he'd ever done for him, because Devon turned out to be a very good painter (decorator).

"On the whole," Calvin said, "it was one of the biggest turning points in my life, when Mama decided to walk out that day, because suddenly everything began to change around me and I was no longer the baby.

"Most of the time I had to wash my own clothes, which was done manually with my bare hands, and I prepared my own meals on the odd occasion, but as time went by I got accustomed to my new life. Nonetheless, covertly I was missing Mama severely, because she would always pamper me when she was around. Mass Percy on the other hand wasn't the sort of father who would read books or spend leisure time with us kids. In fact, the only leisure time I can remember spending with Mass Percy was when he used to teach us how to gamble.

"Sometimes we used leaves for money, but other times we used elastic bands, purchased from the shops, and as time went by we started to use real money.

"I was fascinated by the Pitta Pat, a card game that two, three or four people played, which ultimately became my all-time favourite card game. I also learnt how to play dominoes, as well as Cooncan, another card game that two people play, but I didn't try to learn how to play with the bone dice, which was Mass Percy's favourite game.

"Some Sundays, when Mass Percy wasn't at the gambling house from Friday, instead of spending quality time with us kids, he would rather be underneath a big tree, close to Money Man's house, with Money Man and other like-minded men gambling the day away.

"Sometimes I used to follow my dad and climb the nessberry trees near where they were gambling and shoot birds with my catapult and ate ripe berries. When Mass Percy and the other men wanted cigarettes, ganja, or alcohol, they would send me to the shop and give me pocket money.

"Initially, I used to feel scared when they got angry and began to shout at each other during the bone dice game, but as time went by I realised that it was only the tempo of the game that made them behave aggressively amongst themselves. After a while they would normally change the game to Pitta Pat, and during this game it was mostly the flick of the cards that could be heard, or when they occasionally shouted, 'Come', to use a certain card, which was said with much aggression.

"As time went by, I became embroiled with gambling too, and as I got older, it became a focal part of my life, which eventually caused me to start lying and cheating in order to get money to gamble with the other youths, who were living a similar lifestyle.

"Often times Marika, Devon, and I used to gamble amongst ourselves at the house, and sometimes other youths from around the community would join us too, and at length I began to gamble underneath a tree in various places around the community with other youths and some of the men that Mass Percy used to gamble with.

"Ultimately I found solace in gambling, and it wasn't because I used to win. No sir! I hardly won anything. It was merely because I got the chance to fit in with the other youths, not standing on the outside looking in. To be more precise, I felt I belonged when I was gambling. The other gamblers were like my family. It was like a drug to my soul."

At this stage, Calvin was on his first summer's holiday at the Anchovy Primary School. Earlier when the exam results came out, he came fourteenth out of thirty-six students, and Junior Street, another youth from the same community who sat beside him in class came in thirteenth.

He was getting wiser, but the living conditions were getting tougher each day. Ultimately, it reached that stage when everybody seemed to be thinking about him or her. Percy, Devon, and Marika didn't seem bothered about what he did on a day-to-day basis. The older he grew, the less attention he got, and automatically he became a self-sufficient child, who was swiftly learning how to survive on the island. Equally, he was granted the go-ahead to roam the community with Carl and Monkey or to spend the days on his own hunting for various fruits or gambling with the locals.

It was evident that neither Calvin nor his friends had any fundamental direction, and their main aim was to see the present day through by all means necessary. That entailed finding enough food to eat and enjoying life as much as they could, both of which added up to freedom.

"Notwithstanding, back in those days, most children, both boys and girls, used to build their own toys from scratch, from the natural things that lay around or from things that were discarded. As for me, like other poor boys, we used to observe the toys that the rich kids had and try to come up with our own inventions to make similar copies, or we'd simply use our own ingenuity to build toys.

"As for the toy cars or trucks, we would simply use empty milk or juice cartons for the body with two pieces of sticks for the axles, and four small green oranges for the wheels, or four bottle caps and a piece of string to pull it along, while we made humming sound from our mouths like a truck or a car would.

"Most Jamaican youths grew up with a catapult (slingshot), and for those who lived in the countryside, like I did, the slingshot was a must-have toy. It was commonly use to hunt the wild birds, which were a source of food, and shoot mangoes and berries from the huge trees. On the other hand, as a young catapult owner, you had a deadly weapon in your possession, because you could use it to defend yourself in a fight, to threaten others, or simply to make mischief by shattering other people's windowpanes.

"The marbles weren't made from scratch, but they made for one of the favourite games for boys – and some girls, who were tomboys. It was one of those games that got a lot of boys into trouble with their parents, because they would spend endless hours playing, while they should be at home doing their chores, and it also caused a lot of productive school days to be wasted, not to mention the lunch money that was spent on marbles.

"I had huge knuckles from a child, so it wasn't easy for me to expertly pitch the marbles, but there were always a few dominant youths who could pitch the marbles better than others. Carl was one of them, but oftentimes the bigger boys would beat him up and take away his marbles, and that was when the slingshot normally came into play.

"Most kids made kites with notepaper and the spine of coconut leafs, and I used to admire them when they flew, but I've never tried to fly a kite in the entirety of my life.

"One of the best exercises was running up and down the footpaths and the roads with a hose hoop toy.

"This was a simple toy, but it took great skill to operate it. We would get one meter or three feet of water hose, insert a short stick in one end, and push it into the other. Then we straightened a rigid piece of wire (preferably a clothes hanger) and shaped one end to accommodate the hose hoop. Then we hummed the sound of a motorbike while running along the road or footpath."

*

Not long after Ruby walked out on Percy and her children, Calvin started to experiment with smoking, which in itself was another step in Percy's footsteps.

He'd observed how Percy built his spliffs (joints), but he couldn't get hold of any cannabis, which is popularly called ganja, marijuana, or weed. So he decided to use dried cho-cho leaf.

The cho-cho is a tropical fruit that is native to Mexico and Central America, but in the Caribbean people consume it as a vegetable. There are quite a few varieties; however, they all have a pear or slightly oval shape and a thin skin, fused with its flesh. It also contains a good source of vitamin C and amino acids.

Cho-cho leaves are also believed to contain diuretic and cardiovascular aids, and in some Spanish-speaking countries, the word *cho-cho* means vagina. However, at a close examination of the Jamaican cho-cho, maybe the reason is clear why there is a correlation. Rumour also has it on the island that when one suffers from high blood pressure, the consumption of cho-cho is a good way of treating it.

Calvin used to pretend he was getting a buzz, after he'd smoked the cho-cho leaves, but it wasn't long before he got his chance to experience the effect of ganja, which occurred one day while he was at home playing.

He had a habit of swinging from a piece of board that was nailed above one of the doors on the unfinished section of the house. However, on this day, as he attempted to swung, one hand touched something soft. At first he thought it was a croaking lizard, because there were lots of them at the house. He quickly jumped down, because he was scared of them.

Immediately as his feet touched the ground, what he thought was a lizard also fell, and he shivered. On closer inspection, however, he realised that it was only one of Mass Percy's half-finished spliffs.

It suddenly felt like Christmas to him, and he picked it up and ran straight to Monkey's yard. Fortunately Carl was there too, and after he showed them what he'd found, they all went behind Monkey's house, where they got stoned with the spliff.

"It was an extraordinary experience for me, because even though my living conditions were at the lowest peak and my environment were bleak, after I smoked the spliff I could feel the essence of joy, togetherness, peace, and a moment of freedom.

"Consequently, after much laughter, my friends and I got very hungry and decided to head for a cane field, where the three of us filled our bellies with cane juice.

"I also realised that I could speak more clearly, and it happened to be one of the best days of my life. After a while, I was talking so much that my mates had to beg me to shut up, but I didn't want to stop, in case my inability to speak clearly returned.

"At home, nobody noticed the transition in my speech; nonetheless, from that day onward I continued to smoke ganja."

At that time, Percy's style of living was moving towards a greater obliteration. Sometimes when he decided to go away on his own quest, he would leave a little food and a few dollars to help tide the family over. However, as soon as his back was turned, Marika would share the money between the three of them, and after a few days into his absence there would be no food and no money in the house.

The daily provisions mainly consisted of rice, dumplings, breadfruit, bananas, yams, salt fish (codfish) and ackee, coconut rundung with pickled mackerel, and chicken back (a traditional menu for Jamaicans).

The yam was a very essential sort of vegetable, with various derivative products after it has been processed. It can be barbecued, fried, roasted, grilled, boiled, or grated.

There are many cultivars of yam, and the majority of the vegetable is composed of a much softer substance known as the meat. This substance ranges in colour from white or yellow to pink or purple in mature yams. They are a primary agricultural commodity in West Africa and New Guinea. They were first cultivated in Africa and Asia around 8000 BC.

Due to their abundance and consequently their importance to survival, the yam was highly regarded in Nigerian ceremonial culture and used as a vegetable offering during blessings.

Yams were taken to the Americas by pre-colonial Portuguese and Spanish, on the borders of Brazil and Guyana, followed by dispersion through the Caribbean.

Although it is unclear which came first, the word *yam* is related to the Portuguese or Spanish name, which both ultimately derives from the Wolof word *nyam*, meaning "to sample or taste"; in other African languages and in Jamaica, it can also mean "to eat".

The breadfruit, otherwise called *Artocarpus altilis*, is a species of flowering tree in the mulberry family, which can be found throughout Southeast Asia and most Pacific Ocean islands. Its name is derived from the texture of the cooked fruit, which has a potato-like flavour, similar to freshly baked bread. Before being eaten they are cooked, boiled, baked, or roasted.

The breadfruit trees sometimes grow to a height of ninety feet (twenty-seven metres). All parts of the tree yield latex, a milky juice, which is useful for boat caulking. It is also one of the highest yielding food plants, with a single tree producing up to 200 or more fruits per season. In the Caribbean, it is estimated that one tree produces up to twenty-five fruits per season.

It is said that the ancestors of the Polynesians found the trees growing in the northwest New Guinea area, around 3,500 years ago. They gave up the rice cultivation they'd brought with them from ancient Taiwan, and raised the fruit wherever they went in the Pacific, except Easter Island and New Zealand, which were too cold. Their ancient eastern Indonesian cousins spread the plants west and north through insular and coastal Southeast

Asia. It has, in historic times, had also been widely planted in tropical regions.

It is alleged that, according to a Hawaiian origin myth, the breadfruit originated from the sacrifice of the war god Ku. After he decided to live secretly among mortals as a farmer, Ku married and had children, and he and his family lived happily until a famine seized their island. At length, he could no longer bear to watch his children suffer. So Ku told his wife that he could deliver them from starvation, but to do so he would have to leave them. Reluctantly she agreed, and at her word, Ku descended into the ground, right where he stood, until only the top of his head was visible.

His family waited around the spot where he'd last been seen, day and night, watering it with their tears, until suddenly a small green shoot appeared where Ku had stood. Quickly, the shoot grew into a tall and leafy tree that was laden with heavy breadfruits.

Consequently, Ku's family and neighbours gratefully ate the fruits, which saved them from starvation.

It is also said that Christopher Columbus brought the breadfruit to Jamaica in 1495, and to this day, some Jamaicans strongly believe that the letter C, which can be found when the stem of the fruit is cut, is a trademark of Christopher Columbus. Many also believed that the letter C simply means "Come to save us", because the breadfruit kept a lot of people from starving.

The ackee is one of the unique fruits on the island, but it has to be properly ripened before eaten. It can also be dangerous if prepared improperly, because it is partly toxic.

It is alleged that the ackee was imported to Jamaica from West Africa on a slave ship. Its name is derived from the West

African *akye fufo*. It is also known as *Blighia sapida*. The scientific name honours Captain William Bligh, who took the fruit from Jamaica to the Royal Botanic Gardens in Kew, England, in 1793 and introduced it to science.

Although native to West Africa, the consumption of ackee mainly takes place amongst Jamaicans. It is one of their all-time, best traditional dishes, internationally known as ackee and salt fish, the national dish of Jamaica, which spread to other countries with the Jamaican Diaspora. It is also eaten widely in the United Kingdom, Canada, and the United States.

Ackee was initially introduced to Jamaica and later to Haiti, Bali, Cuba, Barbados, and other Pacific islands. It was later introduced to Florida. Rumour also has it that ackee is often used in Haiti to perform witchcraft (obeah).

When breadfruits, yam, bananas, and ackee were available on Calvin's property, or they could afford to buy a pound of flour or a pound of rice, they couldn't afford to purchase any meat, fish, or poultry. Thus they would consume the provision with butter and ackee, or cook them in coconut milk. When avocadoes were in season, they would use the ripe ones to substitute meat or fish. They were not alone, because most poor people on the island, who couldn't afford to purchase chicken, meat, or fish, would do the same.

In those days, the cheapest meat that was available for the poorer people was the chicken parts, usually only the chicken back.

On Sundays, everybody would make it a priority to prepare a nice dinner. Rice and peas would be the main dish, accompanied by fish, meat, or a whole chicken, but chicken back was a delicacy for a lot of people. They later nicknamed chicken back "the poor people's steak", which the first class citizens would normally use to feed their dogs on the island.

After the fruits were harvested from the trees on Calvin's family land, they would sometimes buy from other people in the vicinity when they could afford to, but because he was always on the prowl, he would have lots of fruits that he had stolen from other people's property.

Lawyer Stenit's property, which was part of the jungle close to Percy's house, became one of the main places where Calvin would frequently go to steal the fruits.

To him, Lawyer Stenit was only a mystery, because he'd only heard through the grapevine when he was growing up that the man who owned the seventy-five acres of land, laden with vegetables and fruits with the big Victorian house on the hilltop, was a white man name Lawyer Stenit, but he never actually met the man.

Lawyer Stenit's house remained empty for many years, and a lot of people used the property as a footpath to get to Anchovy. They would also resort to the property to collect vegetables and fruits.

In the end, Lawyer Stenit's house and his property became for Marika, Devon, and Calvin both a playground and a hot spot to find a meal.

There was a big tank in the lawyer's backyard with lots of black fishes, and frequently Calvin and his siblings would catch the fishes to make a meal. There were also lots of coconuts, sour sop, bananas, breadfruits, mangoes, ackee, avocado, pomegranate, oranges, plums, and yams on the property.

"I used to have lots of fun at Lawyer Stenit's house. It was set magnificently on top of a hill, about seven hundred yards from our house, and although it was isolated from other houses, it could be seen from a distant, from all directions.

"From the veranda I could view miles of the green countryside, and there was always a cool breeze blowing. Oftentimes I sat on the veranda and daydreamed for hours about my other siblings and about having a better life than what I was living. When I got hungry, I used to climb the coconut trees, pick the green ones, drink the water, and then eat the meat. Sometimes I would use the coconut water to wash my hair."

Sometime Calvin would go to Lawyer Stenit's property on the fruit raids alone, and frequently Monkey and Carl would join in. Other times they would go to the farmer's fields, cut down their bananas, and hide them in bushes until they were ripe. They would also go to the farmers' cane fields and reap their sugar cane. The cane juice would provide them with a substantial amount of energy.

Oftentimes they would steal from each other too, by removing the spoil to another secret hiding place of their own. Nevertheless, it was fun to them, because at the time it was about the only thing that they knew. There was nothing else constructive for them to do, because their environment was bare and bleak. Accordingly they were left to their own devices.

When most fruits were out of season, it was hard for Calvin to find sustenance to make it through the day. Occasionally he would get a meal at home in the evenings, when there was food at the house to cook, but at times he and his siblings would go to bed without eating a meal.

Most people in those days had an outside kitchen, where they would prepare their meals on a wood fire, especially during dry season. Those who didn't have an outside kitchen would build the fire on the ground, beside their houses. They simply placed three stones in a triangular position on the ground, four or five inches apart and put dry wood between the spaces of the stones. Then they'd light the wood and put their pots on top of the stones to cook the food. Some people would simply build a wall of stones beside the house, which would serve as their kitchen.

Calvin and his family used to build their fire underneath the unfinished roof of the house, which caused the board and the zinc to turn black from the smoke, and as time went by the whole house started to rot.

Sometimes when Calvin didn't have any food to eat, he would watch the neighbour's kitchen top to see when the smoke went down, which in itself was a sign for him to know that his neighbour's dinner was ready.

When he saw the smoke go down, he would start throwing stones at birds – even at imaginary birds – to work his way round to his neighbour's yard. Sometimes he would tell them a story to win their attention. Other times he would hang out with the kids in the yard until dinner got served.

Some of the kids didn't like when Calvin came around at mealtimes, because it meant their dinner was going to be shortened. Nevertheless, the parents always knew he was hungry and gave him some of their food, especially Cherry's grandmother, Aunty Beck, who loved him with all her heart.

Aunty Beck and her husband had five children, who went their separate ways to make a living for themselves. Her husband passed away when Calvin was only a child, leaving Aunty Beck with Cherry, Audrey, and Maxine.

Calvin was like a member of Aunty Beck's family, because he was always at the house.

Maxine, the youngest of the grandchildren, went to live in Kingston before she later migrated to America to live with her mother.

Cherry and Audrey continued to live at home with Aunty Beck, until Cherry eventually met her husband and moved out of the family home.

Audrey continued to live at home with her grandmother until she met Rema, who later moved in with her. Together they had two children, and after Aunty Beck passed away, Audrey continued to live at the house. At length she and Rema were like brother and sister to Calvin.

There were also a few other houses that Calvin would go to, mainly to get some food, but he wouldn't get called in for a plate of food when the meal was served. Sometimes he would walk away silently like a reprimanded dog, but other times he would stick around until the kids finished eating and continue to play with them. Most times he felt even hungrier when the only sound that was coming from the house was that of the plates and cutleries. It was merely his pride that strengthened him then.

Looking back, he realised now that maybe there was simply not enough food to go around, because there were lots of mouths to be fed.

Eventually, it reached that stage when Calvin's pride forbade him from begging for meals. On the whole, it was getting embarrassing for him, because some of the other kids would tease him about his continuous begging. As a result, he decided to resort to stealing, and his first major act was to break into Mr Bee's house.

From his house, he could see who went out or who came to Mr Bee's house, and he could also smell their food when they were cooking.

One morning he was on his own at the house, wondering where he could go to find some food, and whatever Mr Bee and Miss Cassie were cooking smelt very good. The aroma made him even hungrier, because he hadn't eaten since the previous afternoon.

As he peeped through the hole in the side of his house, he thought about going over to beg a bit of sugar from Miss Cassie, to make a cup of bush tea, but he couldn't muster the will to impose on her.

After a while Mr Bee stepped through the front door and put his boots on, picked up his machete and a bag, and set off for his farm. Minutes later Miss Cassie left the house too, but some of the windows were open. Suddenly, Calvin realised he could go inside the house to steal a bit of sugar and maybe some flour or rice. Without a second thought, he decided to enter his neighbour's house through one of the opened windows.

Inside the house he quickly rummaged through bags, boxes, and cupboards, but he only found half a loaf of hard dough bread. He cut himself two thick slices and decided to make an exit, but on his way towards the window, he spotted Miss Cassie's Bible lying on a table. Like a magnet to steel, the Bible drew him closer, and curiosity got the best of him. He stopped and opened it, and to his surprise, one hundred dollars were smiling at him. Immediately he pocketed the money and jumped out the window.

He ran inside his house and began to consume the bread nervously. The first mouthful went down his throat with ease, but he choked on the second one, so he picked up the jug of drinking water and began to sip with each bite, while peeping through the hole in the side of the house.

When the bread was gone, he left the yard and went in search for gambling, but he was a nervous wreck.

In those days, one hundred dollars had a lot of value, and it was also very hard to pull together.

Miss Cassie cried out when she realised that her money was missing, but up to this very day Calvin never got found out.

At that point, his pride was out in front of his integrity, but he was generating the skills of a criminal unconsciously. Most youths started out by indulging in petty theft around their homes, later taking it to the streets and embarking on bigger missions, such as shoplifting, pick pocketing, robbery, and fraud. Although some do it for a buzz and some because of peer pressure, there are always those who do it because they can't see any other way out. As for Calvin, it seemed like his life was pencilled out since the day he was born into shame and poverty.

CHAPTER FOUR

TIME TO FACE REALITY

At this point, Calvin was well aware of his surroundings, and he had also begun to observe how other families were conducting their lives. He often wished his family could compare to some of them. He also wished he were a part of another family, because he thought his family was uncoordinated and dispirited, which caused a lot of people to look down on them in a discredited way. Ultimately, it tarnished what little self-worth he possessed.

At length, most of the bigger boys from around the area started to take advantage of his vulnerability, because they all knew that he was a victim of a broken home. Having a brown complexion didn't make things any easier for him either, because the colour of one's skin had an effect on how one would get recognised in Jamaica, for good or ill. Most clear-skin (mixed-race) people in the Caribbean are usually in the better position, but those like Calvin, whose standard of living didn't reflect their skin colour, were objects of disrespect.

Regularly the bigger youths used to beat him up and tell him the most repulsive things about his family. The all-time worst insults were when they told him that his mother and father were actually brother and sister or that Percy was having an affair with Marika. Sometimes the youths would hold him down and rub scratch bush all over his body. This left him in agony, and his body turned red in the aftermath. Then when he managed to get away and run, they would hurl stones after him.

One time while he was running away from a group of youths, one of the stones caught him on the head and shattered on impact. He cried out as he fell to the ground, but they continued to hurl stones at him, therefore he had to get up and run to his house. To this day, a bald spot can be found on his head as a constant reminder of where the stone shattered.

Ultimately, Calvin couldn't take the abuse any longer and started to fight back verbally. Sometimes he would curse the other boys when they attacked him and tell them horrible things about their parents; often this only caused them to beat him up even more. At length he had to start defending himself physically, and even though he was sometimes badly beaten, he felt it was always better to fight and lose than to run away.

After a month or so Ruby returned to the family home, but this time she was more unsettled, because she would go out more often than the last time when she was around. In due course, she started to go out with one of Mass Percy's friends, which was a massive low blow for Percy's ego. As a result, for the first time he told her to get out of his house.

"I can vividly remember that morning. It appeared as if it was the end of an era, or a shift in power.

"Mass Percy was like a weary defeated man or a changed person. Even Mama noticed the transition in him and took advantage of it. The neighbours too were shocked.

"It was about nine o'clock, and Mama was sitting on one of the big stones in the yard, close to the footpath, enjoying the morning sun. Mass Percy had been up from early, and he'd made a pot of cornmeal porridge and eaten a bowl, after he had a wash behind the house. He was dressed in his duck egg green trousers, a white long-sleeve shirt, and a pair of black shoes, which were as shiny as a looking glass.

"He was rather quiet that morning, and it put everybody on edge, because we could never tell when he was going to flip and lash out at someone.

"I was sitting at the doorway eating a bowl of the porridge, while enjoying the warmth of the morning sun on my skin. Suddenly, Mass Percy stepped past me and walked towards the gate, where Mama was sitting on the rock. When he got close to her, he stopped and raised his right hand, to point a finger at her, and Mama flinched and quivered with fright. Nonetheless, in the coolest manner, Mass Percy told her in patios, with his finger still pointing at her, 'I want you to take your things and get out of my house before I return tonight.' With that said he walked away and headed towards Lawyer Stenit's property, where he used to walk to go to Anchovy.

"When Mass Percy was halfway up the hill, Mama started to curse him, loud enough for the people on the other side of the village to hear, but he didn't reply. Mama on the other hand continued to unleash her abuse by telling Percy that he was always going down on her (which was one of the most disgraceful things that you could tell a Jamaican man), but Mass Percy ignored her.

Nonetheless, Mama went even further, and this time she told him that he was sleeping with his own daughter, and Mass Percy suddenly stopped, turned around, and took a few steps towards her. But she was already running up the footpath, and he turned around and continued on his way, leaving her cursing at the top of her voice.

"Mama moved in with Mass Percy's friend the same day, and the end of my parents' relationship seemed final.

"There wasn't any need for them to get divorce, because they were not married. That was something that used to puzzle me: I couldn't understand why my mother and father shared the same surname, yet they were not married.

"A lot of people were also baffled about my parents' situation, and eventually they concluded that they were actually brother and sister.

"I didn't know Mass Percy's mother, because she had passed away before I was born, and I didn't know his father either. From a child, I'd only heard Marika and Devon talking about our grandfather, James Riley, who happens to be Mass Percy's dad, and he was living some six miles away from Carey Village. Just like it was with the rest of my siblings, I would often try to visualise what my grandfather looked like and how he was living his life.

"At one point, it was alleged that James Riley had been very ill, and on his dying bed he sent a message to Percy, stating that he shouldn't take anything that belonged to him if he should die. As the years went by, nobody make any more mention of my grandfather.

"I'd only heard about my father's five brothers, but I've never once seen them. Uncle Willy was living at Bakers Stet, and Biran,

Papa Beagle, Freddy, and Melvin were living in Kingston. I knew his sister Ivy, who was living at Anchovy, and once I'd also met his other sister Sissy, who was living at Bogue Hill, in Montego Bay, and who Mama claimed to be her sister also.

"I didn't know anything about Ruby's parents' whereabouts. It was a subject that she'd rather not talk about. However, she once told me that her mum died while she was giving birth to her; therefore she herself did not know what her mum looked like. On the other hand, she didn't mention anything about her dad, and I didn't ask her about him either. I didn't know if my mum had any other sisters or brothers, apart from Sissy.

"As time went by, I felt like I should know the truth about the propaganda of my parents' relationship, but I couldn't find the courage to ask them, because in those days parents were very secretive, and I would surely have got a few slaps across my face, to broach such a question to either of them. Nevertheless, I was desperate to tell them what I'd heard about them being brother and sister and also let them know how traumatic my ignorance of the truth was and how damaging it was to me psychologically, when the other youths teased me about it, but instead I only suppressed my grief.

"Many years later, I overheard my Grand-Uncle Roland and his wife, Millie, on more than one occasion making comments about Ruby's and Mass Percy's situation. They were both convinced that James Riley was the father of Ruby and Percy. In later years it was also revealed that Aunty Ivy, Uncle Melvin, and Uncle Willy, who was fathered by James Riley, was also Ruby's brothers and sister.

"Each time I gathered more information about my parents' background, it seemed real, and I often felt sick, knowing that

I was conceived in an undignified manner. But over the years I masked my inner feelings and tried not to think about it too much, because there is nothing that anybody can do to change things.

"After Ruby left the family home, she decided to stay away from Percy, although she would go by the house every once in a while, when she knew Percy wasn't there.

"Regularly Mass Percy had began to take Devon to work with him, and sometimes they would went off to work for weeks at some faraway places, where painting was in demand, and during that time it would only be me and Marika at home.

"On one of those occasions, Marika got pregnant by a Rasta man who went by the name of Bungo Pully. I doubt if she'd turned fourteen years old at the time.

"When Mass Percy found out that his beloved daughter was pregnant, he blamed me for it."

"'Yuh was supposed to protect yuh bumboclaat sister,' he swore as he told me.

"Consequently, I began to pay the price for my sister's pregnancy, by not getting sent to school regularly until she had her baby.

"During Marika's pregnancy, I remembered one night when she, Devon, and I went to meet Mass Percy at Anchovy. That night, we decided to wait for him at the police station. We were sitting on the steps at the front of the station, with Special Constable Brown, when I noticed the .38 Smith and Wesson revolver in its holster around the officer's waist. Without a second thought I shouted, 'Mi know gun. Mi see it before.'

"The officer turned around and asked me, 'who yuh see wid gun, bwoy?'

"'Mass Percy hab (have) one just like dat,' I told the officer.

Marika and Devon shouted, 'Shut yuh mouth,' in unison as the officer was beginning to take the questioning to another level.

"That night, while we were walking home, Marika and Devon told Mass Percy what I'd told the officer, and it was the first time my dad reacted so viciously towards me.

"From the outset, Mass Percy appeared to be a deeply shaken man, and he was also under the strong influence of alcohol and ganja. It seemed as if he'd lose at the gambling house again, but that wasn't the main reason why he was so angry. It was to do with the fact that his precious daughter got pregnant, at such an early age. For that he was very embarrassed. Moreover, the word was also out that he was the father of his own daughter's child.

"We got off the main road at Cotton Tree, onto a road that runs over a train line tunnel, which takes us through Lawyer Stenit's property and then to our house, at the outskirt of the jungle.

"When we reached the middle of the bridge, Mass Percy suddenly stopped and grabbed me and then swiftly lifted me off the ground and held me over the concrete barrier, with my head dangling down over the train line, and said, 'I feel like jus trowing yuh lickle raasclaat over de bridge!'

"Initially I thought he was only messing around when he lifted me up, but when he swore and said he felt like throwing me over the bridge, and from the tone that he used, I knew straight away that he was serious.

"All of a sudden my eyes felt like they were about to pop out of my head, and I screamed, a sharp shriek, with my mouth wide open, but in an instant fear knocked the air out of me, and I couldn't breathe.

"I knew I was safe when I felt Marika and Devon tugging on my legs and begging Mass Percy not to drop me.

"After they placed me back on the ground, Mass Percy walked away and I curled up myself, at the foot of the barrier and panted, as I gasped for air, while tears were rolling down my cheeks.

"Devon followed Percy, but Marika lingered behind and told me to get up and come on, because I was going to be all right, but from that night, the bond between me and my dad was broken, and I watched him waste away slowly thereafter.

"On the second of April, 1977, Marika gave birth to a little baby boy that she named Andrew Fletcher. I was just under nine years old, but instantly my school days began to diminish even more.

"In mid-1978, Marika decided to move out of Carey Village and went to live with Uncle Roland and his wife, in Mount Salem (one of the rural areas around Mobay), leaving her baby behind in the care of me and Percy.

"Uncle Roland Riley was Mass Percy's uncle by his mother's side. He was one of the most respected members of the family. Nonetheless, it still puzzles me today how he shared the same surname with Percy and Ruby, and they meant to have different fathers."

In that same year, Calvin dropped out of school permanently, months after he went into year four.

Ruby would come around every once in a while to visit, and at length Calvin became the sole baby-sitter, while Mass Percy went to work.

By then the relationship between Percy and Devon had turned pear-shaped. Devon used to spend most of his days on the streets with his friends, but he would sleep at the house sometimes, and occasionally cooked a meal there too, but he always ignored Andrew. Equally, whenever he cooked he would eat the food all by himself, but whenever any of the food was left over, Calvin would have some. On the other hand, when Devon returned to the house he would beat up his brother for taking some of his food. Nonetheless, the beatings were not a problem for Calvin, because by then his belly was full.

Soon after Marika had her baby, Mass Percy got ill, and after he visited a private doctor, he was told that he had ulcers in his stomach. The doctor offered him prescription drugs and advised him to change his lifestyle, but Percy was moving at a fast pace and couldn't slow down.

A few months after Marika went to live at Uncle Roland's house, things went from bad to worse at Carey Village, because Mass Percy was getting sick frequently and was unable to do much work, which meant little money was coming in. In spite of that, most days he got dressed and went to hang out at Anchovy, leaving Calvin alone at home with Andrew; as a result, most of the time Calvin went without food, in order to feed the baby.

As time went by, things got very hard for Calvin, and it became impossible for him to provide food for the baby and himself, while babysitting at the same time. Andrew was also a slow learner, and he was always crying.

Sometimes when Calvin needed a break to play with his friends, he boiled ganja tea and gave Andrew some, which knocked him out for hours. When his nephew finally roused, Calvin would have food prepared for the both of them. Still, while

Andrew was growing up, he suffered from a lot of deficiencies. For example, he found it very hard to release his bowels when he wanted to, and he was always sleeping. His body was also very weak, and he would wet his bed every night. Only when he'd reached the age of about seventeen or so did he manage to overcome his ongoing problems. On the other hand, his sleeping disorder continues.

"I didn't have any intension of hurting my nephew in any way, and I felt ashamed when I looked back on those days, but if I knew then what I know now, I certainly wouldn't have given my nephew ganja tea. Conversely, I was on the battlefield of poverty, therefore I did what I had to do to survive, regardless of how selfish it may seem."

At length, Mass Percy got very sick and was taken to the Cornwall Regional Hospital, where they admitted him on arrival.

After numerous tests were performed on him, they discovered that he was suffering from stomach cancer. After he was operated on, they realised that there was nothing that they could do to save his life, because the cancer had already spread all through his body.

After Percy had been in the hospital for a while, the doctors candidly gave him six months to live and discharged him.

While he was laid up in bed at home, Ruby moved back to the house to look after him.

"I was very happy when Mass Percy came home," Calvin declared, "because I was not allowed to visit him in the hospital. Nonetheless, there was a constant mixture of vibes around the house. There was that horrible feeling of resentment, hatred, regret, revenge, betrayal, and loss, mixed with the smell of sickness and death.

"I knew for a fact that Mama was happy that Mass Percy was no longer able to physically abuse her. I could also see the hatred in Mass Percy's eyes when Mama was helping him, and he always gave her a dirty look when she turned her back. I also knew he was wishing he could beat her up, even on his dying bed."

Uncle Roland and his wife would visit sometimes with food and other stuff for Percy, but every week without fail, Miss Lee, a half Chinese lady, who owned one of the biggest grocery stores at Anchovy, would send bags of groceries to the house for Percy and his family.

It was rumoured at one point that Percy used to have an affair with Miss Lee.

"Miss Lee was one of the kindest people I've ever known," Calvin exclaimed. "While I was growing up, Mama used to tell me that Miss Lee was very fond of me, and she always called me Cheese, because of my complexion.

"When I used to attend Anchovy Primary School, I would go to her shop sometimes, and she always gave me something to eat, but after I got older, I was too embarrassed to go into the shop if I wasn't buying anything. Nonetheless, each time I went there to purchase anything, she would always give me something."

Eventually nature proved the doctors wrong, because three months after Percy got discharged; he got very ill again and was taken back to the hospital, where he died on the eighteenth of July, 1979, and fifty-nine days before his forty-third birthday.

"Even though I was only a young boy, I knew that my dad's death was a complete disaster, in the sense of financial difficulties. I also knew for a fact that things would not be the same again.

"Neither Mama nor Mass Percy had a bank account or any assets. As a result, the funeral arrangements were left to the rest of the relatives.

"Devon and I didn't have any decent clothes at the time to wear on a day-to-day basis, needless to say having any put aside that we could wear to our dad's funeral, but ultimately Uncle Roland and his wife, Aunty Millie, put together and bought us some clothes.

"Thursday, the twenty-fifth of July, 1979, had finally arrived, and everybody was busy preparing for Mass Percy's funeral, which was scheduled to be held that afternoon, yards below Miss Fan's lavatory.

"Many times before I'd seen people preparing for a funeral, but I've never felt such sadness, grief, anger, and loss. I was also frightened, and I felt alone.

"The footpath from our house was cleared, all the way up to Mr Shaw's gate, to allow my dad's body to be transported to the yard where the service was going to be held, because he wasn't a member of any church.

"After I got dressed for the funeral, I went and stood at Miss Dinie's gate, where I waited patiently for my dad's casket, which was being transported by Mother Mira's stepson Junior, in his Ford pickup van, from Madden's Funeral Parlour in Montego Bay.

"As soon as I heard the engine of the van coming over Pan Bottom Hill, my heart started to beat very fast against the wall of my chest, a huge, bitter lump formed in my throat, tears welled up in the back of my eyes, and a fierce flame suddenly ignited in my tummy.

"When the van finally came into view, I felt happy, yet sad. I ran along until it reached Mr Shaw's gate, and I hopped onto it.

"As I sat on top of the casket, I inhaled the freshly sprayed varnish, and without second thought I slid the flap from the glass to steal a look at my dad's solemn face, and although Junior told me to close it, I continued to stare. Finally, I was unable to suppress all the pent-up anger, grief, sadness, and loss, and eventually I hugged up the casket and started to cry until the van reached its destination.

"That night, after the funeral, they held a gathering at the house, which is a ritual that everybody on the island generally does after their loved ones are buried.

"All night long, until daylight, the people who stayed over sang, drank rum, coffee, and tea, and ate corned beef sandwiches and fried fish and bread.

"During the night I asked my grand-uncle Roland and his wife if I could come and live at Mount Salem with them, and they told me yes.

"I was elated, because I knew what alternative was ahead of me, regarding suffering. On the contrary, it appeared as if Papa Beagle, Aunty Ivy, Biran, and Freddy didn't want anything to do with me, Marika, or Devon. The way that they ignored us was proof in itself that something was rather wrong with Ruby, Percy, and us kids.

"It was the first and only time I saw my dad's brothers. I was well excited when I heard that they were coming to the funeral, but I was very disappointed when they didn't greet me. Instead, they acted as if I didn't exist.

"Although Uncle Willy was only living six miles away from Carey Village, he didn't visit Percy while he was sick, and he was also absent from the funeral. It was also declared that Uncle Melvin had purposely refused to attend the funeral.

"Although Mass Percy didn't play the role of a good father, deep down I knew that the result of his death was the beginning of the full struggle in my life, and things would never be the same again. Conversely, his death changed the whole context of my life, because it also gave me the chance to move away from a world that was void where progress was concerned and full of tears, disillusionment, and dishonesty.

"When I looked back, I always considered myself very fortunate, when Uncle and his wife agreed to take me away from my sad world and into another, where the standard of living makes life worth living. I knew from the outset that life at Uncle's house was going to be totally different from the world I had known, but I was prepared to do whatever it took to conform to their way of living."

CHAPTER FIVE

Climbing a Steep Hill

Betrayal is something others do to you;
bitterness is something you do to yourself!

On the morning of Friday, 26 July 1979, Calvin got up very early and prepared himself for the chance of a lifetime: to move to Mount Salem, where he was going to join Marika, at his grand-uncle's house. Gone were the days of babysitting. He was glad to leave all his troubles behind at last.

Ruby had decided to take Andrew to live with her and her boyfriend in Mobay, leaving Devon alone to his own devices at the house.

Mount Salem was a divided community. The main road separated the ghetto from the residential area, but all the residents had three things in common; they travelled in the same taxis, shop at the same shops, and went to the same hospital when they get sick.

Uncle Roland was living at number 10 Crichton's Drive, on the residential side of the district. He and his wife bought the house on the sixth of May, 1968, while they were living in England; the house was initially built as a three-bedroom house with two bathrooms, kitchen, living room, dining room, and veranda. There was also a separate bedroom at the back with its own bathroom.

Shortly after they return to live in Jamaica, they decided to extend the house, by attaching a separate apartment onto one side of it, with two bedrooms, a bathroom, living room, kitchen, and dining room. The veranda was also extended across the front of the house.

"Unlike Mass Percy's house, where no utilities of any kind were installed, Uncle had it all! They also had a four burner gas stove, refrigerator, television and a telephone. It was the first time I saw a telephone, and I was fascinated by it. Each time it rang, I would run to answer it."

Uncle and Auntie were occupying the extended side and they rented out the original section.

It was a dream come true when Calvin arrived at Uncle's house that Friday morning. He couldn't believe he was going to be living in a real house for the first time in his life, with all the features that enabled people to live in peace and comfort.

Living at Uncle's house had always been his fondest dream, from that very first time when his dad took him there, along with Marika, Devon, and Ruby, to celebrate Christmas with Uncle and his wife.

"It was the biggest house that I'd ever been in," Calvin exclaimed joyfully.

"My mouth was constantly agape from the moment I turned up at the gate that Christmas morning, and I was totally mystified by the beauty and the enormity of my uncle's and the other houses around the neighbourhood.

"There was a nessberry tree at the front of the house, and it was laden with ripe berries. In one corner of the garden a big patch of black mint was also growing, and the scent from the fresh mint and ripe nessberries made my belly rumble.

"As we ascended the red, polished concrete steps towards the veranda, my heart started to beat fast, and there were all sorts of things going on inside my belly.

"I subsequently squinted my eyes to create a gleam from the sheen on the glazed veranda floor tiles, when I got to the top of the steps.

"Uncle greeted us and ushered us through the house towards the kitchen, where Aunty was preparing loads of lovely food for Christmas dinner.

"I also observed the lovely design on the carpet and the nice furniture that was placed neatly against the freshly painted walls, and inhaled the fresh, homey smell as I strolled through the house. It was also the first time I'd walked on carpet, and it felt extremely surreal.

"When dinner was served, I admit that it was the best meal I had ever had, and from that day onwards it became my dream to live in Uncle's house.

"The following Independence Day Mass Percy took us there again, and eventually it became a regular routine to celebrate most Independence and Christmas Days with Uncle and Aunty. On the other hand, it was the only good thing I had to look forward to each year. It was also the only time we would get together as a family and celebrate life itself."

*

That Friday morning, after his dad's burial, Calvin gingerly followed his newfound parents up the red, polished concrete steps of 10 Crichton's Drive, with two carrier bags that contained his worldly possessions dangling from his little hands.

Uncle opened the padlocks on the steel gate and entered the veranda with Aunty following closely behind him.

Calvin stood on the top step and looked back awkwardly, not knowing exactly what to do.

After Uncle unlocked the front door, he said to Calvin, "Come on in son. Welcome to your new home," with a passion in his coarse voice.

Aunty stepped past Uncle and entered the house without uttering a single word.

Calvin noticed his grand-aunt-in-law's reaction immediately but shrugged it off and went inside by the command of his uncle.

"The feeling I experienced as I walked through the house that Friday morning was quite the opposite of what I'd experienced on my initial visit. It was such a funny feeling, and it suddenly felt like it was my first time at the house, and I'd felt lonely and afraid. It was similar to being in a dream, at a strange place, and you didn't know how you got there. Overall, the experience was dreamlike, and it frightened me in a way that is hard to explain," Calvin concluded sadly, as tears began to trickle down his cheeks.

However, it didn't take long for him to get settled in his new home after the initial shock.

The joy he felt then showed on his face as he reminisced and declared, "I can still distinctly remember the fresh smell of my grand-uncle's house.

"There was a different smell in each room, and I would often sit on the veranda for long periods and count every single car that went by.

"When I wasn't counting cars, I would walk around the yard counting the windows and the burglar bars that they installed over the windows.

"Breakfast, lunch, and dinner were a must for me, and there was no need to worry about what I was going to eat or where it was coming from, because food was in my grandparents' house in abundance. The food was also good, and my belly was filled to capacity at every mealtime. For once I could have a shower inside a proper bathroom, without having to catch a bucket of water to wash my body at the back of Mass Percy's house. When the rain fell I could walk around the yard for once, without having any fear of the mud covering my little feet.

"At Mount Salem, there was the luxury of a proper toilet inside the house. Toilet paper was available for me to use, and there was no longer any need for me to crouch behind a cluster of bush to have a poo or any need to make do with some bush or stone as toilet paper.

"Inside the house and around the whole yard was clean. My skin and clothes were clean too, even though most of my clothes were handed down. Regardless of that, I felt clean, comfortable, and alive, and it was a damn good feeling. On the whole, it was absolutely the best time in my young life, and I embraced it with a passion."

During Calvin's second day at Mount Salem, Marika returned from Mount Carey. She had stayed behind to help tidy up the place after the funeral and the gathering. At the time she was attending evening classes in downtown Mobay.

In the second week, Aunty decided that they should all go to Carey Village and visit Devon.

That was music to Calvin's ears, because he wanted so much to go back to his old world and show off his new look.

That Sunday evening Aunty cooked rice and peas, brown stew chicken, and pork chops for dinner, and before they left Crichton's Drive, she packed a little basket with a portion of the food for Devon. Then they hired Mr Dove (one of their good friends) to drive them to Mount Carey in his taxi.

The car couldn't get to Mount Carey fast enough for Calvin, because he was dying to see his little friends, but when the car finally reached the district he was suddenly full of mixed feelings, and he could see clearly for the first time how bare and gloomy the place where he had been living all his life must seem to people. Those he passed on the way, that he'd known all his life, also looked out of place and odd, compared to the people he saw around Mobay.

He felt good then, knowing that he was no longer a part of that isolated world, even though everybody was pleased to see him, most of all his little friends.

He wanted so much to play with his friends and tell them about his new life, but he was afraid to get his clothes and shoes dirty.

Devon was hanging out with his friends at the roadside when they entered the district. Calvin noticed the happy look on his face that he was trying to hide when he saw them coming.

That night, before they returned to Mobay, Aunty told Uncle that it wasn't right to leave Devon at the house all by himself. As a result, they made a decision and told him to pack his things and come to Mobay to live with them.

It seemed like a good idea to Calvin, because he was beginning to get lonely at Uncle's house, even though he knew that some beatings were in store for him, because Devon seemed to get pleasure from punishing him.

Two days later, Devon arrived at Mount Salem. Calvin could see that he was having a similar reaction on arriving to Calvin's own, even though Devon was trying very hard not to show it. However, Calvin knew Devon wouldn't last as long as a snowball at that house, because there was no way he was going to endure living the type of life that their grandparents wanted them to live.

From the outset, Devon was a rebellious kid, as Calvin can remember, but his lifestyle was partly fuelled by the upbringing that he'd got, and having two notorious bigger brothers as role models didn't make things any easier. Overall, it appeared as if his outcome in life was expected of him.

He had been Percy's number one enemy. It was plain for everybody to see that Mass Percy hated him with a passion. For that reason, on his dying bed he'd told Devon exactly what James Riley had told him; that he shouldn't take anything that belonged to him, if he should die, but nobody took his wishes seriously. So Devon took some of his clothes anyway.

The atmosphere at the house changed, as soon as Devon arrived at Mount Salem. For instance, there were no rats in the house before he arrived, but suddenly a big one appeared from nowhere.

They set traps in every possibly places for the rat with coconut, bread, and cheese, but the rat just wouldn't take the bait. What really amazed them was that the rat wouldn't touch anything in the entire house. It wasn't scared of anybody either. When it was seen in an open space and anybody made an attempt after it, the rat would just walk away like a person would.

Calvin always stayed clear of the rat, because he didn't want anything to do with any rat; after all was said and done, it wasn't doing him any harm. Nonetheless, before long he got exposed to what his grandparents strongly believed were Percy's ghosts.

"Devon and I used to sleep on a single bed in Uncle's living room. At night the streetlight illuminates the room, thus anybody could easily read a book without having to turn the lights on.

"I used to sleep at the front of the bed, but on that particular night Devon took my space at the front.

"I suddenly woke up at about three o'clock in the morning, but I was comfortable in my warm bed, thus I lay where I was on my back, watching the shadow of a car on the wall of the room as it passed by. Some minutes later I saw a big black bird appeared in the room and it flew straight at my face.

"I was terrified, and I quickly pulled myself out of the bed and screamed out with all the strength that I could muster.

"Uncle and Auntie's room was adjacent to the living room, thus they heard the screaming and rushed in to investigate. No doubt they'd thought I was getting a whipping from Devon.

"I told them what had happened, and although there were no sign of the bird, they confirmed that they too had seen a shadow passing through their room.

"At the time I didn't know what to make out of all that was happening around me, but my grandparents took out their Bible and began to read a psalm. Afterward, at their command, Devon and I knelt down while they prayed.

"At the end of the mini ceremony, Aunty told Devon to pack up all of Percy's clothes and take them back to Carey Village in the morning, and throughout the rest of night I couldn't sleep.

"At daybreak Devon returned Percy's clothes to Carey Village, The rat disappeared, and no unusual event ever occurred again.

*

Aunty and Uncle were very strict, and unselfishly they tried to rearrange Percy children's lives.

Aunty didn't hide the fact that she didn't like Calvin and Marika, and she would blatantly treat Devon better on the whole, because he was just as cunning as she was. Nonetheless, when she was in a good mood, she wouldn't hold back her love and devotion from the three of them.

Uncle on the other hand loved Marika and Calvin very much. He loved Calvin even more, because they resembled each other. Conversely, it was also plain to see that Uncle wasn't really into Devon. Still, every weekend without fail, Uncle always gave him and Marika one dollar each for their pocket money, and Calvin would get fifty cents. It was a gesture that Mass Percy hadn't shown when he was alive.

On Sundays, everybody had to get dressed up and go to the Burchell Memorial Baptist Church, and at mealtimes everybody would take turns to bless the table. Also, every night before they went to bed they would have to pray, and in the mornings everybody would join Aunty and Uncle at their bedside to read the Bible and pray.

On Sunday evenings when they were not at church, they sat down together on the veranda and played a Bible game called Proof.

The kids were not allowed to go on the streets except to go to the shops, church, or wherever their Aunty or Uncle sent them.

For Calvin, the transformation was good in every respect, because the things that his grandparents were teaching them were exceptionally good. Most important, he believed that the path they were leading them on was the way that any child should be led. On the other hand, no one could vouch for Devon, whether he appreciated what Aunty and Uncle were doing for them are not, albeit, Calvin knew deep down that Devon wanted to be in a world of his own.

Uncle Roland was highly respected by everyone in and around the community. He wasn't just an ordinary member in the Burchell Memorial Baptist Church. Uncle was an honourable deacon, who was also the best singer on the church choir and a member of the Brotherhood Group. The late Doctor Reverend Leon Robinson (the Burchell Baptist pastor) used to hold him in high regard for the role that he played in the church and around the community.

*

Although Devon was rated as a good painter, he was also interested in mechanics, and shortly after he arrived at Mount Salem, Aunty and Uncle got him an apprentice job at the Blue

Danube Bus Company – but at the end of August he got turned out of the house.

Apparently the bus company was owned and operated by Aunty and Uncle's church sister and brother, who told them that they were having problems with some of the garage staff regularly using ganja on the premises. They'd also told Uncle and Aunty that they were suspicious of Devon's involvement in that practice. Conversely, Aunty and Uncle were having their own suspicions too, that Devon was smoking weed. Therefore, one evening they decided to search Devon's pockets when he got home from the garage and in the process they found some weed and a knife in his possession, which was against their religion. As a result they turned him out of the house.

Calvin was left grieved and lonely after his brother went. Moreover, it was getting more difficult to communicate with Aunty, if only because he knew she didn't like him. Therefore, a few days after his brother got shown the door, he took it upon himself to run away, back to Carey Village.

"When I arrived at Carey Village, after walking over ten miles from Mount Salem, I found nobody at my dad's house. All of a sudden, the place where I'd once lived seemed lonely and deserted, and it made me shiver deep within my soul.

"Cautiously I opened the door and placed the carrier bag with my clothes inside on the floor, and then hurriedly stepped outside and closed the door behind me.

"Out of the blue, it suddenly felt like I was being watched and it made me very afraid, and without any delay I ran down to Aunty Beck's house to seek refuge. They gave me food and allowed me to sleep there that night."

A few days later, Ruby and Aunty Ivy came and took him back to his grandparents' house at Mount Salem.

Ruby said she did not approve of the idea of him staying at his dad's house all by himself. As for Devon, nobody knew where he was at the time, even though they wouldn't have allowed Calvin to stay at the house with him, because of his continuous bullying. On the other hand, Calvin was really enjoying the few days of freedom that he had with his own little gang of boys. Therefore he wasn't really keen on going back to his grandparents' house. However, it didn't take much persuasion to get him to go back.

Calvin felt embarrassed on his second arrival at 10 Crichton's Drive. Nonetheless, Uncle welcomed him back with open arms, but Aunty suggested that they shouldn't force him to come back if he wanted to be at Carey Village instead.

Uncle told her that the boy was confused and it was their duty to guide him.

Angrily Ruby told Calvin to behave himself and stay with Uncle, because there was nothing at Carey Village for him, and she couldn't afford to look after herself, let alone looking after him too.

While Ruby was saying her piece, a boy around Calvin's age appeared on the veranda from inside Uncle's house.

Proudly Uncle turned to the boy and said, "Paul Boggle, this is my grandnephew Calvin. He will be living here with us from now on."

Calvin felt better instantly.

He and Paul Boggle checked out each other, and in an instant, a bond was formed. Before long they were inseparable friends.

Paul's parents were living at a place called Appleton, in the district of St. Elizabeth, about eighty miles from Montego Bay.

Aunty did business there for many years, and she often allowed some of her friends' children to come and live with her, to enable them to find a better life by way of working or going to school.

Paul was one of such children, and he was attending the Mount Salem All Age School, but he had been on vacation with his family on Calvin's initial arrival.

The following week, after Calvin returned, his grandparents got him enrolled in the Mount Salem All Age School.

"It was one of the happiest times in my life, and at that stage, it seemed like I was finally heading in the right direction.

"At school I fitted in easily, and before long I had a whole heap of friends, both girls and boys. In my class, I was one of the top pupils, because only three girls and two boys were brighter than I. At recess times I could hang around the vendors outside the school, because I could buy some food to eat. On the whole, for once in my life I felt like I was on the inside and not on the outside looking in."

In October 1979, Marika got kicked out of 10 Crichton's Drive. Apparently, she was having an affair with a man Aunty and Uncle did not approve of. So they decided that it would be best for her to go and live the life that she wanted to live.

Calvin felt sad when his sister made her exit, but he had enough distraction at the time that it didn't bother him too much. Nonetheless, the atmosphere around the house changed after Marika left. For one thing, he and Paul were given extra duties around the house and had to wash their own clothes (by hand).

Uncle was working as a sales clerk at Crichton Brother's Hardware Store, downtown Mobay, and he used to leave the house at 7:45 a.m. from Monday through Saturday to work from

8:00 till four o'clock in the evenings, apart from Thursdays and Saturdays when the store closed at one o'clock.

Most evenings Uncle would either go to choir practice at his church or go out visiting the sick, but when he was at home he would sort out his songs, drink beer, rum, and red label wine, and sleep.

Aunty was the boss around the house. Occasionally Uncle would put his foot down when he did not agree with some of her decisions, but most times he would let her have her own way.

Aunty was in charge of collecting the rent from the tenants and sorting out the bills. Also, she was always busy collecting old clothes from all over to sell at jumble sales, and she usually used the money that she made that way to buy food. She turned around and gave the food to the less fortunate church sisters and brothers and to others around the community.

From Monday to Wednesday Aunty would shop, pay the bills, and prepare herself to travel to St. Elizabeth on the train or bus, on Thursday mornings, to sell clothes and food and collect "Partner" money. Then she returned on Friday nights.

The "Partner" was her favourite hobby; she spent most of her life doing it, because she got the chance to handle a lot of money and helped a lot of people in the process.

A "Partner" is a form of banking system, which the poor and a lot of small business people on the island, depended on to give them financial stability and keep their heads above water. Many of them managed to give their children proper schooling and built their homes with the help of this form of banking system.

The system required one trustworthy person to be the banker, and the banker's only tool was a book where he or she would jot down the names of the people who joined the "Partner".

The number of people who joined a "Partner" could range from five to fifty or more.

Everybody in the "Partner" was required to pay the same amount of money each week, which could be fifty or a hundred dollars, for an example.

The sum of money is called a "Hand". However, any one member could have more than one "Hand" if he or she could afford to pay it.

When an individual couldn't afford to pay the full "Hand", two people usually got together and shared one.

The length of time the "Partner" lasted depended on how many people joined it.

Each week, one person would get a draw, which consisted of everybody's money that had been paid to the banker for that week. If two people shared a "Hand", the draw was shared between them.

Everybody who got their draw was required to continue paying every week until the last person got his or her draw.

The names of the members were placed in the banker's book in no particular order, so the banker could give anybody a draw, if he or she wished to do so.

The banker sometimes got one week's money from every individual, when they collected their draw, but that was left to the compassion of the individual.

The "Partner" that Aunty ran was really big, because it was mostly businesspeople and taxi drivers who joined it.

During those Thursdays and Fridays while Aunty was away, Paul Boggle, Uncle, and Calvin used to have their own way behind her back. Paul and Calvin would regularly turn the whole of Mount Salem and Mobay upside down, while Uncle cheated on his wife.

Most Thursdays, one of Uncle's church sisters or Auntie's dressmaker would visit him at the house after he got off work. Sometimes he would share his lunch – which Aunty prepared for him before she went away – with his church sister. Other times they would only have a drink, and later he would lead the woman into the matrimonial room and remain there with her until late afternoon.

At times Calvin and Paul would hang out in the front yard until Uncle and the women resurfaced. The women used to smile at them on their way out, while Uncle sat on the veranda rubbing his fat belly. The tenants also knew about Uncle's infidelity, but nobody told Aunty about it.

One day Paul Boggle and Calvin were sitting in the garage at 10 Crichton's Drive, wishing for things that they would like to have, such as a football, boots, and socks. Out of the blue, Paul suggested that they should steal some of Auntie's money from her chest of drawers. It was a suggestion that changed every aspect of Calvin's life.

At the time football (soccer) was the leading trend on the island, and most youths, both young and old, were crazy about it. Everywhere you could see the game being played, even on the streets.

About a quarter of an acre of land was situated across the road from Uncle's house, and almost every day, the youths from the ghetto side of the district would play football on it.

By then Paul Boggle and Calvin had managed to form their own little gang. Sometimes they also played football on the field opposite the house, when the youths from the ghetto weren't playing, and at night when the streetlights came on, they also played on the street in front of the house.

The least chance they got at school they would also play football. It was even more fun at school, because they had the big fields to play on.

Calvin was happy playing the game barefooted or occasionally in the one pair of shoes that he owned, which he'd grown accustomed to from when he was living at Carey Village.

Paul Boggle was very good at football, and he wanted to play the game in style. Calvin on the other hand spent the entirety of his life wishing for things that neither he nor his parents could afford. Thus the idea of seeing some of his wishes granted seemed like a dream come true. After all, he was fresh out of the country, and he wanted so much to explore and indulge. As a result of Calvin's eagerness to experience new things, when Paul suggested that they steal his aunt's money he said, "Yes," without thinking about the after-effects.

Now many youths got caught up like Calvin did, but one should always think about the after-effect and the consequences before making a decision, because you cannot undo what already has been done.

Many years later, Calvin unravelled the obnoxious plot behind the proposed scam. He believed Paul Boggle lured him in on the plan mainly because he had staged such robberies for a long time, but because Calvin was around, it would be impossible for Paul to continue, which left him with only one alternative and that was to get Calvin to do it too.

On the whole, although Aunty was very cautious and methodical, it was easy for the boys to steal from her without her knowing.

Basically, she stored all her money in the top drawer of her chest of drawers, (bureau) and in a separate bag she would put each individual account's money.

Most of the money in the drawer was stocked into bundles of a thousand dollars, and whenever she made a mistake and put down her bunch of keys, the boys would rob her. She could always put her purse anywhere she pleased, because they wouldn't take any money from it, even though it was always full of money.

In the beginning, whenever the boys were stealing from the drawer, one of them would watch while the other stealthily went in for the kill, but it reached a stage when Calvin didn't need any watchman, and he felt safer working on his own than with Paul watching.

Each time he went to take some money from the drawer, he would slip out a hundred-dollar bill from two or three of the bundles, which was the biggest banknote in Jamaica at the time. He would also dip into the bag where Aunty kept the Partner money and the bag that she would take with her to St. Elizabeth.

"I still have a vivid memory of the distinctive smell that came from the drawer each time I opened it," he declared.

Ultimately, he and Paul began to live it up large among their friends at school. Paul had his own gang, and Calvin had his.

They bought the best football boots and socks, and they each had a football at all times, but they had to ask their friends to keep the football boots at their houses, because they could always tell Aunty and Uncle that they borrowed the football, but there was no explaining the boots.

At school, Calvin became a king. He was able to buy lunch for the girl that he fancied in his class, and he could also buy anything he wanted to eat, but his reign did not last very long.

After months of stealing his grandparents' money and living the life of Riley with Paul Boggle, guilt took over, and Calvin finally got tired of it and sometimes felt lonely and empty. All of a sudden he didn't want to live that kind of life anymore, and at length he felt like he was being stifled, because the guilt was ever present and left him feeling as if he had a heavy load on his head constantly.

One Monday morning in March 1980, he was at home confused and lonely, while Paul was at school and Aunty was in her bed sleeping. He decided to have a little Monday morning treat, so he went to the shop and bought himself a big tub of Napoleon ice cream.

After he went back to the house, he sat in the garage and tried to consume the whole box of ice cream, but it was impossible for him to eat it all. Besides, his heart wasn't in it anymore. Finally, to obliterate the surging feeling of guilt and loneliness that he was experiencing, he took that opportunity, packed his things, and fled the scene, back to his dad's house, leaving behind his new friends, the easy money, and the life of luxury that he loved and hated at the same time.

By then Ruby had returned to live at Mass Percy's house with Marika, Andrew, and Devon, and they were shocked when Calvin turned up at the house with his bags that day.

He told them half the truth when they asked him what had happened.

He told them that he was lonely and so he ran away, but the following Sunday, Uncle Roland, Aunty Millie, and Paul Boggle turned up at Percy's house.

When Calvin saw them coming down the footpath his initial thought was that they were there to take him back to Mount Salem, but a big surprise was in store for him.

Also present were Ruby, Marika, Andrew and Devon. The neighbours were there too, just like when Percy used to beat Ruby.

Calvin noticed that Aunty and Uncle weren't smiling when they got closer to the house, and from experience, he knew, by the look on his grandparents' faces, that something was terribly wrong. He braced himself for what was to come.

Aunty was the first to speak.

"Weh mi money deh wah yuh teef from out a mi draw?" Aunty barked at him angrily.

Translation: "Where is my money that you have stolen from out of my drawer?"

Before Calvin could respond, Aunty continued, "Paul Boggle tell we seh you tell him seh you a guh teef mi money and bring it to yuh ma, becah she naah work," Aunty concluded.

Translation: "Paul told us that you told him that you were going to steal our money and bring it to your mother, because she wasn't working."

The place suddenly went silent after Aunty completed her opening remarks. It was a kind of silence one could hear and touch; the type that made you wants to run and hide.

Uncle broke the silence and spoke, with a soft but harsh tone in his voice. "I did not expect this from you, Calvin. Look on all that my wife and I did for all of you, and now you turned around and threw it right back into our faces."

Calvin started to defend himself by saying that he didn't take any money when he was leaving the house. He also told them that he'd only decided to run away because he wanted to be with his family.

Aunty got very angry at that point and started to cursed Ruby and the others too, even swearing at Calvin (even though Christians were not supposed to swear).

Uncle told her that the swearing wasn't necessary, but Aunty was in a rage. She had blood in her eye and vengeance in her heart; thus she continued with her onslaught.

Without any warning, Aunty marched into the house and began to gather up all of Calvin's clothes.

Calvin tried to stop her, and Uncle tried to hold him while undoing his belt from around his waist, but Calvin wasn't having any of it and ran away from his uncle's grasp.

While Aunty continued to hurl her obnoxious abuses at them, Ruby didn't say a single word.

The neighbours were watching the drama in amazement, because it was unlike Ruby to keep quiet when there was a verbal battle going on, because she had a tongue that spit fire.

Calvin was really mad with Paul for betraying him to his grandparents and telling such dreadful lies about his mother, because at the time nobody knew he was going to run away. He also felt embarrassed about the whole situation, and it made him very angry.

Uncle made another attempt to grab him, but he slipped away from his uncle's grasp and tried to take a knife from Devon, who was sitting nearby. However, Devon stopped him from getting hold of the knife, and Ruby tried to hold him, but Calvin ran away and went to lie on Mass Percy's grave. There he cried tears of hate, sorrow, pain, and anger.

On the whole, Calvin was angry with Uncle, because he didn't want to come to terms with the fact that Aunty didn't like his family and that she would have done anything to humiliate them.

Before they went back to Mount Salem, Aunty made sure that Calvin didn't have many clothes to wear, apart from a few pieces of rags.

After Aunty, Paul, and Uncle went away, Calvin saw his mother cry for the first time without being beaten by Mass Percy, but at the time, he didn't know what to make of the crocodile tears she was shedding. However, during the night when he started to reminisce about his dad, his life at Uncle's house, and where he was again (at the beginning where he first started), he realised then why his mother was so upset.

Eventually, he concluded that his mother was too embarrassed to respond to Auntie's obnoxious abuses earlier, because the whole story seemed real, beginning with the mere fact that she wasn't working at the time. He could also fathom the pain and humiliation that she felt, and he could imagine the jumbled thoughts running through her mind, because she was unable to provide for her children and give them direction that she herself didn't have.

He also realised that he would have to start making some serious plans for his own life, but like his mama, he didn't know where to start. All he could do was dream about where he would like to be and the kind of life that he would like to live, but making his dreams into reality was far, far away.

CHAPTER SIX

The Turning Point

Calvin was happy to be back with his family, although the living conditions were nothing compared to what he gave up at Mount Salem.

Ruby wasn't working, but it wasn't really a big issue, because she didn't have to worry about Devon or Marika. Calvin wasn't a big problem to her either, because by then he knew exactly how to fend for himself, but she always gave him whatever she could to make life easier for him.

Ruby would also help Marika with Andrew, who wasn't getting any support from his father.

Back then, Ruby used to have a lot of men friends, and frequently she would visit them; on her return, she would have money and food. Nobody used to question her actions, but later in life Calvin put all the pieces together.

When he looked back on the whole scope of things, he couldn't find any reason to blame her for doing what she had to do to survive. After all, she wasn't alone, because single women all over the world find themselves in similar situations, without much prospect of putting one foot in front of the other. Thus they do what they must to survive, regardless of the circumstances.

At length things got really hard for Ruby, and she could no longer afford to buy clothes for herself, let alone for Calvin. Sometimes she would take Calvin with her to visit families and they used to give her yams, bananas, and breadfruits.

One day Ruby decided to visit Uncle Willy at Bakers Stet, and she tugged Calvin along.

Calvin used to hear stories about his uncle Willy, but he didn't get the chance to meet him, even though he was only living six miles away. Nonetheless, he always visualised him as a rich man, on account of what Ruby had told him.

She'd once told him that his uncle had a lot of money, but because he was so selfish he buried it. How she knew that still baffles Calvin. She'd also told him that Willy's father had left him two big concrete houses, which he rented out, as well as another property and a house some distance away.

That day, Ruby and her son walked the six miles to Bakers Stet, but Calvin was disappointed on their arrival, and all the enthusiasm went out the door when he met his uncle. He was also afraid to go near him.

Uncle Willy was a short, stocky, dark brown–complexion man with a bald head. He was living in a little old board house on his property, surrounded by a lot of bushes. There were lots of oranges, bananas, mangoes, coconuts, breadfruit, cedar, and mahogany trees on the land. He would sit on his veranda most of the time and make clothes, as he was a tailor.

He was about to have his lunch when Calvin and his mum arrived, and he offered his nephew a piece of roast breadfruit with a piece of roast salted mackerel, but Calvin didn't accept it.

Instead, he told his uncle that he wasn't hungry, even though he was quite hungry.

While Ruby was speaking to Willy, Calvin went outside and sat on a stone, because he couldn't stomach the foul smell that was coming from his uncle's mouth and the house.

When he saw what Calvin did, he said to him, "Son, never sit on a cold stone; it is best to sit on a cold piece of iron, because it will draw cold from your body, but you will only catch a cold from a cold stone."

Those are the only words Calvin can remember hearing from his uncle's lips. Nonetheless, he learnt a lesson from those few spoken words.

Before Calvin and his mum left, Willy gave them some oranges, breadfruits, and bananas.

Calvin never returned. That was the first and last time he beheld his uncle.

*

In due course Marika got pregnant with her second child. Her boyfriend Budget was living at Mount Carey; as a result, she moved in with him.

Budget was born and grew up in Mount Carey. He was from a big family and had many brothers and sisters. He also had a few other children from different relationships. His youngest son, Rowan (Kaka Waller), came to live with him and Marika after a while. Andrew would also stay with them sometimes, but he spent more time with Ruby, who took care of him more often.

As for Devon, he was out most of the time doing his own thing, which he had grown accustomed to by then.

Daytimes, Calvin would run around the whole community making mischief and securing what little food he could and money to gamble with the rest of boys.

In September 1980, Ruby tried to get him enrolled in the Anchovy Secondary School, although normally the students were transferred there from the primary schools. His last school was at the Mount Salem All Age School, and it was his choice when he walked away. As a result, the family were told that there was no vacancy, and Ruby didn't bother to try anywhere else.

Deep down Calvin knew that his school days were over, and although he'd just turned twelve years old, he also knew that his future was resting in his own hands.

Ruby would offer him a little food when she could afford to, but most of the time he was left to his own devices. To him, it was cool to have the freedom to do whatever he wanted to do.

At that time, he couldn't purchase many things from the shops, even if he had money, but he wasn't alone, because most people on the island were in the same position. They were all experiencing the vile, chaotic changes on a day-to-day basis, with the bloodiest election of all time in progress.

Previously, it'd got more intense in January 1980, when the then prime minister, Michael Manley, leader of the People's National Party (PNP) announced that 11,000 public sector jobs would have to be cut to facilitate the $500 million budget. However, not long after that statement, 300 public sector workers went on strike, leaving 70 per cent of the island without electricity, which continued regularly, without warning, throughout the year.

That action was the beginning of a string of sabotages on the island, and each political leader was blaming the others for the instability, which only made the economic situation worse.

During that time, flour, rice, salt, sugar, milk, bread, cooking oil, matches, kerosene oil, and soap, just to name a few, were in short supply. As a result, the shopkeepers would bundle those essential items in the shops. As an example, to purchase a bar of soap, people would have to buy a number of other items that they didn't need, before they could get it. Partly as a result, cornmeal (polenta) became one of the main sources of food for many people, when no yams or breadfruits were available.

Calvin and his family regularly used warm water to bind the cornmeal together and then made dumplings out of it. Other times they would make turn cornmeal.

To prepare the turn cornmeal, they would put coconut milk in a pot and pour the cornmeal into it, with onions, peppers, and thyme, and then continually mix it until the cornmeal was cooked.

It was a healthy meal, but consumed too often, it was likely to lead to bad indigestion.

Meanwhile, Prime Minister Michael Manley came under immense pressure, from the opposition leader, Edward Seaga, of the Jamaica Labour Party (JLP). Ultimately, it was almost certain that the prime minister would be forced to call an early election that year.

In February 1980, Prime Minister Michael Manley announced that elections would be held later in the year. In the months that followed, the political hostility that sparked inner-city violence throughout the 1970s spilled over into 1980.

In his speech in Barbados, in March 1980, Michael Manley blamed the JLP for using economic destabilisation as a tactic to win the voters over. On the other hand, the PNP party was slowly falling apart, because earlier, senior members David Coore and Vivian Blake had resigned, and two weeks after Manley's speech in Barbados, Finance Minister Eric Bell also called it a day. Nonetheless, Manley was adamant that he could resolve the situation, because he was always highly popular amongst the Jamaican people.

Meanwhile, the mood in the JLP camp was strong, and they had high motivation, which was reflected in their campaign slogan, "Deliverance Is Near". Moreover, at the beginning of 1980, the polls showed the JLP were in the lead.

In April 1980, five people were killed in what became known as the Gold Street Massacre, in Central Kingston. In that same month, the Hannah Town Police Station, in West Kingston, was attacked, which resulted in the death of two people, including a policeman.

Suddenly, the People's National Party (PNP) and the Jamaica National Party (JLP) were engaged in a bitter ideological war, which spilled over to the streets and got very ugly.

A strict colour code was implemented. The PNP's colours were red, orange, and black, while the JLP supporters wore green and white.

Anybody who got caught wearing a specified colour in the opposition's zone would most likely be beaten up or killed. Conversely, activists would sometimes confront people, even when they weren't wearing the specified colour, and ask them to declare what side they were on.

The best answer one could give was to say that they were neutral.

As a result, many people began to sell their homes for next to nothing and migrate to other countries to find a safe haven. Some moved away, leaving their homes behind.

Going into Election Day, there were several tragic incidents.

Manley's motorcade was fired on in May Pen. Roy McGann, the PNP's candidate for East Rural St. Andrew, and his bodyguard, acting Corporal Errol White, were killed in Gordon Town. Gunmen also killed seven people on National Heroes Day, in Kingston. Two children were also killed in Top Hill, St. Elizabeth, where the JLP and PNP group clashed. Twelve members of the Workers Party of Jamaica, including Lambert Brown, were arrested in Lucea, Hanover, for possession of bombs.

The police on the other hand were often outgunned by criminal gangs from both political parties, and they were at a distinct disadvantage, because the weapons they had were inferior to the weapons with which they were often attacked. M16 assault rifles were introduced to the police, and the locals soon dubbed it "Wahdat", because it was the first time most of them had heard such a powerful weapon being fired.

Overall, close to one thousand people were killed in the prolonged election run-up period.

On the evening of 5 October 1980, Michael Manley announced the date for election at Sam Sharpe Square, in Montego Bay, in front of a massive crowd. The date was set for the thirtieth of October, that same month.

It inspired a fiery Manley to predict victory with his famous declaration that "50,000 strong can't be wrong."

On the Election Day, the Jamaica Labour Party, led by Edward Seaga, whipped the PNP fifty-one seats to nine, the biggest margin of victory in elections since Jamaica gained independence from Great Britain in 1962 and ending the chaotic eight-year term for Michael Manley, the island's fourth prime minister.

The JLP victory was welcomed island-wide, with many people participating in the daylong celebration. Many schools and places of business also remained closed.

Not only were there celebrations amongst the middle-class citizens, who had feared a Communist takeover, due to Manley's socialist leanings. The poor, many of whom benefited from the PNP's grassroots programmes, had also voted against Manley, who came into power in late 1972, with a mandate to elevate the island's impoverished masses.

Manley, who came into power as champion of the poor, was a beaten man. In his concession speech, he declared that his decision to stand by Cuba and other Third World countries, which were not popular with the United States government, proved his government's downfall. In his own words he exclaimed: "Maybe what I did wrong was to challenge the power of the western economic structure, and for this I will remain unrepentant and unreconstructed."

Two days after the election, Edward Seaga was sworn in as the fifth prime minister of Jamaica. Within days, he expelled the Cuban ambassador to Jamaica, Ulises Estrada, severing ties with that country, and attempted to rebuild Jamaica's ties with the United States of America.

On the other hand, the violence that had escalated during the election period continued, signalling the birth of a violent nation ruled by a corrupt government, members of the judiciary, and the police force.

CHAPTER SEVEN

A Traumatic Experience

It reached a point when Ruby would regularly join some of her heavy rum drinker, female cousins in Mount Carey, to party the nights away, and she would sometimes tug Calvin along with her too.

Calvin didn't have a problem with that, because he would get money from his mum's friends or from some of his dad's old friends, to buy soft drinks and play the jukebox. The only problem was when he wanted to sleep, and Ruby was just ready to drink rum and dance with her male friends.

One particular night, one of Ruby's male friends accompanied them home, and on their arrival at the house, Calvin went straight to bed, because he was exhausted, leaving his mama and her friend outside talking.

During the night he was roused out of his sleep by the sudden shaking of the bed. Even though he was just over twelve years old, he knew exactly what was going on, which was enough to traumatise and rivet him to the spot.

While Ruby and her man were having sex beside him, his little heart kept pounding in his chest, and he was also afraid that they might find out that he was aware of what they were doing. At the same time, he was vexed with his mama, because she had no respect for him. Conversely, it would have been better if they did what they were doing and went away, but when the shaking stopped Ruby asked the man, "Yuh enjoy it?"

"Yeah," the man replied.

Ruby giggled and asked him again, "Yuh want more?" but suddenly Calvin coughed and turned in the bed, and at that point they must have come to their senses and realised what they were doing, because they both got up and went outside.

For the rest of the night Calvin couldn't sleep but lay awake and prayed for morning to come.

At daybreak he got up and took his slingshot and left the yard.

He went to Carl's yard to see what he had planned for the day, but on his arrival he saw Carl in the middle of his morning chores, therefore he whistled for Carl to know that he was around. Carl's grandparents wouldn't have let him out of their sight if they knew Calvin was around.

After Carl completed his chores, they both went off to hunt the early morning birds.

Calvin wanted so much to tell Carl what he had experienced during the previous night, but he couldn't divulge such a story to him, Monkey, or anybody else for that matter, because he knew they would only laugh at him. Therefore, he carried that burden with him until he was in his twenties before he could divulge it to Marika and Budget, who are still his closest friends in his family.

From that night, his respect for Ruby began to deteriorate, even though he has never really disrespected her in any way. Nonetheless, he could no longer look her in the eyes anymore, and he didn't want to be around her as he had before.

Ruby's reaction was the complete opposite, because she continued to treat Calvin as if nothing had happened, or maybe she thought what she had done was a normal thing to do. Maybe she was drunk and had no recollection of what she had done. In any case, Calvin continued to live with those bad memories, which left him feeling insecure and confused, for many years. On the whole, it remained a central point in his life, in respect of how he saw himself. Deep in his heart he felt as if he was the one to be blame and not his mum. Frequently he would tell himself that he shouldn't have been in the bed that night, because he was only invading his mother's privacy. Regardless of that, as he got older and wiser, he forgave her for her ignorance, even though that night had changed his life completely.

On the whole, he knew his mum was a good woman, because she was more honest than a lot of other parents around, who often turned their noses up at Ruby and her children. He could vouch for her any day, because she was the type of mother who would turn her own children over to the police – unlike many parents he knew, who would cover up for their children when they went out and stole things and then brought them home.

If he or Devon should bring anything into the yard, Ruby would demand to know where it came from, and if she didn't get a positive answer she would shout very loud for them to take it back to wherever it came from. Sometimes a few good licks encouraged them to move faster.

The following is only an example of how seriously Ruby took dishonesty.

One day Calvin was roaming around the community, and ended up a few miles away from his house. At one point he spotted a hopping dick bird in a tree and threw a stone at it. The stone caught the bird and it fell in some bushes and he picked it up.

The bird was partially alive, thus he tied a string on its leg and brought it along as he began to wander again, and suddenly he came in view of a house where they had converted one room into a shop. Some younger children were playing in the yard, and he stopped and joined them.

He enquired about their parents' whereabouts and realised that the children were all alone. By then the bird had died, so he gave it to the kids and told them to take it around the back of the house and clean it up.

Back then, it was fun for most kids in Jamaica to roast a bird, and they were very excited. However, he didn't follow them; instead he went inside the shop and took a pint of Cremo full cream milk from out of the fridge. He'd also noticed a tray under the counter with about eight fifty-cent coins on it. He took one coin, slipped it in his pocket, and headed for the gate, but as he stepped through the gate, the woman who owned the shop was just coming home in time to see him leaving with the milk.

"Hey Ruby bwoy, you pay fi dat?" she asked.

Calvin told her yes he had, and the kids put the money under the counter, but he didn't hesitate. Instead, he headed for the train line at a run.

When he was some distance away, he stopped running, opened the milk, and began to drink. Later, though, when he reached home, he wished he hadn't gone roving that day.

Unbeknownst to him, the woman found out what he had done and went to his house, where she complains to Ruby.

While he was on his way home, Ruby secured three good-sized sticks and a piece of electrical cable and put them underneath the bed. When he got home, she called him inside the room and locked the door.

It was the first time Ruby beat him so badly.

When all the sticks got broken up on him she pulled out the piece of electrical cable and continued to unleash her anger on him. However, at one point, he held on to the cable and wouldn't let it go, because by then he was aching all over, and blood was dripping from his body.

There was a big wooden carving of a man's head hanging on the wall, and Ruby took it down and hit him with it over his head, knocking him to the floor. At the same time, she tried to yank the cable from his grip, but he held on firmly, because the licks from it were more excruciating.

Some of the floor tiles at the bedside were sinking, exposing the sharp edges of other tiles. In the uproar, one of his heels was resting on a sharp edge. Ruby stepped on his foot and ground it till the skin tore from his heel and began to bleed. Then she went outside, leaving him soaking in blood and tears.

He lay where his mother left him and cried until his tears dried up, and after a while he pulled himself up and went outside.

Later Ruby offered him a plate of food, which he gladly accepted.

"On the whole, I was vexed for the way Mama beat me up badly, but on the contrary I wasn't mad with her, because I knew a sound beating was inevitable when I went out of place."

As time went by Calvin became very angry with himself and everybody around him. By then he was disheartened, and he didn't want to be around his family and friends as much as before. He also developed the attitude that life was meaningless, and he would often go out of his way to pick a fight, mostly with the older youths, who beat him up most times, but he didn't care, because he only wanted to feel pain.

He and Devon regularly fought as well, because when his brother wasn't bullying him they would have a disagreement about something, which ended up in a fight.

The house they lived in got punished in the process, because most times Devon would hit him and then run inside the house and lock the door. To unleash his anger, Calvin would throw stones at the door, through the windows, and against the zinc housetop.

One day in particular, they were fighting for about an hour nonstop. They were both covered in blood from the cuts that they inflicted on each other in the process. At one point, Devon slashed Calvin dangerously at his left side with a knife. Instinctively Calvin reacted swiftly and disarmed his brother, who then ran inside the house to take cover. But just as he closed the door, Calvin threw a big stone exactly where he knew Devon's head would be behind the plywood door. Suddenly, the door reopened, and Devon stepped outside with his face covered in blood.

Even though Calvin was badly wounded, he felt sorry for him, so he threw down the remaining stones he was holding and walked away. A very big mistake!

While he was walking away, Devon came up from behind and used a piece of firewood to hit him on the head and knocked him out right on the footpath in front of the house.

When Calvin finally regained consciousness, he initially felt like a different person, but all of a sudden, the buried pains stored up in his brain were brought back to life, and he started to cry. Then he struggled to his feet but fell at once back to the ground, too weak to stand. He didn't bother to try getting up again; he merely lay on the ground and cried for dear life. At length, he heard a voice saying, "Get up and take the piece of rope that you have hidden behind the house and hang yourself." He was startled and looked around to see who was speaking to him, but there was no one in sight. The voice seemed to have transformed and revitalised him, and instantly he obeyed and got up with little struggle. There was only the pounding pain on his head where his brother had hit him. He touched the spot with his fingers and felt the moisture of blood and a big lump, but he ignored it and continued to follow the instruction of the voice. He ran to where he'd hidden the piece of rope, which he'd stolen from a farmer.

Still in a daze, he picked up the rope and began to make the slip knot that he was going to put around his neck, whilst walking towards the big breadfruit tree at the footpath, some ten yards from the remains of Miss Fan's house.

Unfortunately there was nobody around that day. It was one of those afternoons when the sun sat in the middle of the blue sky in all its glory, glowing down on the beautiful land of Jamaica.

When he reached the foot of the breadfruit tree, he placed the slip around his neck and proceeded up the tree.

There was an old, dried, broken-off limb about twelve feet above the ground, and the first green limb was about five feet above the dried limb. He stood on the old limb and began to tie the other end of the rope around the green limb, but what happened after that caused him to stop what he was about to do.

Abruptly there was a flash of lightning and a thunderclap; then a shower of rain began to fall. It felt as if he'd been sleeping during the time he was preparing to hang himself, because he suddenly realised what he was doing and scrambled down from the tree.

"The confirmation of what had happened appeared after some days, when the breadfruit leaves on the limb from which I was going to hang myself began to fade and eventually fell off weeks later.

"The limb was partly shaded by another breadfruit tree, on the opposite side of the footpath; therefore, everybody was shocked when they saw the leaves on the limb began to dry up.

"I was in my twenties when I told Marika and Budget what had happened to the breadfruit limb, and Marika cried when I told her.

"The rest of the breadfruit tree continued to yield fruit for many years after, but the tribulation that I was facing continued.

CHAPTER EIGHT

Trying to find the way

Calvin had just turn thirteen years old, but it seemed as though he had lived most of his life before he became a teenager. With the passage of time, he would sometimes remember his lost sorrows, his beliefs, the love that he did not get as a child, and the absent pleasure of growing up in a good home with his brothers, sisters, mother and father.

Unlike the way one remembered the aura of a pleasant dream without recalling a single detail or image, he could always remember every single detail and the images of all the suffering, humiliation, deception, and brutality that he'd experienced from childhood.

After a while Ruby met another man and moved in with him, but she regularly visited Carey Village and gave Calvin whatever she could. During that time he was like loose cannon, and his daily routine was to survive by any means necessary.

Halfway down Pan Bottom Hill, on top of a hillside, some seventy yards or so below Mr Smith's and Miss Heffy's house lived Mr Street and his wife, Miss Liddy, with their eight children, in a four-bedroom semi-concrete house. Below Mr Street's house, at the roadside, Moth, one of his sons, decided to build a ten-by-ten-foot grocery shop out of bamboo. At length, the bamboo shop became the front line in the village, and most days both young and old men alike would converge in front of the shop to gamble. It was also cool on the hill during the hot days, with the huge fruit trees towering over the road from either side.

Miss Liddy used to bake coconut tooto (a Jamaican cake), coconut drops, and coconut grater cake and sell them in the shop.

Regularly Calvin would steal dried coconuts and sell them to Miss Liddy; then he would gamble with the money.

During the days there was a lot of traffic in both directions on Pan Bottom Hill, more by pedestrians than in cars.

Many times Calvin would sit on the hill and watch everybody and everything, and even though he was only a young lad, most people who passed him by knew him as Ruby's and Percy's bwoy.

A lot of outsiders, who came from as far away as America, Canada, England, and Australia, to name a few places, also travelled on the road during weekdays. Their destination was Mother Mira's yard (the local bush doctor) that used to predict their future and give them various types of bushes to boil and use for medicine, as well as manufactured oils and charms, for a fee. She would also dress cuts and wounds for the locals.

Mother Mira wasn't one of those ordinary bush doctors (obeah worker, or black magic, or voodoo practitioners) who invoked evil. She was what they would call a healer.

Before she started to work each day, she conducted a service in her church that was only footsteps away from the front door of her house.

The practice of obeah is associated with the folk religion of the African Diaspora, which is called the Revivalist Zionist or Poco Church in Jamaica.

This practice went to Jamaica with the slaves, who were taken from a variety of African nations, with differing spiritual practices and religions. It is mostly referred to as black magic, voodoo, or hoodoo, but in the West Indies the people called it obeah.

Those who practiced this act in Jamaica normally attached *father* or *mother* to their names, but the locals simply referred to them as *Obeah Man* or *Obeah Woman*. Although many people on the island were strictly against the use of obeah, there were many who pretended to be against it but indulged in it covertly. On the whole, there have been many visible proofs of what obeah working can do to mankind. It wasn't illegal to participate in such an act on the island, and over the years it remained a vital form of folk magic. In addition, many people believed they had gained wealth and other benefits by using obeah. On the other hand, it was rumoured that the participants in obeah had to make a sacrifice in order to gain their heart's desire. Such sacrifices might often be the life of a loved one, whether by death or the loved one ending up with a mental disorder.

Mother Mira and her family were considered the richest people in the community of Carey Village, and a considerable number of the locals also attended her church. Her only son, Dooba, fell victim to one of the most gruesome car accidents in Mount Carey, where the car tumbled nearly fifty yards down a steep gully. He survived, but ultimately they had to cut off one of his legs, and eventually he ended up half mentally ill.

Calvin frequently hung out on Pan Bottom Hill and begs money from some of the people who came to visit Mother Mira. But at times, while he was hanging out on the hill, his heart would bleed when he saw the other children going or coming from school. Sometimes he would stay off the road until all the schoolchildren were at home.

At that point his life was at a standstill. Nobody was making any effort to point him in the right direction, and he didn't know where or towards whom to turn for assistance. Every day he would wake up to the same thing: being at anybody's disposal to cut his or her lawn or go to the shops, to scrounge a few dollars for his pocket to gamble and buy a decent meal. In the process, he would be on the lookout for anything worthwhile to steal.

Back then, the drinks bottles for the biggest brewery on the island, Desnoes & Geddes (D&G, makers of the renowned Red Stripe beer), were valuable, and people used to collect them and exchange them for money.

Regularly Calvin would walk the streets and search the waysides for those empty bottles, which people would sometimes throw out of cars.

One day, he and Monkey were searching for D&G bottles, while walking the five-mile journey from the sea, where they'd gone to catch fish. Suddenly a passenger bus drove by, and someone threw a disposable lunch box out the bus window. The box fell on the road with a thud, and the lid flipped open – exposing the remains of rice and peas and chicken skin and bones.

Both boys were quite hungry. Their lips were dry, and they couldn't summon the saliva to moisten them. Immediately both of them ran their tongues over cracked lips, gave each other a questioning look, and wordlessly moved towards the lunch box. Monkey picked it up, and together they devoured the remains of the lunch and every single bone. From that day onward, each time Calvin went in search of D&G bottles, he would also be on the lookout for discarded lunch boxes.

Ultimately, he got fed up with his daily routine. One day, therefore, he boldly got up, went back to his grand-uncle's house, and begged them to take him back. Miraculously they did so.

Paul Boggle was no longer living there, and the only other people living at the house were the tenants. Aunty and Uncle didn't mention the reason Paul Boggle was no longer living there, but Calvin came to his own conclusion; they must have eventually caught him stealing their money. Also, they didn't issue him any warning about what had happened the last time he was living with them, and over the years that followed, he never once stole from them again. Nonetheless, the memories of what had happened were still vivid.

Uncle wanted Calvin to go back to school, but Aunty told him that it would be best for him to get the boy a job at the hardware store instead. Uncle was a bit reluctant, but eventually he did what Aunty had suggested.

At the time Calvin didn't know what was best for him, because his life was at a dead end, and he was desperate, so anything they told him to do he would have done gladly. Fortunately a vacancy was available at the store, and with the respect that the owners had for his uncle, he got the job.

The following Monday morning Calvin woke up early and prepared himself for his first job, and with packed lunches in their hands, he and his uncle set off for work, looking like father and son.

"I felt very proud that morning, and as we walked toward the main road, to get a taxi, I deliberately copied my uncle's gait, with pride.

"When we got to the hardware store, I was taken aback by the enormity of it, but I wasn't nervous, because I had my uncle as a shield.

"As soon as we got inside, Uncle introduced me to Mr Spence, the supervisor, who gladly shook my hand and genuinely welcomed me, and then called Martin and told him to escort me to the baggage booth, where I was going to be posted.

"The baggage booth was an open top board box, five feet high and eight feet wide on each side. Martin told me to ask the customers to leave their bags on entering the store, give them a numbered ticket, and pin a copy on the luggage. He also told me to keep an eye out for potential shoplifters, before he scurried away, because two staff members began calling him from separate sections of the store.

"Martin was the errands man for the store. He was a Christian, and most people thought he was gay, because of his effeminate mannerisms. Apart from being the errands man, he was in charge of cleaning the floor and the windows, stocking the shelves, working in the baggage booth, and he would also help to serve the customers occasionally.

"At the time, Crichton Brothers Hardware Store was the biggest of its kind in the Parish of Saint James. Every day was busy in the store. People came from miles to shop there. The company, which initially started in a small board shop, yards away from the present one, was founded by a white Jamaican man, and his four sons. They sell almost everything under the one roof. They had a household department, an auto sales department and the hardware department itself. The store rooms at the back of the building were huge, and they also had their own lumber yard, tile and building block factory at a different location. It was also the only place I knew on the island that sell guns."

That Friday, when Calvin got his first wages, he went and bought himself a fancy lunch, which consisted of rice and peas and fried chicken, with a huge glass of carrot juice.

After he got home that evening, Aunty and Uncle summoned him to the veranda.

"How much did you get paid today?" Uncle enquired, while he took a swig from his concoction of Gordon's gin and Red Label wine.

"Forty dollars, sir," Calvin replied cheerfully, still feeling the buzz after collecting his first ever wages.

"Where is it?" Aunty asked, with a not-so-happy tone of voice.

Calvin ran to his room, picked up the envelope with the wage slip and the rest of his wages, returned to the veranda and handed the envelope to Uncle, who took it and checked the contents then handed it to Aunty.

"How are we going to work this out now?" Aunty asked, as she took the envelope from Uncle.

"He will need money for his taxi fare to go to work for the week," said Uncle, "and the rest you can save for him," he concluded, as if Calvin wasn't present.

After Aunty calculated how much Calvin needed to pay on the taxi for the week (about six dollars), she told Uncle that she also needed some money to help run the house.

Uncle's reaction was the total opposite. It was evident that he wanted Calvin to save his money, but whatever Aunty said was final. Eventually he told her to take whatever she wanted and save the rest for the boy.

Again, Calvin didn't have a problem with what they had chosen to do with his money. The most important thing at that time in his life was that he was no longer living a gloomy life at Carey Village.

At the store, a month or so later, Calvin became Martin's sidekick, and oftentimes he would do Martin's job when he wasn't at work. Later he also started to help out in other areas, such as in the storeroom and serving customers occasionally.

Some of the staff was doing backdoor dealings at the store, but Uncle didn't forewarn Calvin against such activities, and eventually, after he'd got acquainted with some of the other youths, he was tempted to participate in the backdoor dealings too. However, he was very naïve, and because he was going through a difficult stage in his life, he was easily led, and without thinking twice he jumped on the impure bandwagon.

Consciously, he knew that he was entering a forbidden world, but the temptation was too strong to resist, and he didn't want the opportunity of getting a little bit more to pass him by. He also knew that he would lose everything if he got caught or if his uncle should find out his secrets. Accordingly, he couldn't purchase anything to take home with him; so the only way to get rid of the backdoor dealings money was to spend it – and the only things he could spend it on were food, weed, sometimes alcohol, and going to the cinema during his lunchtime hour.

Back then he didn't have any knowledge about putting money into the bank. In fact, even if he'd known about saving money then, he still wouldn't have saved any, because all he wanted to do was have fun. But as with everything in life, all things do come to an end.

Unfortunately, he couldn't sense when all the raving was coming to a climax. Ultimately, after working at the store for eight months, he got into a fight one day with one of the older staff, in which he had to pull his knife on the guy. The repercussion of his thoughtless action was the end of his job.

The following day, after Uncle got home from work, he summoned Calvin to the veranda. Gladly he ran to the veranda, because he thought his uncle had found another job for him, but Uncle's reason for summoning him was something else.

After Calvin was seated, Uncle said, "Son," and then he paused. "Now dat you're not working" – he coughed and continued, "mi an' mi wife can no longer accommodate yuh here," he wrapped up, getting straight to the point.

Calvin sat motionless where he was, as if struck by something really hard, and he couldn't comprehend what his uncle was saying to him.

"As yuh already know," Uncle continued, "mi an' Millward are getting older, suh yuh ha fi guh." (You have to go.)

If Uncle had used a knife to cut him then, he wouldn't have bled.

"I couldn't believe what my uncle had told me that day," exclaimed Calvin. "I thought to myself, even though they didn't have a child to support and I was the only kid living there with them, they still were heartless enough to turn me out, regardless of what I'd done.

"I wasn't expecting them to give me much financial support, because I was willing to fend for myself. They didn't need anybody to tell them that either. They just couldn't see that I was a disturbed child, who only needed a place to stay, with people who were able to watch over me and gave me some guidance.

"I knew there was nothing that I could do or say to justify my inexcusable behaviour at the store, but damn, I was only a loose, mixed-up kid who needed counselling and reprimanding. Maybe they couldn't be bothered. Nonetheless, I didn't argue with them. I simply packed the few pieces of clothing I had, collected the money that Aunty had saved for me, and went back to my dad's house, where Devon was living by himself."

At the time, Devon was working next door, painting Aunty and Uncle's neighbour's house, so that evening Calvin returned to Carey Village with his brother.

"While I was sitting on the bus going towards Mount Carey, I kept looking out the window with that familiar, sickening feeling of vanished hope burning inside my belly, and fear of the inevitable suffering and brutalizing that was sure to come before long."

Because he was naive, he made another silly mistake and let Devon know that he had some money with him.

That same evening, after they got off the bus at Mount Carey, Devon took his little brother to a club where they were playing reggae music. Here, everybody, no matter their age, was allowed to smoke weed and drink alcohol.

Feeling like a man who had come of age, with a few hundred dollars in his pocket, Calvin decided to purchase weed, alcohol, and food for himself and his brother.

During the night, Devon approached him and asked to borrow some of his money until payday, and without thinking twice, Calvin gladly handed over his money. But when Devon got paid, he drew a card on him (told him a story) and promised to repay him the following week.

Because there was still some money left in Calvin's pocket, he accepted his brother's story, but the following week Devon gave him a different story and another promise. By now, Calvin's money was almost finished. As a result he started to screw up his face (got vexed), and he let Devon knew that he wasn't pleased with his false promises and was fed up with his stories.

Devon didn't like the way he was being spoken to. So an argument developed, which resulted in Calvin getting his backside kicked. This began a string of beatings, which would occur every time he enquired about his hard-earned money.

After the little money he had ran out, eventually the few suits of clothes and shoes he had started to deteriorate, and before long he was back at square one with no money, no good clothes, and – the most essential thing – no food.

At length he became dependent on mainly fruits to survive, but there wasn't much on Percy's half-acre of land. In due course, his only chance of surviving was to steal fruits and raid the farmers 'fields.

Back then there were lots of other fruits around, apart from the popular breadfruits, bananas, ackee, mangoes, and coconuts, although most of them were on other people's property.

Sour sop, custard apple, sweetsop, genep, papaya, otaheiti apple (regularly called coco plum in Jamaica), and star apple, just to name a few, were also on the island.

The sour sop is very popular around the world but it can only be cultivated in areas of high humidity. This seven-to-nine-inch-long fruit can be harvested throughout the year in most tropical areas. The sour sop fruit supplies a lot of significant nutrients, such as vitamins C, B1, and B2. It is also high in carbohydrates, particularly fructose.

The skin of this special fruit is green and leathery, covered in small knobby spines that easily break off when the fruit is ripe. The thin, inedible skin also cuts or breaks easily when the fruit is ripe, and inside the skin there's a large mass of edible white, somewhat fibrous pulp and a core of indigestible black seeds, and the pulp is juicy and creamy with an unusual aroma.

The sour sop is consumed when it is ripe, by peeling away the skin and eating the creamy pulp.

Throughout Jamaica, the natives normally place the seeded pulp in a bowl with water and wash it, then press it in a colander or sieve or in cheesecloth, to extract the rich, creamy juice, which is then sweetened with condensed milk, vanilla essence, and nutmeg. It can also be sweetened with sugar or honey and lime juice for a refreshing drink.

Sour sop is also used to make ice cream and sorbets, and the leaves are widely used in Jamaica to make tea.

Research published in the *Jamaican Gleaner* in recent years shows that extract from this miraculous tree may now possibly be used to attack cancer safely and effectively with an all-natural therapy that does not cause extreme nausea, weight loss, and hair loss, but instead protects the immune system and combats deadly infections.

On the other hand, the star apple is the worst fruit to consume when one is hungry. It does kill the hunger, but at the cost of a prolonged bellyache. Calvin used to eat it when there was nothing else around to eat.

The star apple also prefers to grow in high humidity. There is a propaganda surrounding its origin. It is commonly stated that this special fruit is indigenous to Central America, but others strongly believe that it belongs to the West Indies.

Many Jamaicans believe the fruit is a symbol of the birth of Jesus Christ, only because it ripens near Christmas time.

The trees are erect and grow in different dimension, from twenty-five to a hundred feet (8–30 m) tall with short, stocky trunks. The fruit is round, ellipsoid, or somewhat pear-shaped, two to four inches (5–10 cm) in diameter, glossy and smooth, with a thin leathery skin. It comes in two varieties, a red-purple and a pale green.

Both varieties have a soft, white, milky, sweet pulp surrounding the gelatinous, fairly rubbery seed cells in the centre, which when cut through crossways; resemble an asterisk or many-pointed stars.

The skin of the star apple is inedible and contains bitter latex; therefore it is best to cut it before consumption, but when Calvin climbed one of those trees to pick the apples, he used to bite into it and then tear it open to devour the pulp.

The star apple is also used for medicinal purposes, against diseases such as pneumonia and diabetes, and the bark of the tree is used to make tonics and stimulants and also taken to halt diarrhoea, dysentery, and haemorrhages.

*

The jungle adjacent to Lawyer Stenit's land was owned by Miss Eve, a white woman who was living at Anchovy. Over the years, the origin of Miss Eve has never been told, nor did anybody know the extent of the land that she owned. Nonetheless, people used to take over sections of her land to farm, and in later years they started to build houses on it too.

Lots of white yam (renta yam) used to grow wild on Miss Eve's land in those days. It was said that the slaves planted a lot of white yams all over the country, which eventually grew wild. The yam season ran officially from mid-December until March and during late July to September, mangoes would be around in abundance, which was an ideal source of food for many poor people too.

A lot of people used to search the jungle for the wild yams, and some would replant the heads of the plants after they reaped them, which would increase the yield the following harvest season. However, in recent years, people more often transplanted the head of the plant to their own fields. Others started to make money from it by searching for the heads and selling them to farmers, which eventually caused that source of food to become scarce and eventually created more hardship for many people who were dependent on the wild yam crop.

Calvin used to go into the jungle regularly with other youths to search for renta yam and mangoes, but sometimes he would go alone.

On one of those occasions he was on his way home from the jungle with a group of youths, including Carl, when he found a wallet on the track with three dollars in it.

He thought it was his lucky day, and he showed it to the rest of youths and gave Carl one dollar.

After he got home and put away his yam, he decided to go to a house below the back of Miss Maude's house, where youths would gather to gamble. He was in the middle of a Pitta Pat game when Devon turned up and accused him of stealing his wallet. Calvin admitted that he had found a wallet with three dollars, but he didn't know that it was Devon's. The others who were with him confirmed the facts, but Devon was furious, because Calvin had already lost the two dollars in the card game. As a result, a fight broke out between the two brothers.

Some of the other youths began to cheer them on, while Calvin and his brother were throwing punches at each other. One of Calvin's punches caught Devon in the face, which sent him into a rage and he went to his waist and produced a ten-inch knife.

When Calvin saw the knife, he froze. Devon made a swipe at his face with the blade, but he swiftly backed away. Devon slashed at him again, and this time he tried to open his brother's belly and with more conviction.

There wasn't much room for Calvin to jump out of the way, because by then his back was close to the house. However, instantly his survival instinct chipped in, and he stretched his arms out and pulled his belly in as far as he could, to reduce the impact of the blade. Still, he felt the cold steel catch his left side, as Devon dragged the blade around to the middle of his belly in the same motion.

He screamed out in agony and held on to his side and his belly with both hands. Devon moved in on him and grabbed his neck, while pointing the tip of the blade in his face and threatening to kill him.

Some of the other youths went silent, though some kept cheering as if they were watching a movie. By then Calvin was standing on weary legs, because all the fight had left his body.

Suddenly, one youth from out of the audience jokingly told the others that he could see Calvin's liver hanging out through his side, and the rest of them laughed.

Calvin could feel a burning sensation where the blade had made contact, and blood was dripping through his fingers. At that point, some of the youths began to show concern, and suddenly Devon released his hold on his brother's neck and walked away.

Calvin removed his hands slowly from his wound. He was happy when he realised that the blade hadn't gone deeper than he thought, but there was a twelve-inch cut running from his left side to the middle of his stomach. The gash at his side was opened, but the rest of it trailed off faintly to the middle of his belly.

Quickly he got some mud and used it to stop the bleeding, and the rest of youths were praising him for his skilfulness, but deep down he knew that his life had been spared.

Now there are two scars at his left side, as a constant reminder of Devon's brutality.

At that point, Ruby was living with a different man in Mobay, but she would go to Carey Village some Sundays and bring groceries and a cooked dinner for Calvin, and she would also give him some money before she took her leave.

After Ruby went back to her life in Mobay with her boyfriend, Devon would start acting like the beloved brother, and Calvin would share with him whatever Ruby had brought, because he was happy for the loving attention that Devon would showed him.

The goodies that Ruby brought Calvin didn't usually last long, and Devon's loving attitude would also go out the window when the goodies were done. In spite of that, Calvin wasn't really bothered. In fact, he was happy, because he had a good life with his brother for a few days in a row.

At that stage he was becoming more concerned about the difficult circumstances that confronted him every day. He also felt like he wasn't a part of the world that he was living in, because he had grown accustomed to the type of life which Uncle and Aunty used to offer him at Mount Salem. On the whole, the only good thing about living at Carey Village was the freedom that he had to roam the whole community, because there wasn't much in place for him to do.

During the days it was all about hunting for food to eat and money to gamble. Evenings, he would hang out with the other boys on top of Pan Bottom Hill, where they used to play football along the level unpaved road, or a game that they called chase. It was even more fun when they built a big fire and put a lot of breadfruits in it to roast, which they then ate with butter.

Some nights, he would either hang out at the shop on Pan Bottom Hill until it closed, or go to Mount Carey with Carl and Monkey to enjoy the nightlife.

Most evenings he wouldn't bother to go home and change his clothes, because it wouldn't make much difference; in any case, most of his garments were rags, but he didn't care what anybody thought of him, Overall, at that point in his young life, pride wasn't of much significance to him, because he was accustomed to walk without any shoes on his feet and wear his trousers even with the seat ripped.

"The little town of Mount Carey used to livened up most nights, with reggae music playing in most of the bars and clubs. The smell of rum that whiffed through the doors of the bars and clubs were welcoming to one and all. The aroma from the jerk chicken, jerk pork and roasted corn on the cob that a few men would prepare at the roadside, on top of metal drums, was also welcoming.

"Women used to sit at the roadside selling fruits from baskets, and there was one man with a big pot of soup, another with hot roasted peanuts, and another with his sons selling sugar cane from a pushcart.

"It was fun hanging out at Mount Carey, and it was even more fun when I had money to buy sugar cane, hot roasted peanuts, soup, jerk chicken or jerk pork."

Sometimes Calvin would go "down de ole (a bamboo dancehall in a gully, below the main road at Mount Carey).

During the days, they would keep basic school 'down de ole', but at nights they used to gamble and show movies there.

In those days, they usually used a projector to show the movies, but in later years when the colour television and video recorder got prevalent, they started to use them.

Sometimes Calvin could afford to pay the $1.50 to watch the double bill, but other times he would have to peep through the gaps in the bamboo to see the film.

At one point, two brothers from Lethe (one of the communities adjoining Anchovy) started to show movies "down de ole". They were the first people to start showing movies on a colour television.

One brother was in charge of sorting out the movies, and the other would collect the fees at the door.

The new showmen were less strict with the fees than the previous operators, and oftentimes the one at the door would let some of the youths in free.

Calvin used to stand at the side of the door, peeping through a hole, until one night the showman told him that he could get in free. From that night, the man continued to let him in without charging any fee.

One night, the brother who used to collect the fees at the door turned up on his own to show the movies, and he asked Calvin to collect the fees at the door for him, while he set up the television and the video recorder.

Calvin was happy to get the opportunity to perform such a responsible task, and when the show ended, he also helped the showman to carry the television and video recorder to his car.

The showman gave him a few dollars and told him that he was happy for the help. He also told Calvin that he could give him the job of collecting the fees at the door, because his brother was occupied with other business. Calvin told him he would like that very much.

Before the showman drove away that night, he gave Calvin directions to visit him at his house where they could sit down and discuss business.

Calvin, who was very excited, told the man he would visit him, and that night he went home on cloud nine. He also told his friends about the conversation that he had with the showman, and they were happy for him.

"A few days later, I got up and prepared my best clothes and the only pair of shoes that I had left from the last time I was living with Uncle and Aunty, and at midday I began to walk the three miles or so to the showman's house.

"When I reached the road that I was directed to turn on, I realised that it was where the renowned Rockland's Bird Sanctuary was situated.

"I always looked out the bus window whenever I passed by that particular area, but it was the first time I'd been to that part of the community on foot.

"The Rockland's Bird Sanctuary is a tourist destination. It is home to one of the most unique nature tours and wildlife experiences in Jamaica and all over the Caribbean. For decades, the caretakers of this unique property have been hand feeding the endemic wild birds of Jamaica, to the point that many of them are tamed and will eat seeds right from your hands.

"While I walked up the hill, I was amazed to see how beautiful the houses were, and I kept looking from one house to the other until I reached the house that the showman described to me.

"I was astonished to see the well maintained garden and the house, which was in pristine condition.

"The showman was standing on the veranda smiling, as I stepped through the gate, and he beckoned to me to proceed up the steps, towards the veranda.

"I felt good at that point, because I was convinced something good was about to happen, and my miserable life would finally change for the better.

"The man opened the burglar bar gate and welcomed me, and I was dazed by the exquisiteness of the house's interior.

"He ushered me toward a massive lounge and asked me if I was hungry, and I told him yes. In actual fact, I'd only drink a cup of sour sop leaf tea during the morning hours, so I was very hungry.

"The showman offered me a seat on a big brown leather sofa and then turned on the biggest colour television set that I'd ever beheld in the entirety of my struggling life. It was also the first time I'd got offered a seat on a leather sofa.

"Delicately I sat down on the edge of the sofa, with my mouth agape, watching the television, while the showman disappeared into the kitchen.

"Minutes later he reappeared, with a pack of cream crackers and a cold bottle of Red Stripe beer, which he handed to me, and I gladly took them and began to sip the cold beer.

"'How did you get here?' he enquired.

"'I had to walk all the way, because I didn't have any money,' I told him, and suddenly he took out his wallet and gave me a twenty-dollar note, which I took and stuffed way down in the only pocket of my trousers that didn't have a hole.

"He noticed how uncomfortably I was sitting on the edge of the sofa and told me to sit back and relax, but I told him that I was okay and put a cracker in my mouth.

"He picked up the remote control, sat himself down beside me on the sofa, and then asked me what I wanted to watch.

"'I don't really mind what is showing,' I told him. In fact, I was more concerned about discussing some work at the show house, because my life was in peril.

"He set the television on a music channel, and suddenly moved closer to me on the sofa, but I shuffled away, while continuing to stuff crackers and beer down my hungry belly.

"He moved closer to me again, and this time, before I could shuffle away he placed his right palm on my left thigh. I quickly moved my thigh, and his hand fell off, but he replaced his hand again, while continuing to move even closer towards his prey.

"Suddenly I jumped up and asked him what he was doing, and he laughed and told me to sit down and relax.

"'Yuh a batty bwoy' (a homosexual), I protested angrily, as I quickly headed for the door that I'd come through earlier, with the beer and crackers still in my hands.

"The man got up and followed me toward the veranda, while begging me to stay, but by the time he got to the veranda, I'd already let myself out and was running down the steps.

"He called out to me, and I turned around and threw the beer bottle at him and told him that I didn't want anything to do with any batty bwoy.

"He made an attempt to follow me, but I started to run down the steep, rough hill, and I didn't stop running until I was close to the main road.

"By then I was limping, because one of my shoe heels had fallen off while I was running, down the hill, and I stood at the bus stop anxiously gasping for air.

"My heart was beating at a very fast pace, and I kept looking back up the road where I'd run from, in case the showman was following me, until the jolly bus (passenger bus) turned up.

"Hurriedly I got on the bus and it suddenly seemed like everybody was looking at me as I struggled to the back seat, and before I was seated, I overheard one woman saying to another, 'Nuh Ruby and Percy bwoy dat?' Translation: Is that Ruby and Percy boy?

"The other woman answered and said, 'It seems like su'mady (somebody) wen deh run im dung (was running him down).

Look how de bwoy deh pant like im jus done run a marathon,' she concluded.

"'Yuh nuh se him boots?' the first woman asked. 'Ah wonder wah (what) or who 'im wen deh run from?' she concluded resignedly.

"I braced myself, swallowed my pride, and ignored the comments as I tried to gather my thoughts. I was angry with myself for acting like a fool and going to the showman's house, but on the other hand, I was only looking for a way out of my daily struggles. In addition, I knew that the earlier event was something that could never be told to anybody. I also knew that if such a story should get out on the streets, I'd be branded as a batty bwoy for the rest of my life, and the mere prospect sent shivers down my spine.

"When the bus reached Cotton Tree, I got off and headed towards Lawyer Stenit's house. Halfway up a hillside I stopped and sat down underneath a big mango tree to rest. Suddenly I started to cry, and as I cried, my weary body got weaker. Eventually I fell into a deep sleep, in the same position.

"While my weary body, heart, and mind were resting, I heard Mr Shaw say, 'Wake up, manity,' but I didn't move, because I was too weak. I slowly opened my eyes and looked up at him pleadingly, as to say, *Please leave me alone.*

"'Why don't you go home and sleep, manity?'Mr Shaw asked.

Mr Shaw, (Barber) otherwise called Manity, was Monkey's grandfather. He was a deacon in the Mount Carey Baptist Church, and people all over the communities respected him. He would always tell stories about the day he met the Bishop of

Canterbury and about his visit to Asia, and most times when he spoke he would add 'ity' to the end of his words.

"I folded my arms tightly around my belly, to reduce the stabbing hunger pain, and mumbled a few croaky words in reply to Barber's earlier question.

"He shook his head from side to side with an emotional expression on his face, and, just like what Bob Marley told us in one of his songs: 'Wake up and live,' "Mr Shaw told me,' 'Wake up and live, son. Wake up and livity,' "and as he turned and walked away, he began to sing 'Amazing Grace,' and I deliberately fed my soul on every single word as he sang, until he disappeared over the top of the hill.

"Even though I was badly shaken by the earlier event, I was suddenly filled with a renewed energy, and I got up slowly and began to walk towards my dad's house, thinking about what I was going to cook, because by then I was well hungry.

"Months after the showman attempted to abuse me, he made a similar attempt on another youth from Mount Carey, but this time some of the older youths caught him and beat him up badly, and he never returned to Mount Carey again.

"For many years I was weighed down with guilt for acting like a fool and going to the showman's house, but I managed to blot out what had happened, and I also tried not to think about what could've happened if I was a lesser person. Conversely, the experience changed the way I trust people, and I've spent my life believing everybody I come in contact with has an ulterior motive."

CHAPTER NINE

Finding a Solution

It was the beginning of 1982, and although the Jamaican economy was slowly getting back to normal after the turmoil of the last election, Calvin's living condition was going from bad to worse.

Ruby wasn't visiting as much as she normally had, and Marika, on the verge of having her third child, was living her own life with Budget, at Mount Carey.

"It was only Devon and I living at Mass Percy's house. I didn't know the whereabouts of Salomon and Babs, and it was only by chance that I heard any news about Van. For many years I was ignorant about what had happened to him after he went back to Kingston, but finally I heard through the grapevine that he was in prison, on death row. It was alleged that he was wanted for a number of murders and other crimes, and it was also said that he'd eventually got sold out by one of his friends. Apparently he and the friend killed a man, and the friend got caught and decided that he wasn't going down alone for the murder. It was also revealed to me that Van had played a vital role in the killing, because he'd held the man by one of his ears with a plier, and his accomplice used a knife to cut the man's throat. In court, he was found guilty for the killing of the man, as well as for other killings. Ultimately he was charged with four counts of murder and got sentenced to hang.

"When I acquired the news about my brother, I was sad to know that he would be killed at some point, but I also thought it was trendy and cool, because my bad brother was in prison, and oftentimes I bragged about it to my friends and foes.

"During that same time I'd also received some disturbing news regarding another sister. Although I was very confused when it was initially revealed to me, that I had two other brothers and a sister, I was even more confused when I was told that I also had another sister named Janet. Just as with the others, I also wanted to know about Janet and her family's whereabouts, but the only information I got was that she was living in Mobay, and her father's name was Mr Beckford.

"After it was revealed to me, I approached Mama one day and asked her about Janet, but she acted as if she didn't know what I was talking about and changed the subject. Another time I asked her again, and she only ignored me."

At that point in Calvin's life, the struggling had begun to take its toll on him, and the physical and mental abuse was on the rise.

Lawyer Stenit's property was no longer accessible for him to steal fruits, because it was sold to a man called Buchanan (Mr Buck) from Trelawney, whose brother was an inspector of police. Regardless of that, it served its purpose for a while, because lots of men from Trelawney were staying at the house, while they refurbished it, and Calvin used to hang around them in order to get food to eat.

After some time Mr Buck started to raise lots of goats, cows, and pigs, and he gave Calvin the job of helping to look after the animals. The whole thing only lasted for a short time, though, because Mr Buck eventually brought his own people in to look after the animals, and before long Calvin's back was against the tall wall of poverty again.

The government on the other hand didn't do handouts, unless of course it was election time, when they would come out in numbers to brainwash the people for their votes.

Devon, who had inherited most of Percy's clients, would occasionally get big painting jobs, but when he got paid, he would buy the latest clothes, cook the best meals, and squander the rest of his money amongst his friends, but he wouldn't offer anything to his little brother.

Ultimately there was nobody to offer Calvin any help, and he felt alone, hopeless, and confused, but he knew that he had to survive by any means necessary.

"At that point, most youths in and around the community of Carey Village were planting ganja, and eventually I decided to embark into the cultivation too, without any prospect of what I would achieve out of it?

"For instance, I didn't have all the required things that I was going to need; such as a machete or ganja seed. Nonetheless, I was adamant to survive, regardless of the circumstances.

"Initially I borrowed a machete from one of Money Man's sons, and secured the piece of land that I was going to farm on. The latter wasn't a problem for me to acquire, because Miss Eve had lots of wasteland around the area. When the land was ready,

I asked the older farmers, who were cultivating ganja, for some of their ganja seedlings, which they gladly gave to me.

"Months after I started farming the herbs, I got hungry one day and decided to roam through the jungle in search of mangoes and other fruits, and I ended up at Cotton Tree.

"The little district at Cotton Tree was a prime place to live, for those who could afford to purchase a plot and build a big concrete house on it next to the existing ones. At the time, a number of houses were being built on some of the plots, and Osburne and his younger brother Melvin were in the process of building one for the both of them.

"Osburne and Melvin were Mr and Mrs Tinglin's two sons. They were a pedigree family, one of the most respected throughout the regions. Together they operated an all-inclusive shop in the centre of Anchovy, where they supplied almost everything from food to building materials and clothes. They also had a rum bar built next to the store, and they used to sell fresh patty and folding bread (coco bread) to the schoolchildren.

"I can vividly remember the atmosphere in the shop, when I used to attend the primary school, and went there occasionally to purchase my lunch. It was one of the most electrifying moments I'd experienced as a child, when all the kids were shouting Osburne's name and their order at the same time.

"Osburne, like everybody else around the region, knew Mass Percy well when he was alive, and just like with everybody else, he also knew Percy's children too. Therefore, that day when I went to his building site and half-heartedly asked him for some work, he gladly gave it to me.

"Austin, one of Aunty Beck's grandsons, was living yards away from where Osburne was building his house, on the ghetto side of the community, and he was also working on the site. Osburne's girlfriend and her family were also living next door to the site, and her dad, Mr Boswell, was working on the house too.

"I was very happy and surprised when Osburne employed me as the building site's handyman. To be honest, when I asked him for the job, I was expecting him tell me no, and although I didn't have any experience, the builders showed me what to do, and I always did it right.

"Although I was the youngest one in the team, everybody treated me with love and respect, and before long I was promoted to the site's chef.

"During that period, I fell in love for the first time, with Susie, one of Mr Boswell's younger daughters. She was a year older than I, and she was attending the Montego Bay High School.

"Susie was medium built and about five feet tall, with a light brown complexion. She was very mannerly and pleasant, and the first time I saw her, I couldn't stop myself from looking at her. When she wasn't around, I thought about her all the time, with a fire burning in my belly continually.

"I was afraid to tell Susie how she made me feel, but somehow she realised I liked her after a while, and she liked me back. Nonetheless, neither of us could find the confidence to tell the other how we felt about each other, until one night the truth came out.

"It was late 1982, and we were at a party that was being held at Austin's house. Michael Jackson's album *Thriller* was getting played over and over, and everybody was having a good time.

"I was having a good time too, because Austin had killed a ram goat, and they cooked Manish Water (goat soup) curried goat and boiled rice. Lots of liquor and weed were there too, but covertly I felt embarrassed, given that my clothes were shabby. Nevertheless, while I was standing underneath a cedar tree smoking a joint, sipping cold Red Stripe beer, and dancing to one of Michael's hit songs, Susie joined me.

"I suddenly felt extremely high after she came to me, and I threw away the joint when she began to dance with me.

"When the song was over, she held my hand and led me to a wooden bench, under a mango tree, where we both sat in silence. Minutes later she told me that she liked me, and I stuttered and told her that I liked her too. Another silence ensued, and then she took off a fake gold chain that she had around her neck with a crucifix attached and gave it to me, as a token of her love, quickly planted a warm, juicy kiss on my cheek, and got up, saying she had to go. I watched her walk away, wondering if I'd said and done the right things.

"After that night, Susie and I would always meet at Austin's house, but my low self-esteem wouldn't allow me to take our relationship to the next level, and eventually we ended up just being friends.

"Eventually I started to hang out at Anchovy regularly, and when I wasn't gambling at the back of the community centre or playing dominoes for Red Stripe beer in Mr Thomas's grocery shop, I would be seated at the far corner of Osburne's rum bar on a stool, watching his television.

"Every night without fail, as soon as I entered the bar, Osburne would give me a bottle of ting, a Jamaican grapefruit carbonated drink.

"Almost everybody who drank in the rum bar knew me. My presence always seemed to bring back the memory of Percy, and most times a conversation would ensue about him.

"I used to feel very proud as I listened to them talking about my dad. Even though he was dead, his memory was still strong. However, the atmosphere changed one night after they mentioned Ruby in the conversation.

"I was watching a James Bond film for the first time, when an old man walked into the bar and came to where I was seated at the back. As soon as he recognised me, he shouted, 'Wait, nuh Percy bwoy dis? Wah yuh deh duh a treet dis time a night, bwoy?' Translation: 'What are you doing on the street at this time of the night boy?' "Before I could answer, a conversation started up about Percy amongst the patrons, and one man from the other end of the bar suddenly said he couldn't recall the last time he saw Ruby, and laughter filled the bar.

"By then I was trying to shrink deeper into the shadows of the corner, because I knew exactly what was coming next. A second man replied to the first and said, 'How come yuh askin' about har (her) an' me hear sey yuh an' har did have someting going on at one point?' "A third man was standing close to the first, and he picked up his drink from the bar and was about to walk away, but someone stopped him in his tracks and asked him about Ruby, and another round of laughter erupted. Before long fingers were being pointed from one man to the other and some was denying sleeping with my mother while some admitted that they had slept with her once or twice.

"One man said, 'But me nuh hear sey Ruby and Percy a breder (brother) and sister!' and instantly everybody went silent. Although the television was on, you could hear a pin drop.

"I couldn't listen to any more of the conversation at that point, so I cautiously got up and slipped out the back door, but I didn't go far, because I was keeping an eye on Papa Seeta, who I used to depend on for company to go home.

"Papa Seeta, who was living on his own some forty yards below Percy's house, was a painter (decorator), and almost every night he would drink lots of liquor at Anchovy and go home drunk. Although he wasn't keen on having me follow him after the bars closed, nonetheless, I would trot behind him, until that particular night, when it all ended.

"It was a Saturday night, and everybody was in high spirits at Anchovy. I drank two bottles of Red Stripe beer and smoked a few spliffs, and I was feeling rather tired when Osburne decided to close the bar at half past three in the morning. On the other hand, Papa Seeta had one too many to drank, and as soon as he staggered out of the bar and I began to follow, he stopped, swayed from side to side and back and forth, and then stood still. After a few more sway he made it clear to me that he didn't want anybody to follow him, because he wasn't afraid.

"I walked away in the opposite direction, hid behind a building, and watched him stealthily as he tottered from side to side along the deserted road. When he was a little distance away, I began to follow again.

"I caught up with him at Cotton Tree, because from that point, to get to my house, everywhere was obscured in darkness.

"He grumbled a few distasteful words, but I ignored him and continued to walk behind, while trying to avoid bumping into him. Minutes later he stopped abruptly, and we almost collided, and he swore and rocked from side to side as he searched his pockets for cigarettes. After he found the package he began to search for his matches. He was taking forever to find the packet of matches, and at that stage I told him to hurry up, because I was tired.

Big mistake! He swore at me and told me not to follow him anymore, because he wasn't my keeper, and I should go and find my mother who was getting drunk and sleeping with every man she came in contact with.

"I'd never seen Papa Seeta get so angry as he did that night, and I felt ashamed and petrified at the same time, and although I was afraid of the darkness, I walked the half mile or so to my dad's house and I never looked back.

"On the contrary, although I was hurt when Papa Seeta vented his anger at me, I later thanked him in my heart, because unbeknownst to him, he had done me a favour, in view of the fact that I'd overcome my fear of the dark that very night. From there on, I got very brave and I didn't need anybody's company to go wherever I wanted to go at night."

A month or so later, Calvin was busy preparing lunch at Osburne's house when a motorbike suddenly pulled up outside the gate. Minutes later Sarge, Austin's brother, sauntered through the door of the unfinished house and greeted everybody enthusiastically. When he noticed Calvin, he went over to him and shook his hand gleefully. He said it was good to know that Calvin was hanging around the right people and before long stories were being told about Percy, but they didn't mention Ruby.

Sarge and Austin had grown up together in the same neighbourhood with Percy, and Sarge was Aunty Beck's favourite grandson. He was living at Mount Salem, but he used to visit his relatives regularly. While Aunty Beck was alive, he used to give her anything that her heart desired. After she passed away, he would visit her granddaughter Audrey at the house occasionally, but most times he would hang out at his brother's house.

Sarge was the type of man who loved to talk a lot, and wherever he was, you could hear his voice from a distance. Whilst he spoke, the side of his mouth would froth, and spittle that looked like snowflakes would occasionally fly from it. He was also a member of the infamous Popsy gang, one of the most feared gangs in Mobay at the time. Often times he struck fear in a lot of people, by telling them about his experiences with the gang. Still, he was well liked by most people, because he was a man of principle and very kind. The only thing people could say about him was that he talked a lot.

"I used to love when Sarge came around, because he would always buy food and drinks for everybody to partake of. Sometimes he would send me to the shops and on my return I got rewarded with money and ganja.

"One day I was sitting in Austin's house eating corned beef and crackers and drinking lemonade with him, his wife, and Sarge. Out of the blue, Sarge suddenly mentioned that he would like to plant some weed in the hills opposite Cotton Tree. His brother's wife told him that he could take me on as his apprentice, if he was serious, but the conversation was cut short when someone came to visit Austin.

"Ultimately, Osburne's house was completed, and I went back to my weed field permanently, but I'd only managed to produce a few kilos of herb that year, and it was only by chance I'd sold some of it, which enabled me to buy a suit of clothes and a pair of shoes.

"The following year I linked up with Sarge, and he made a deal with me. He promised to provide the tools and seeds and give me money to buy food, but I would have to prepare the land and do most of the work in the field throughout the season.

"It may seem like a lot of responsibility for a fifteen-year-old youth, but it was a tremendous advantage for me, to move up a notch out of poverty. Moreover, Sarge told me that he was an expert in producing some of the best quality herb, so I was convinced that I would be prosperous come the end of the weed season.

"Everything was going to plan for the most part of the year, until a man decided to raid the farm."

It was a bright Saturday afternoon. Rain had just ended, and the sun was out in all its glory. Calvin decided to go to his field to transplant some of his seedlings. On reaching the nursery, he noticed that a big patch of his seedlings was missing, and that was when he saw the footprints that the intruder had left behind.

After he backtracked the footprints, he found one of his mother's former lovers in the process of transplanting them and he confronted him and asked, "Yow, wah mek yuh ha fi guh teef out mi weed sucker dem star, an' yuh done know sey if yuh ask mi I woulda gi yuh some?"

Translation: Hey, why did you have to go and steal my seedlings, when you know that if you asked me, I would've given you some?

The man moved towards Calvin with his machete in his hand, and Calvin ran to an open field and stopped. The man sauntered closer to him and stopped, while Calvin was venting his anger at him.

Suddenly, history repeated itself, because the spot where Calvin was standing was exactly where the man had a farm during the 1980 election period. At the time, Calvin was hungry, and he had gone there to reap a few yams when the man crept up from behind and grabbed him. That day, he was so hungry that he didn't hear the man's footsteps when he approached him. The man often bragged that he'd dropped a bundle of firewood behind Calvin, when he caught him digging his yams, but he didn't hear it because he was too engrossed in what he was doing.

The man had cut a piece of stick and beat Calvin badly, before taking him, along with the bag of yams, to hand him over to Ruby, who also gave him another course of beating on the already bruised body. The only good thing to come out of it was that the man gave Calvin the bag of yams after Ruby had finished beating him.

Calvin, whose body was aching from the two courses of beatings, was very hungry at that point. Although he was embarrassed for getting caught stealing yams, nonetheless, he began to prepare the dried coconut that he was going to use and cook the yam, and in no time he prepared himself a meal.

The memory of that day was still vivid to Calvin, and he began to hurl more abuse at the man, but before he knew what was happening the man suddenly moved towards him with his machete raised in his hand.

Calvin was taken by surprise, so he had no chance to prepare himself for the attack.

When the man was close enough to Calvin, he gave him a wicked slap across his chest, throwing him off balance.

Calvin wasn't wearing any shirt; therefore the impact of the slap burnt the skin from off his left breast.

As he stumbled backwards from the impact of the blow, the man moved in and grabbed him by the waist of his trousers. "A kill yuh waan mi kill yuh, bwoy? Yuh tink sey yuh cyan talk to mi like how yuh talk to yuh lickle frien' dem?"

Translation: "Do you want me to kill you, boy? You think you can talk to me like how you talk to your little friends?"

Calvin had a knife tucked in the back of his trousers waist at the time, and he made an attempt to draw it, but the man held his hand and the knife fell to the ground.

Suddenly, the man began to drag him towards a cluster of bushes, and he thought his life was going to end at that very moment. The thought of losing his life triggered a sense of endurance in him, and he began to fight for his dear life. The man was much stronger than he was, but he kept fighting him. Nonetheless, the man managed to cut down a piece of stick and began to beat him with it.

While the man was landing some vicious blows on Calvin's head, in his face, and all over his body, he managed to escape and run away.

He was a little distance away from the man when a huge stone flew past his head and collided with a tree, breaking off a limb. But Calvin didn't look back; he only continued to run towards his house.

The man was in his forties, so he had most of the advantages, but Calvin was adamant to get his revenge, and while he was running towards his yard he kept rehearsing aloud what he was going to do to the man.

When he reached his yard, nobody was at home, therefore he began to search around the house for something to use as a weapon, He found an old claw hammer and decided to take the handle out of it and use the iron as a weapon. He then lay in wait for the man behind some shoeblack flowers (Chinese hibiscus) that his dad had planted close to the wayside.

About an hour later when the man was passing by, Calvin attacked him.

At first when he saw him coming he was very nervous, but nothing could have stopped him from getting even with this man, so he waited patiently until the man had passed where he was hiding. Then he moved in as close as possible and hurled the hammer at him with all the strength he could muster, hitting the man in his back.

When the man received the blow he cried out and Calvin watched him go down on his knees, but he didn't linger to see what happened next, because he panicked and ran.

Unbeknownst to Calvin, Ruby took the man to the police station and the hospital.

Later that night, when Calvin returned to the house, he heard that the man had suffered a fractured bone in his spine. He was also told that the police were looking for him, in connection with causing grievous bodily harm to the man, but Calvin, for his part, was only happy to hear that he'd done some damage to the man.

Calvin continued to hide from the police, but on the fifth day after the encounter, he decided to go to Anchovy to meet Sarge, who had promised to bring him some money. Without any concern whatsoever, he was seated in the shadows of Osburne's rum bar watching a movie, while waiting on his partner to turn up, when suddenly Constable James, otherwise known as Horse Mouth, approached him. "Wah yuh name, yout'?" Horse Mouth towered over Calvin and enquired angrily, with his coarse voice. Nervously Calvin stuttered and told the officer his name. "Ha long time mi ha look fi yuh, lickle raasclaat," bellowed Horse Mouth. "Get up off ha yuh raas. Yuh under arrest for causing grievous bodily harm to a man," he concluded.

Calvin made an attempt to speak, but he was stammering very badly.

"Shut up yuh mout', bwoy, an' gi mi ha search," Horse Mouth demanded.

Calvin had a flat stainless steel knife in his trousers waist, but the officer didn't find it during his search, and after the search was completed the officer grabbed him from behind by the waistband and led him out of the bar, to the amazement of Austin, Osburne, and the rest of the patrons.

Together they walked about five hundred yards down the street to the police station, where the officer handcuffed him onto the gun box (a big metal box) where they kept the guns in the reception area.

When the officer's back was turned, Calvin stealthily took out the knife with his free hand and slipped it underneath the gun box. Not long after that a lot of people started to gather outside the station, including Austin and the presumed victim.

Unknown to Calvin at the time, Austin had telephoned Sarge and told him what was going on at the police station.

Fifteen minutes or so later, Horse Mouth started the interrogation in front of all the people who were present. His domineering presence alone was enough to throw Calvin off balance, and when he posed the first question Calvin got very nervous and started to stammer with the answers.

Suddenly, Horse Mouth picked up the cat-o'-nine-tails (which the police used to beat prisoners). When it lands on the body, it peels the skin off. Horse Mouth slapped his palm playfully with the device as he sauntered closer to the prisoner, but Calvin gave all who were present a surprise before the officer could land the first blow.

"To be frank, I didn't really want him to use that thing to hit me, because I had seen what it did to many other youths' bodies before," Calvin disclosed.

Whilst the cat-o'-nine-tails was dangling in the air waiting to land on him, he used his free hand to tear open his shirt. At that point Horse Mouth, the other officers, the presumed victim and the civilians in the station could see the burn he had on his chest, and the whole place suddenly went silent.

The wound was as raw as a piece of meat, because he was on the run, and he had been unable to get treatment for the burn he'd received from the machete slap.

Horse Mouth broke the silence and said, "Wahapen (what happened) to yuh chest, yout'?" Calvin didn't hesitate; he told the officer exactly what had happened.

He told Constable James that he was a ganja farmer and had caught the presumed victim stealing his herb. When he asked the man why he had to do it, he decided to beat him up.

Horse Mouth told Calvin that he would have to take the police and show them where the man had planted the seedlings, come the following morning, and he also told the presumed victim that he too would have to take the police and show them where Calvin had his field.

Without having second thoughts, Calvin told the officer yes, because he knew that he didn't really have anything more to lose, and before water could warm, the man disappeared out of the station.

Sarge turned up at the station about midnight with some money and gave it to the policemen who were present. They in turn set Calvin free, but before they let him go, they told him to be careful of his mother, because she was the one who had insisted that they lock him up.

The following morning while Calvin was on his way to his ganja field, he looked where the man was planting the seedlings, but there was not one to be found. It seemed as if he'd gone there in the night and pulled everything out.

The police didn't bother Calvin again. Sarge, however, wanted revenge, because the man's action from the outset had cost him dearly. It was also going to cost him even more, because the police now knew he was involved in ganja cultivation.

The following Sunday, Sarge turned up at Carey Village with his gun to kill the man, but Calvin begged for his life. After all, the man was Monkey's father.

CHAPTER TEN

FIGHTING TO SURVIVE

As Calvin reminisced, he experienced an indescribable feeling of sadness and joy at the same time. It reminded him of the times when he used to travel miles on foot with Monkey and Carl to the Great River to catch crayfish and swim. He would always sit on the hillside and watch the silky water as it washed over the rocks, and he could feel an indefinable sense of the infinite as he looked down on the clear, dreaming waters of the Great River.

"I used to dream and wish a lot then, and sometimes I would wish I could fly away to a place where everybody was living in peace and harmony."

Just as Dr Martin Luther King once said, "I have a dream," Calvin had only dreams to sustain him throughout his struggling life.

*

After the episode with the police and Monkey's dad, Calvin continued to grow his crop, and the cops didn't intervene. But Sarge no longer had much interest in the farm, and as a result the crop didn't turn out as expected.

Calvin would reap some of the plants and take them to his house, while Sarge would pass through occasionally and reap a little. On the whole, it was obvious to Calvin that his back was still going to be against the wall at the end of the weed season. He also knew that he would have to survive by all means necessary, even if he had to do something drastic. It was a life-or-death situation.

At that time he was already feeling the pangs of hunger, because no money was flowing, and it was obvious that Sarge had lost all interest in the ganja farm.

One day he was very hungry, therefore he decided to pick up his machete and a bag and head for the jungle to search for some old renta yam.

He wasn't having much luck finding any yam, but he bounced upon a mature ganja field in the process. He couldn't believe how beautiful the plants looked in the sunshine. However, he walked away from it, but as darkness set in, he was on his way back to visit the ganja field. This time he decided to help himself to a number of the mature plants, but he also left a trail of ganja leafs, which enabled the owner to follow him.

The following morning he was fast asleep in bed when he suddenly heard a man calling him by name. When he didn't answer, the man continued to call him. Eventually Calvin recognised the voice and answered.

When he opened the door and looked outside, he saw one of Mass Percy's friends standing on the footpath holding a machete.

At the doorway in only a pair of shorts, Calvin yawned and rubbed sleep from his eyes and then asked the man what was the matter. The man said he had come for the weed Calvin had stolen.

Devon, who was lying in bed listening to the conversation, decided to get up and intervene. He asked the man what was wrong, and the man told him that Calvin had stolen his weed, and he wanted it back. But Devon told him that he didn't see his brother with any weed, and the man shouldn't accuse him like that.

The man got angry and started to swear at them, but Devon threatened to hurt him if he continued, and the man went away fuming.

By defending Calvin, Devon had assumed part ownership of the stolen weed, which was of top quality, and it generated some money for the both of them. Suddenly, Devon realised that he could make a living from stolen ganja. As a result, he encouraged Calvin to steal more weed and occasionally they would go together to stage those robberies on the ganja farmers.

At one stage they had the bedroom full of stolen ganja, but they were perched for a fall.

At that time they had a war going on with Base, a wannabe bad man who was living in the area. He was one of Miss Lidy's older sons, who would always get into trouble with the locals. The war had started one evening after Base tried to bully Calvin, while he was having a shower at the public standpipe.

By then a few people had started to possess the luxury of water attached to their homes, but most youths still went to the nearby spring to have a bath or shower at the public standpipe.

That evening in question, Calvin and Monkey went to have a shower at the public standpipe, which was situated at the foot of Pan Bottom Hill.

Darkness had already descended upon the land and the boys were planning on hitting the streets of Mount Carey that night.

Monkey had his shower first and was waiting on Calvin to have his, when Base turned up and started to bully him for the use of the pipe. Eventually, an argument developed, and both were trying to win it by using the foulest words. In the process, Calvin told Base, "Go and suck your mother," which is one of the most insulting things one can say to a black youth. In response, Base attacked him and shoved him to the ground.

Such an act wasn't going to be tolerated by Calvin; as a result he decided to take it to another level.

The only streetlight was near the top of the hill, so it was dark at the bottom. Calvin hurriedly picked up his clothes and he and Monkey went up the hill, and they didn't have to say to each other what they were going to do next, because they already knew what needed to be done.

Halfway up the hill the boys stopped and waited until Base started to shower. While he was showering, he kept on singing aloud some chanting songs. Obviously he'd thought he had won the confrontation, but a big surprise was in store for him.

Without any warning, the boys began to hurl stones at Base, but he was bigger than they were and much tougher. Therefore, when he started to chase them up the hill, they ran, but on reaching the top of the hill, they decided to ambush him.

They hid in the cluster of shrubs on the embankment and waited for their pursuer, who was racing up the hill at bird speed, and when Base appeared on top of the hill, the boys let him have it all; every stone that they could lay their hands on got thrown at him. He ran away as fast as he'd come – but towards the boys' homes.

They decided to head for Mount Carey instead, where they would possibly get protection from Devon and his friends.

At the time, Devon used to hang out with Lee and Clarkie. Lee was one of Money Man's sons, and he used to work at the Anchovy police station. Clarkie was Lee's brother-in-law, who was married to Grace, Lee's sister. Clarkie was a butcher, and he used to work in Mobay.

Monkey and Calvin would occasionally associate with them and indulge in some of the things that they would do, but that night they ran out of luck, because they couldn't find Devon, Lee, or Clarkie when they got to Mount Carey, which left them with no choice but to head home alone.

When the boys reached the foot of Pan Bottom Hill, where the fight started earlier, they began to walk silently and close to the side of the dark, deserted road.

They were petrified at that stage, because Base had the strategic advantage. After all, he was living opposite the shop on the hill with his family.

Calvin was relieved when they reached his gate and he was nowhere in sight. However, Base had a different plan in mind for them. He had decided to lay in wait for them at the same spot where they'd ambushed him earlier.

When the boys got to the top of the hill, unlike them, Base gave them a warning before he cast the first stone.

"Yuh bloodclaat, unoo," he bellowed, "unoo tink seh unoo deh get weh dis time?"

Translation: "You bloodclaat, you. You think you guys are going to get away this time?"

Before the last word left his mouth, he began to hurl stones at them.

The boys were completely taken by surprise and on impulse they run towards their homes, but it wasn't possible to dodge all the stones that Base was hurling at them.

Calvin was the unlucky one, because one of the stones caught him on his right heel. The pain was excruciating, and it pulsated as if he'd been hit by a thousand volts of electricity. Nonetheless, he couldn't stop to inspect the injury. Therefore, both of them continued to run until they reached Monkey's home, where they say their goodbyes, and Calvin continued on home.

When he finally reached home and looked at his heel, he nearly fainted, because the impact of the stone had shattered the spot where he got hit, and the sight of the damage ignited more pain, which ran throughout his shuddering body.

When Devon got home later that night, he found his little brother in pain, and asked him what was wrong. Calvin filled him in on the whole episode.

"It was the first time I'd seen Devon got so vexed when something bad had happened to me," Calvin exclaimed.

In the morning Devon told him that he was going to kill Base, and Calvin told him that he was coming too, but Devon said no. Even so, after he went away, Calvin followed behind him stealthily.

Initially, Devon went to Lee's yard and told him what had happened to his brother. Without delay, they both hurried off in search of Base.

By then Calvin's heel had swollen badly, and it was paining him very badly. It was still bleeding profusely, and he didn't have any form of medication to dress it himself. Therefore he had to tie it with a piece of cloth to stop it from bleeding. He'd planned on getting it looked after by Mother Mira, but that would have to be done after Base got sorted out.

Calvin hopped on his injured leg to Monkey's house to inform him about what was going down, and after he found his friend they both headed for Base's yard.

On reaching close to where Base lived they met Victor, one of Lee's younger brothers. "Have you seen Devon and Lee?" Calvin asked.

"Yes," replied Victor, "they're on their way down to Dr Airance's house, where Base is working as a gardener."

They didn't hesitate; hurriedly Calvin and Monkey headed for the doctor's yard.

Dr Airance was a white man who lived in a big old Victorian house on top of a hill, between the border of Mount Carey and Carey Village, with Miss Molly, his mixed-race secretary, who became his lover after his wife died, and he was working as a medical practitioner in Montego Bay.

Just as with all the white settlers, Dr Airance's land was of prime quality and rich with various types of fruits.

A lot of the youths around the area were scared of Dr Airance, for the mere fact that he was a gun owner. He was renowned for the many times he'd fired shots at youths, who went on his property to steal his fruits. It was also rumoured that he buried his wife and other family members in the house, and the house was believed to be haunted. Nonetheless, Calvin and many other youths would frequently reap his fruits.

*

That morning, Calvin and Monkey reached the doctor's yard just in time to witness Devon unleashing some vicious blows on Base with a piece of wood, but Base got away from Devon and ran; however, he had another plan up his sleeve for his pursuers.

Devon and Lee led the chase after Base, but he was much faster than them. On the contrary, Base had a reputation for making trouble, but when trouble came his way, the first thing he did was run to the police station. As a result, they thought Base was heading there, but this time he wasn't.

There was a bridge above the train line, close to the Mount Carey Baptist Church, that everybody had to cross to get onto the main road. Base lay in wait for them behind the bridge with his machete, ready to kill.

Calvin couldn't run fast enough with his injured leg and was left behind eventually, but when he finally caught up with them, it was too late.

On reaching the bridge, he found his brother lying on his back in the middle of the road, covered in blood and suffering from machete wounds.

He asked the few people who were standing over Devon what had happened, and they told him that Base had ambushed him and inflicted many cuts all over his body.

When Calvin looked down on his brother lying in the pool of blood, he suddenly forgot the surging pain that he was feeling, and he asked the onlookers where the culprit had gone. They pointed towards the main road.

He looked that way and saw Lee and Monkey chasing Base. He didn't hesitate; he raced after them with blood in his eye and vengeance in his heart.

There was a house close to the main road and Base ran through the yard, towards another house on a hill, with Lee and Monkey close behind him.

When Calvin reached the house at the main road he didn't bother to open the gate. He jumped over it like an athlete, forgetting that his heel was badly injured.

Base ran inside the house on the hill to seek refuge, and the occupants decided to call the police.

When the police came, they arrested Base and took him to the Anchovy police station.

Devon, who had received chops all over his body, on his head, arms, and back, was taken to the Cornwall Regional Hospital for treatment and later released.

The men decided not to press any charges against Base, and the police released him without any charge.

As it goes, rude boys never get the police involved in an affair, no matter what another person or a gang might have done to them. Devon, Lee, Monkey, and Calvin were adamant to live up to the laws of the street in a shrewd way, but two weeks later the war started afresh.

By then Devon's wounds were healing nicely, but Calvin's badly damaged heel had caught an infection and begun to suppurate. The constant pain he experienced was much worse than when he'd got injured initially.

Base thought that accounts were even, because of the initial dropping of the charges, but he was to be proven wrong.

To begin with, Devon got a piece of metal pipe and waited for the right moment to launch another attack on Base, and nobody knew when he was going to attack the antagonist. It was a spur of the moment thing.

The whole crew was sitting at Lee's gate one afternoon, smoking weed and listening to the stereo, which Lee had connected to the public electrical pole by a single string of electrical wire.

Out of the blue, Base came strolling down the road boldly, while singing a Bob Marley song.

Ever since he'd wounded Devon and Calvin, he began to exert himself a lot, and he would regularly walk around with a machete in his waist and sang chanting songs whenever he saw them.

That day, Devon waited until Base was about to pass before he attacked him.

Base was taken completely by surprise, and before he knew what was happening, Devon gave him two licks, one at the base of his neck and the other on his left arm. Although he was wounded, he still managed to run away swiftly, and nobody saw him after that for many days.

When Base eventually resurfaced, he was sporting a bandaged left arm and a neck cast, but that was not to be the end of the war, because a few weeks later he decided to launch another attack on Calvin.

It happened one Saturday morning, while Calvin was standing at a light pole with his back against it, opposite the bush doctor's gate, waiting to go and get his rapidly decaying heel dressed.

It was his second visit to Mother Mira in two days. Before then, he had gone to the public clinic at Mount Carey to get his heel dressed each Monday, Wednesday, and Friday, but whatever the nurses were using to dress his heel wasn't working. As a result, he'd decided to ask the bush doctor to heal it for him.

Her one-legged, half mentally ill son, Dooba, was standing there with him that morning.

To his left was that rough, unpaved road that went down a slope towards Miss Dinie's gate. On the other side was that straight, rough unpaved road, which connected to Pan Bottom Hill.

Calvin saw Base sauntering down the straight, rough, unpaved road towards him with his good arm behind his back, but he didn't pay him any mind, because he knew Base was licking his wounds like he was.

"Hey, Calvin, watch yuhself, yuh nuh," Dooba suddenly warned. "De bwoy Base have a machete behind him."

When Dooba saw the machete and alerted Calvin, Base was only five or so yards from where he was standing, but Calvin didn't flinch, instead he decided to stand his ground and fight him if he had to, because he wasn't going to let that fool scare him.

When Base got close to his victim, he slowly produced the machete in front of him and said, "Hey, pussy," but Calvin didn't respond. "Yuh tink seh mi ha guh allow yuh Breda fi brok mi up an' nuh duh nutten 'bout it?" he continued.

Translation: "You think I'm going to allow your brother to break me up and not do anything about it?"

"Ah gwine kill yuh bloodclaat dis morning."

Translation: "I'm going to kill you bloodclaat this morning."

With that said, Base raised the machete and took a step closer. Calvin instinctively ran off to his left, down the rough slope.

After taking a few huge strides, he impulsively dived feet first, with his injured right foot, and as he dived, he heard the machete whistle over his head.

Base was moving fast, and his momentum carried him down the hill.

Calvin got up swiftly and made his escape down the rough, unpaved road, where Base had appeared from. Base turned around and began to chase him, but when Calvin reached Lee's gate, he held onto the gatepost and swung himself into the little track, quickly picked up a few stones, and began to hurl them at Base, who was gaining distance on him by then.

Base didn't stop, he continued to run towards his house, and Calvin gave him chase with stones until he turned into his gate.

When the chase was over and Calvin checked his right thigh, which was burning by then, to his surprise, he found all the skin missing from one large area. Mother Mira had more than his decaying heel to dress that day.

On the contrary, Base got cold feet that morning and decided to report Calvin and Devon to the police, and this time he let on to them about the weed that his rivals had at their house.

Early one afternoon, a few days later, the cops raided the house, and on their arrival they found Calvin and Devon with over ten kilos (22 lbs) of prepared ganja.

Calvin recognised a few of the officers; Sarge had paid them to set him free on the night when he was arrested for the wounding of Monkey's dad. So without thinking of the consequences, Calvin blurted out that the weed belonged to Sarge, even though Sarge had nothing to do with the stolen weed. Nonetheless, that was good news for the police, because that meant they were going to get paid twice for doing their job.

A lot of people gathered around when the police came, and consequently they had to make an arrest.

Quietly the corporal asked the boys who was going to take the rap (take responsibility). Calvin was the first to hold his hands up, but the corporal told him that he was too young and eventually took Devon instead. They also took about one kilo of the weed for exhibit and told the boys to get rid of the rest once all the people who were present had left the scene.

Devon got bailed out the same day, and when he went to court a week later to answer to charges for possession of ganja, they charged him $70.00 Jamaican and set him free.

When Sarge heard what Calvin did, he was furious with him. Still, he gave the policemen some additional money for their trouble.

The fighting eventually ceased without anybody calling a truce, but the tension in the community was always visible.

"Looking back, it was a senseless war, which could have gotten worse easily, but that is just an example of how a lot of gang wars develop in the ghettos on the island of Jamaica and around the world.

"Sometimes one could easily take someone else's disrespect, or simply walk away from an argument, but on the streets of the ghetto that can be dangerous. For instance, one of two things will happen in such a case: either the offender takes this for weakness and continues to show disrespect to the offended, or the offender starts to brag about it around the neighbourhood, which sometimes attracts other wannabes, who help make the offended's life a misery. In turn, the offended can either be weak or strong. If he is weak, he may take the continuous disrespect until it blows off. Equally, he may choose to move away from his present residence, but oftentimes you may see it on the newspaper or hear it on the news that such victims have killed themselves. On the other hand, the strong will not do that. He will do whatever it takes to regain respect, and the outcome of it most times is the loss of lives and the breakdown of community spirit. On the whole, however, if most youths would think about the after-effect of taking revenge, a lot of lives would be spared and a lot of youths would never end up with a criminal record."

*

A few months after the fighting ceased, Devon, Lee, and Clarkie decided to steal some of the villagers' goats. The following day Calvin was captured by some of the disgruntled members of the community, convinced that he'd also played a role in the robbery, only because he was in the same crew.

After he was caught between Sitta's and Money Man's houses, the residents decided to beat him up with sticks, machetes, kicks, and punches.

Initially, he didn't know what they were beating him for. Still, he tried to fight back, but he was unable to defend himself against the angry mob, while they were raining blows on him from every direction.

While the vicious blows were landing on him from left, right, and centre, some of the frustrated people were shouting, "Kill him! Kill him! Him too fucking teef," and that was when he realised that he was being crucified for something he hadn't done.

Audrey was also amongst the irritated crowd, and without hesitating she came to Calvin's rescue and said, "No sah! Last night Calvin was in Mother Mira's church wid mi, an' im went straight home after dat," but before Audrey could utter another word, Asley (otherwise known as Bad Man), the biggest man in the crowd, gave Calvin one last punch in his mouth, smashing his top lip and knocking him flat out on his back.

When he regained consciousness, the crowd was standing over him, some with their mouths agape, looking concerned. Slowly he pulled himself up from off the ground and staggered on weary legs. At that point his whole body was aching, and he couldn't close his mouth, because his already fat lips were three times their usual size. Suddenly tears started to flow from his eyes, mixing with blood as they ran down his cheeks.

He took a few unsteady steps, and the crowd parted to let him through. Still determined to defend himself, he made a sudden motion as the crowd parted, as if he was going to launch an attack, but someone slapped him viciously on his back from behind with a machete, which sent him sprawling onto his stomach. Without hesitating, he got up quickly and ran straight to the police station to hand himself in.

On reaching the police station, he was denied the chance to clear his name, because another wretched group of people from the same community was present, who also knew he was a member of the infamous crew; hence they held him steadfast as an accomplice of the accused culprits.

"Se one ha dem deh, lock im up too," the dissatisfied crowd began to shout to the policemen, and Detective Minto didn't need a second telling. Roughly he grabbed Calvin and searched him, and then led him into the reception area of the station.

Calvin, who was weary from the beating he'd received earlier and the distance he'd travelled on foot to the station, began to plead his innocence, "Off-off-officer," he started to stammer, while struggling to speak with his swollen and aching lips, but Detective Minto only looked him hard in the face with his bloodshot eyes as he tightened one bracelet of the handcuff around his right wrist, and then do the same with the other on the handle of the gun box.

Calvin shivered from intimidation, but he continued nonetheless, "Mi . . . mi nuh guilty, yuh know sah," (I'm not guilty you know Sir) but before he could utter another word, Minto responded by cocking his right fist and slamming it into his already aching face.

Minto was a very big man, and the impact of his fist was like another jolt of electricity.

Calvin fell sideways off the stool that he was sitting on, and with his handcuffed hand dangling from the gun box, he half curled up his body, whilst awaiting the inevitable kicks, but the officer only stood over his quivering body and said, "Onoo too bloodclaat teef. Onoo fi guh luk wok duh."

Translation: "You guys too bloodclaat thief. You guys should go and find work to do."

Calvin was surprise when Detective Minto, suddenly turn and walked away, leaving him in the same position, where he cried silently until his hungry, aching, shuddering body ceased from trembling.

While Calvin was being held at the police station, Clarkie got caught with the remains of the goats at the butcher shop where he used to work in Mobay, and he was subsequently arrested and held at 14 Barnett Street Police Station, one of the roughest jails on the island.

Not long after that, Lee and Devon also got caught in Mobay and were transported to Anchovy. On their arrival, the police locked them in separate rooms for interrogation.

After what seemed like an eternity, the corporal walked into the guard's room and released Calvin and then told him that they had concluded that he was really innocent.

Calvin was very happy, and he didn't ask any questions, nor did he hesitate. But as he was about to walk away from the station, the corporal stopped him. He was frightened, because he thought they were going to arrest him again, but he was relieved when the officer asked him if he wanted a job.

He was shocked by the officer's offer, and he didn't know what to say, because he knew what job he was being offered. He also knew a lot of people were going to brand him as an informer, if he was to take the job (just as they'd branded Lee), but at the time he was struggling to make it through each day. Ultimately he thought to him, *"it's better to be earning a living than to continue suffering because of pride.'* Eventually, he told the corporal that he would take the job, and without any delay the officer sent him to wash the police jeep. On the other hand, he didn't expect things to move so fast, after all that had happened, but '*There's a reason for everything that happens*,' he thought to himself.

Although he was a bit embarrassed washing the jeep at the side of the station, in front of everybody, especially his earlier accuser, at the end of the day he had the last laugh.

While he was washing the jeep, the police started to beat Lee and Devon.

There was a deafening silence, after the first crack of the cat-o'-nine-tails, but after a few more cracks Calvin heard Devon cry out in pain, and from that moment his blood ran cold from every blow his brother received.

Slowly Calvin picked up the water bucket and went to fetch more water at the back of the station, and on his way toward the water tank, he looked through an open door and beheld Devon standing between Horse Mouth and Detective Barns. He was wearing only his trousers, and the officers were taking turn to hit him all over his body, even on his face and head. Devon was twisting with each impact of the blows and bawling like a baby.

Later that same evening, Devon and Lee were transferred to 14 Barnett Street Police Station, where they were held in custody, and a few weeks later, along with Clarkie, they were charged with the theft of the goats and later sent to prison for nine months each.

It was the first time in prison for the three of them. During their time in prison, Ruby and Marika occasionally visited Devon and brought him food, money, and clothes. On the whole, they thought they were doing him good by supporting him while he was behind bars, but years later he threw it right back into their faces, because he certainly wasn't the type of person that anybody or prison could tame.

CHAPTER ELEVEN

Dishonouring

Although Calvin started to work at the police station in the middle of the month, the corporal sent in his wage slip and he got paid at the end of the month.

He was on top of the world when he got his first wages. Suddenly he felt like a grown man, and he didn't want the feeling to go away.

His job description consisted of washing the police jeep, but he also washed the officer's private cars. He was also responsible for the up-keep of the premises. Later he was called upon to cook for the officers, and at length they also asked him to clean the guns, under the watchful eyes of District Constable Brown.

An elderly woman worked there too, who was in charge of cleaning the inside of the station.

Day by day Calvin began to enjoy working at the police station, and although some of the officers were a bit arrogant at first, others were cool, and gradually all of them grew to like him, or so he thought.

Eventually he fitted perfectly into his new job, but even though he was working at a police station, it wasn't doing much good for him, in the way of transforming him into a law-abiding citizen. Consequently it'd only make him an accomplice of the corrupt (JCF) Jamaica Constabulary Force.

Halfway through the second month, he was called upon to assist two officers in loading five big bags full to capacity with ganja, into the van of a well-known don (drug dealer).

Calvin knew from experience that the police were corrupt, but he didn't know how bold they were or how far they were taking the corruption. Nonetheless, he simply did what he was asked to do and pretended what he was doing was normal.

"At that crucial stage in my life, I was in no position to say, 'No, I'm not getting involved in the corruption,' because doing that would surely cost me my job, which I was most grateful to have. Furthermore, I didn't want to become an enemy of the corrupt members of the JCF, for the simple fact that I was trying to stay alive, and not being suicidal at that point."

That same afternoon, after Calvin loaded the weed into the Don's van, he got two hundred dollars from an officer, and the same officer also drove him home in the police jeep.

The following week he was called upon again, and this time he was told to put two bags of the weed into the car of a well-respected, prominent member of society. Most youths, Calvin included, used to regard this man as one of their role models in the community.

As time went by, when the police went on raids at the ganja farms and sometimes at the ganja storehouses, they would bring the weed that they seized back to the station. In the process, if they captured anybody at the farms, or at the storehouses, they would bring them back as well, and if those people were working for a don, the don would go in and give the police some money. In return, the arrested person or people would walk free, and later the don would drive his van into the station garage, and sometimes Calvin was asked to load the weed into the vehicle for them. Again he still didn't have a problem doing whatever he was asked to do, and as time went by he still didn't have a problem preparing the herbs for sale, after the police returned from a raid on a ganja farm. He would also put aside some of the best weed for him, when he was preparing it for sale, and most times an officer would drive him home with his share.

It reached the point where he thought he had gathered enough power amongst the police, to stop them from raiding some of his acquaintances' farms. He thought doing so would earn him some respect from the local boys and some money too. Therefore, one morning he seized his chance, when he realised that the police were about to go on a raid in his area.

Many ganja farmers would grow the late plants, which they reaped in December, but this one grew his early, and it was near harvest time.

The officers heard about it and decided to reap it before the farmer, but that morning while they were planning their attack Calvin overheard them, and as soon as they got into the jeep and drove out of the station, he headed for the jungle to forewarn the farmer that the police (beasts) were coming.

He took a shortcut through the hills and reached the ganja field before the police did, and when he got to the field he was breathless.

The farmer and his accomplices were startled to see Calvin, and when he told them what was about to happen, they panicked in confusion. He calmed them down and told them to leave the field and let him handle the situation when the police arrived.

"Yow! Ha mi dis yuh nuh," he shouted, as soon as he saw the six policemen coming up on the other side of the hill. They were on the alert and all aimed their guns in the direction of his voice.

"Ha wah de raas yuh ha duh, bwoy?" the corporal asked, "Yuh nuh 'fraid yuh get a shot in ha yuh raasclaat?"

Translation: "Hey, what the raas (swear word) you think you doing, boy? You not afraid you get shot in your raasclaat?"

Calvin remained calm, whilst they hurled a barrage of abusive language at him, and when they were satisfied with the verbal onslaught they went away fuming, and later that day when he returned to work the corporal told him that he was lucky he hadn't been locked up. The corporal also told him that if he did anything like that again, he would shoot him or lock him up.

On the whole, Calvin knew that his safety wasn't guaranteed, regardless of the fact that he worked with and for the policemen, not to mention breaking the law with them. Nonetheless, he humbled himself and continued to do what he normally did.

Later that same day, Calvin met the farmer on Pan Bottom Hill, who promised him some of the herbs and money on the completion of his harvest. The news of what he did earlier was also hot on the street.

"At that point I felt good, because after all was said and done, I was doing the opposite of what many people thought of me, because I was protecting the locals from the police."

The harvest was successful, and the farmer made a lot of money, but in the process he forgot the promises he'd made to

Calvin, and worst of all, he also began to spread rumours on him, that he was an informer.

Calvin refused to take the farmer's disrespect and decided to get even with him for breaking his promise – even though what he planned to do was against the ethics of a down-to-earth street youth: he was about to become an informer, exactly what he initially feared people would expect of him when he took the job at the police station. But this was simply business at its best, and he didn't felt any remorse whatsoever. After all, he was living in a dog-eat-dog world, where everyone did what they had to do to survive. It was a matter of conforming to the whole concept of the mendacious system and staying alive. In other words, you either played the game by muddling your soul in deceitfulness, or getting out while the going was good. He had nowhere to go, because he was trapped on a beautiful island, framed by lush mountains and shimmering waters, in a nation of people that continually killing each other off for no apparent reason, and a shady government who care only for themselves and their followers. On the other hand, the police were expected to uphold the law to the utmost, but they were no exception, because they were using the power of the law to rape and conduct numerous robberies and atrocities.

Sometimes Calvin would sit on a stool in the garage and watch the police in amazement, as they set up roadblocks after their monthly salary began to run out. They behaved like hungry lions, and they came up with all sorts of reasons to impose a fine on the motorists, who regularly pay the police to get off their backs. No matter how small the money was, the police would accept it, and once a motorist paid, the police continue to bombard them continuously.

The bus and taxi drivers used to get targeted the most, because they always overfilled their vehicles. The fisherman who sold his fish from his van had to stop at the station every time he passed by, because he once got let off for a minor fault with his vehicle. The bread man had to do the same thing also – just to name a few. Calvin also used to benefit from the bread and fish that they received, because he would occasionally get portions to take home with him.

On the whole, because he knew how greedy the police were and how easy it was to bribe them, after their monthly pay ran out, he decided to use them to get even with the ganja farmer.

He didn't need to beat around the bush to put his plans into action; he got straight to the point and told a few officers what he wanted them to do.

Before the policemen headed off on the mission, Calvin demanded that no arrest or any physical harm should take place. The officers agreed, and the raid was successful.

The herbs that the officers confiscated were shared between Calvin, an acting corporal, a detective, and a district constable. From that day his respect seemed secure amongst the officers, and he was now a major part of the corrupt system.

The police also used Calvin for their own advantage, because when they arrested someone for smoking weed, they would ask Calvin to make a spliff, smoke half of it, and give them the rest to take to court as evidence.

"I didn't like that part of the job, because it felt like I was the one responsible for sending those people to jail or issuing them with a fine, but I was in no position to refuse. After all, I was on the team, and I was playing my part."

After a while, Calvin started to visit his grandparents regularly at Mount Salem. They were proud of him for having a job, but they weren't proud of where he was working.

Devon, Clarkie, and Lee got released from prison after serving four and a half months each, but none of them returned to live at Carey Village. Lee went to Bogue Hill to live with other relatives, while Clarkie returned to Mobay, and Devon went to 10 Crichton's Drive.

"Although I was conscious of the wrongdoings that I often took part in at the station, nonetheless I continued to work there, wheeling and dealing with the policemen, and along the way I'd also started to impersonate them."

One day, while Calvin was in the station garage cleaning an officer's car, he saw a buck knife (a hunting knife) the size of a .22 pistol, lying on the floor of the car. He picked it up and began to inspect it.

The officer, who was also present, asked him if he liked the knife. Calvin told him yes and asked if he could have it. Instantly the officer said, with a laugh, "Yes. Go ahead and have it. You can't say I never gave you anything."

The knife became a major part of Calvin's impersonation of the police, and at times while he was at work, he would tuck it in his waist, under his shirt, which made him look as if he had a gun. On the streets it was the same, until one fine day when he decided to model his imitation gun, while he was on his way to Crichton's Drive.

Initially, he got off the passenger bus at the clock tower, on Barnett Street, and decided to walk the two miles to Mount Salem, because he couldn't afford the taxi fare. However, while he was walking toward his grandparents' house, it seemed someone spotted the bulge at his waist and reported him to the police.

At the house, Uncle was in bed sleeping while Aunty was out shopping, and Calvin, Goodall, Wade, and Devon were at the back chatting.

Goodall and Wade were brothers. They born and grew up in Manchester, near ST Elizabeth. They were tenants in the back room at Crichton's Drive.

That day, the boys heard a car suddenly pull up at the gate, and they thought it was Aunty arriving home in a taxi. Calvin ran toward the veranda with the intention of helping her with the shopping.

As soon as he got on the veranda he saw a man in civilian clothes, with a machine gun in his hands, jumping over the six-foot metal gate that led to the garage. Another similar man was already on his way toward the back of the house, and a huge black detective was struggling through the small main gate with an M16 assault rifle in his hands.

"Instantly I realised that the men were police, but I wasn't scared, because I was used to being around them.

"As soon as the huge policeman saw me he aimed his M16 in my direction and I automatically held my hands in the air. With a commanding voice, he told me to walk towards him slowly with my hands in the air.

"When I got to the bottom of the steps, with his gun aiming inches from my belly, he asked me if I was the last one to walk through the gate, and I told him yes. In the same instant, I was also about to tell him that I was one of them, because I was working at the Anchovy police station, but before I could open my mouth he pulled back his arms and rammed me in my belly with the nuzzle of the M16.

"The impact of the blow hurt, and I half curled up myself while trying to hold my hands in the air, and the officer nudged me with the nuzzle of his gun at the same spot where he'd just hit me and told me to walk towards the back of the house.

"When we arrived at the back, I saw Devon, Wade, and Goodall standing with their faces toward the house and hands in the air, while the two policemen aimed their guns at them. At that moment, I realised I was in big trouble, and I suddenly felt intimidated.

"My escorting officer demanded to know where my bedroom was, and when I showed him the room I occasionally shared with Devon, he told one of his colleagues to search it. After the search was completed, the officer found the knife I had in my possession and a photograph of Devon, posing amongst some mature ganja plants in a weed field. At that point, Devon started to screw up his face and one of the officers was about to gun butt him, but out of the blue Aunty appeared and asked what was going on in her yard.

"The huge officer told Aunty that they were acting on information they'd received about a young man who appeared to be carrying a gun, and he showed her the knife and the photo.

"Aunty told him we were good boys who got caught up with the wrong crowd, and he told us that we were lucky, because the situation would be completely different if Aunty hadn't turned up.

"After the officers made their departure, I smiled, but I was badly shaken, and I made a silent vow to discontinue the impersonation."

Back at the police station, things had taken another turn, because a young policewoman came to join the crew.

Debby was about five years older than Calvin and fresh out of the police training camp. It was her first assignment, and she was a bit naïve, but she had enough sense to stay far from her colleagues' beds.

Calvin liked her at first sight, but he didn't have the courage to tell her until one day Debby looked him deep in the eyes and asked him, "Do you have something to tell me?"

He picked up on the hint, but he was taken aback. Still, he composed himself and told her that he liked her. Her response was a haughty belly laugh, one to touch a man's soul, but they were suddenly interrupted. Their closeness didn't go unnoticed, and it also created animosity between one of the policemen and Calvin.

The officer in question fancied Debby also, but she had no interest in him, and when he became conscious of that, it hurt him very badly. As a result, he decided to take it out on Calvin. This occurred one day whilst Calvin was cleaning the gun box.

Debby stood watching Calvin as he cleared some old ganja from out of the gun box, and as usual, they were talking and laughing. Suddenly the obsessed officer appeared on the scene and decided to throw his weight around. It seemed as if he was trying to gain self-importance or simply to show Calvin that he was bigger – which was already clear, because he was the law. On the contrary, he wasn't a better man, and Calvin make sure to tell the officer that.

The policeman went into a rage and dragged the brush from Calvin's hand, but he stood his ground and the officer used the brush to hit him across his chest, and that's when all hell broke loose.

Calvin launched out at the officer with both hands and grabbed him around his midriff, and both of them ended up on the floor, rolling over and over in the reception, while Debby kept shouting; "Leave him alone," to her colleague.

The officer had chosen the wrong time to throw his weight around, because Calvin wasn't going to let him overpower and humiliate him in front of Debby. Moreover, he wanted her to see that he was a man and that he was also capable of defending himself. On the other hand, he and the policeman had a few things in common; they were both stammerers and determined to show the power of their masculinity.

The other officers, who were on duty, including the corporal, stepped in and tried to tear them apart. When they finally succeeded, Calvin was fuming like a mad bull.

"Yuh se if mi did have a gun, bwoy," . . ."Wah yuh woulda duh wid de gun?" (What would you have done with the gun?) The officer stammered, not allowing Calvin to complete his sentence.

Without thinking where he was or who he was speaking to, Calvin said, "I woulda shot yuh ina yuh face wid it, bwoy." Translation: "I would have shot you in your face with it, boy."

Suddenly the corporal intervened angrily and said, "Yu better watch wah yu deh say to de officer, yu know, bwoy. Yu deh guh too far now."

Translation: "You better watch what you are saying to the officer, you know, boy. You are going too far now."

"Yu se anywey me se yu bwoy, yu ah guh have it," Calvin concluded.

Translation: "You see anywhere I see you, boy, you going to have it."

But that was a silly thing to say, because if anything had happened to the officer, he would have been in big trouble. That was one of his worst persistent faults; whenever he got angry, he would say the first thing that occurred to him.

That same day, he'd gone to visit his grandparents, and he told them about the fight he'd had with the officer, (just in case there was a repercussion) – but he didn't tell them that it was over a policewoman.

Aunty didn't like the bit where the officer used the brush to hit him, and so she decided to go to the police station and sort it out.

That night, he stayed at Crichton's Drive, and in the morning he went with his aunt in-law to the station to rectify the situation.

He was a bit tentative about the idea of her coming in with him, but he decided that, on the whole, it was the best thing to do. He also knew that he was making enemies with the police, by allowing Aunty to intervene, but he also wanted them to know that someone cared about his welfare.

Officer Obsessed wasn't at work when they got to the station. However, Aunty told the corporal that she was only there to let them know that her grandson was somebody's child and that she wasn't pleased with what had happened.

The corporal told her that he'd spoken to the officer already, and he would have a word with him again.

It was evident that Calvin's service was no longer required at the station, and he didn't need them to tell him so. Instead, he told the corporal that he wasn't coming back, and they didn't ask him to stay.

Occasionally he would bump into Debby around town. Each would enquire about how the other was getting on, but they never went beyond that.

The same week that Calvin packed in his job at the police station, he returned to his grandparents' house to live. As usual, things were all right between them for a while, until they switched back to their old "do it our way or else" customs.

By then he was used to changes in his life, and he also felt he was a man who had come of age in his own right. He was older and wiser, and he'd begun to see things from a different standpoint.

Suddenly, he realised that his life was the same wherever he went; only the situation was different. On top of that, every other person seemed like a figment of his imagination.

On the whole, there wasn't much that he could do to eradicate the mental torture, so he humbled himself and became his grandparents' maid. His days were consumed with chores, but his nights were sleepless, filled with an endless yearning to be what he wanted to be and not what others expected him to be.

Calvin used to enjoy doing his grandparents' chores, but at length he realised that they didn't have any future plans for him. Thus he decided to do something meaningful for himself. As a result, he asked one of the neighbours to get him a job where he could learn a trade.

The neighbour got him the perfect job, in an electrical store, where he could work and learn the trade at the same time. However, the first morning when he was ready to go to work, his grandparents gave him an ultimatum. "If you take the job," they told him, "nuh bother return to our house."

He'd thought about moving on before, but he wasn't prepared to return to his dad's house and the riotous lifestyle that was stifling him. Neither did he want to be loose on the rugged streets of Mobay. So he was left with only one choice: forget about gaining employment and securing stability for his future, and continue to be his grandparents' humble maid.

That morning, Calvin saw all his little plans of turning his life around going down the drain, and there was nobody else to turn to for support. Just as before, he was left to his own devices, so he tucked his tail like a mangy dog and went behind the house, where he used to hide and smoke his spliffs.

Initially, he built up a spliff and began to smoke it, without caring whether one of his grandparents happened to patrol the yard that morning (as they often did) and catch him in the act.

As he puffed on the spliff, with tears rolling down his cheeks, he kept whispering, "Why me, God? Why me of all the people in this world have to suffer like this? Duh God, please open a way for me, because I can't take this kind of living anymore." The intensity of the pain he experienced that morning was indescribable.

"Later as I got older, I became aware of the fact that in reality, although my grandparents' were good in many ways, nonetheless, it's parents like them who cause their children to pick up guns, live on the streets, and put their own and other people's lives in danger.

"I used to feel infuriated when I reminisced about those days, and I also wished over and over for the memories to go away and the wounds to heal. At one point I almost concluded that my life would never change, but later on I came to realise that although no one has control over their destiny, one can still move forward, regardless of circumstances, and although you can't change what has already been done, you can still make a difference regarding to what happens next."

Still, regardless of his grandparents' selfish actions, he had a lot of respect for them. If nothing else, they had taught him a lot of good things. Uncle Roland was the first person to introduce the Bible to him and teach him how to read it. They were also the ones who taught him how to sit around a table and eat with a knife and fork. They taught him how to pray, to say good night to the members of his household at night, and say good morning the next day. His uncle also taught him how to dress and act like a gentleman, even though Calvin used to get vexed when he had to tuck his shirt into his trousers and buckle the waist around his belly button. Last but not least, they taught him to love and honour God with all his heart, even though they weren't doing what they were teaching him to do and he wasn't sure who the God he was supposed to serve was. Neither was he sure if his grandparents themselves knew the God that they were serving, because the walls inside their house were like a shrine, covered with pictures of a white man with blue eyes who they claimed was Christ.

"I used to believe they were really pictures of Jesus Christ, but many years later I found out that they were only paintings, done by the famous master artist, Leonardo da Vinci."

CHAPTER TWELVE

The Battle Gets Hotter

At the age of eighteen, Calvin was still living at his grandparents' house, but he was more like a live-in helper than a family member. His days were mainly taken up with chores, and at night he would lie wide awake in bed, dreaming of a better life that was completely beyond his reach.

At that stage, he'd started to imagine what having a home, a car, good clothes to wear, and food on one's table really felt like. Although his grandparents offered most of those amenities, he wanted to have his own things.

He didn't have the wherewithal to gain all those things for himself, and he was still clinging to the belief that his family and his environment had failed to nourish him adequately. At last it reached the stage where he could no longer tolerate the kind of life that he was living, because the constancy of suffering seemed irresistible. Thus he decided to go in search of a better life. After all, he didn't want to continue being sheltered and patronized in his grandparents' house.

He got up one day and decided to go on an impossible mission, because he thought he could find the love, stability, and security he craved.

He knew that he didn't have the will to achieve his heart's desire by being kind, loving, and, most of all, honest. Also, he didn't have the demeanour necessary to live his life the way he wanted to, because he could not find a good job, so he could not afford to dress in an immaculate way. Besides all that, he was often unintelligible. Most important, he did not have a home, but he was determined to change his lifestyle, regardless of the circumstances that hemmed him in.

After leaving his grandparents' house for the umpteenth time, he decided not to return to his dad's house, which was one of the biggest decisions he'd ever made.

At first it was daunting, because he didn't exactly know where he would sleep the first night. At the time he was familiar with a lot of the youths from the ghetto side of Mount Salem, but he couldn't pinpoint one who might afford him a place to sleep. On the other hand, he didn't want to hang around Mount Salem, in case he bumped into his grandparents.

Ultimately, he decided to go to the local food market, where a lot of youths were actually living. Nonetheless, the initial thought of living on the edge of danger constantly made him shiver. However, the market was one of the few places where he'd always felt at home, because he could easily identify himself with most of the youths, who came from all over St James and other parishes to find a better way of life in the city.

Some of the youths at the market hustled during the week, sleeping in the market at night, and returned to their homes on the weekends. For those who didn't have a home to go to on the weekends, it was all about scrounging throughout the days, and at night they slept in the market. Others slept in various places around the city where nobody would disturb them. They would sleep on or under cardboard boxes according to the weather.

Most of the market youths possessed only a handcart, which they would use to transport people's goods from the market to the bus stops and vice versa. The farmers who came from afar with their produce to sell in the market were dependent entirely on the handcart youths, to transport their goods from the bus stops to their stalls inside the market.

Some of the youths would sell sky juice on the pushcarts (a small plastic bag filled with shaved or crushed ice with syrup poured over it). This drink was always in great demand by the locals, because the weather was always hot, and it was cheap to buy.

The ambitious youths would save up their money, often cooking their meals on charcoal to avoid spending too much. The rest would squander theirs by buying expensive food and drink, smoking and gambling the rest.

Calvin didn't want to push a handcart, because a lot of people looked down on the handcart youths. Moreover, too many people around town knew him as Brother and Sister Riley's nephew. Conversely, he didn't want to be in the position where he had to explain himself to those people when they saw him pushing a handcart, simply because they would surely want to know why he wasn't living with the precious Brother and Sister Riley. He also knew some of them wouldn't understand his reason, because his grandparents' house was meant to be his, according to Sister Riley. She told everybody that Calvin was born on the same day that she bought her house, so the house was his.

Therefore everybody expected him to stay at 10 Crichton's Drive and look after his uncle and aunty, but what's theirs was theirs, and he wanted what was his.

Occasionally he would use his closest mate Kingman's cart to push a load or two to the bus stops. He would also partake of the meals that they cooked in the market, but gradually he wanted more, and he chose an easy but dangerous way to achieve it.

It was a rainy Friday evening, and he knew that he was about to bark up the wrong tree, but he was determined to survive, whatever it took. He'd witnessed a lot of guys doing it before, but it never occurred to him that one day he would be doing the same thing too. Although he felt guilty after he'd committed the crime, he couldn't see a better way out.

It wasn't trendy and it wasn't cool, because the first and every other pocket that he picked, he was putting his life in danger. Also, it was like a drug: the first time, he felt an exhilaration he thought must be like heaven. Later, though, sometimes it took every bit of his energy to pick one pocket, even though it felt good afterwards.

He and other pickpockets used to hang out at the bus stops and scrutinise everybody, especially on Thursdays and Fridays, when most people got paid. Those who were careless enough to have their wallets or their purses unsecured were the main targets. When the buses arrived and everybody started to push to get in first, the pickpockets would select those particular targets.

Some of the other pickpockets worked in groups, but Calvin didn't want any companion, because he didn't trust anybody.

He continued for a while until one day he heard the news about another pickpocket youth who got gunned down by a policeman. The youth was much younger than Calvin, yet his life got blown away like the wind. From that moment, Calvin realised that he had to find another way to survive, because he could easily have been the youth who got killed.

As he reminisced, he declared, "I feel nothing but shame and remorse when I look back on those days, but it was just the way of life for me then. Conversely, I knew all along that I was breaking the law, but I was only doing what I had to do to survive. Nonetheless, when I think about all the people I've robbed of their hard-earned bread, I often wish that I could turn back the clock."

Calvin was now confused, scared, and unsettled, because he didn't have many choices to survive the day-to-day life on the streets, outside of crime. His needs were also increasing, because he'd started to have more interest in girls and material things, unlike before when his main purpose was to find food to eat and money to gamble.

At length he began to do things to forget some of his fears, pains, sadness, and sorrows. Occasionally he went down by the Barnett River for a whole day, to swim and catch fish with some of the guys from the market. Sometimes he went alone. He also took walks into the jungle, where only the singing of birds were present, to hide from fear and from the people who had abandoned him, but he always clung to the desire to be a good man.

He also wanted to be able to make changes in his life and to be different. On the whole, he was enthusiastic about learning positive ways to live, in order to be a positive person himself. Most of all he wanted to give his love and to be loved.

Regularly he recalled the times when Uncle Roland used to quote words of William Shakespeare: "Son," Uncle used to say, "Life is what you make of it." At the time Calvin couldn't discern what his uncle was trying to tell him, but later on his journey, he suddenly realised that his uncle was simply trying to tell him to wake up and make a living for himself, instead of waiting on other people to help him.

Uncle also told him the story of his own life, how he had struggled, and what he had done to be in his present position.

Uncle Roland was born to Miss Fan on the twenty-fifth of February, 1919, her last child of six. His only brother died while he was a child, leaving him with his mother and four sisters.

Like Calvin, life was hard for Uncle, because his dad died while he was only a baby, but he was a bit luckier than Calvin, because he had a house full of women who spoilt him by doing everything for him.

Uncle said he was not just the last child, but also the only living son for his mother and the only brother for his sisters. However, at one stage, he could no longer tolerate the life that he was living at Carey Village, so he ran away to Kingston, where his big sister Bee was living. He also told Calvin that although he wasn't happy with how his sister Bee treated him at times, he still swallowed his pride and stayed with her until he met Aunty Millie, in the mid-fifties.

After he moved in with Aunty his life changed completely, and from there on they struggled together to achieve what they had. Uncle also stated that he used to be a heavy alcohol drinker and cigarette smoker, but he allowed his wife, who was ten years older than him, to take full control of whatever they were earning.

Covertly, Uncle wanted Calvin to follow in his footsteps. For that matter, in a special way, Calvin used to admire his uncle and wanted to be like him when he grow up, but his life was moving in a different direction altogether. All he knew then was how to survive by any means necessary.

Throughout his life, Calvin had to fraternise to survive, but that was just a part of the game that we all have to play at some point in this life.

He had an immense mind to learn, therefore he could not afford to live his life duplicating that of other underprivileged youths, or even his father and brother's lifestyle, and he definitely didn't want to continue to be complacent with his present lifestyle, even though there were lots of illusions in his way. On the contrary, even though he was fed up with waiting on his enigmatic environment to sustain him, he didn't want to end up dead on the streets or in and out of prison like his brothers or many other black youths.

He was conscious of the suffering of others, and he'd also seen people killed in the process of finding food to eat or merely because of greed.

Initially, he couldn't fathom the real reasons behind it all, but when he stopped and scrutinised the whole scenario, he came to realise why most youths had to do what they were doing. On the whole, he believed first and foremost that a lot of them got trapped by all the illusions that surrounded them, habitual poverty and mental slavery. Although in general, their ancestors were brainwashed with a psychological addiction by the colonial system, which was implanted in their minds that "good things will come to those who wait". That same ideology was later adopted by other nations (mainly by the poorer people within the nations). Now many of those youth's parents had waited and waited, and still nothing good ever came their way. Nevertheless, most parents continued to teach their children the same doctrine, even though most youth today refuse to submit their minds to that indoctrination or teach their children the same thing.

Bob Marley gave a similar warning in one of his songs, where he told us to emancipate ourselves from mental slavery, because none but ourselves can free our minds.

However, for all the unstoppable fighting, killing, and psychological and political mystification in the societies today, it all boils down to survival, power, and control.

Calvin looked around again and noticed what the majority of the people were fighting for and killing each other for. Fundamentally, some fought for power, which they used to manipulate and destroy the population. Some fought for land, even though there are not enough people to fill the earth. Others fought for money, even when they didn't really need it. Conversely, women fought over men and vice versa, yet they never seemed to come to any understanding amongst themselves.

Calvin often asks himself these questions, "What happens to the love that people are supposed to have so strongly? What happens to the unity that is supposed to bind them together?"

Eventually, he concluded that love and unity seemed to vanish from within the hearts and minds of mankind.

*

At length the going on the streets got too tough, and Calvin couldn't accomplish what he'd gone in search for. Ultimately he got fed up with the day-to-day struggles and decided to return to his grandparents' house.

By then Devon had returned there to live also. Andrew, Marika's son, was also living there at that stage, along with Ann Marie, a little girl from St. Elizabeth that Aunty was helping.

At that time they were occupying the bigger side of the house, and Mass Vick and Miss Delta had rented the smaller side; Mass Vick's two brothers were also living there with them.

Mass Vick and Miss Delta didn't have any children between them. Miss Delta had a son from a previous relationship, but he was living with her parents at Lucea, close to Negril Bay.

Goodall and Wade were still living in the room at the back. They were some of the good boys, and they lived in that single room for a very long time.

On the whole, all the people living at Uncle's house were like one big family. Otherwise, things had changed dramatically since the last time Calvin was living there. He was still eager to afford himself a lot of things, in the face of doubtful prospects. On the other hand, it was a major come-down for him too, because he had grown used to being in control of his own doings, going wherever he wanted, and doing mostly what he wanted to do, whenever he felt like it. Overall, though, his lack of self-reliance was having a major impact on his self-confidence, because no matter how incessantly he tried to associate himself with other people, he just couldn't get comfortable with them. Even so, he was very good at masking his inner feelings, which enabled him to blend in comfortably with the people that he used to move with.

For example, whenever he was with any group, he always managed to create a pleasant atmosphere, whether by organising a game or starting a conversation for everybody to participate in. However, as soon as everybody got engrossed in whatever he'd started, he would find an excuse to make an exit – unless gambling was going on, something he could never resist.

His lack of security had the biggest impact on his self-effacing attitude. For example, he was scared both of rejection and of being considered a pain to anybody. As a result, he always tried his best not to impose on anybody. However, living with so much uncertainty didn't do him much good, in the sense of bonding with any individual or simply believing in anyone. His fear of attachment also had an effect on his relationships with the opposite sex, making it hard for him to have a steady relationship. He would chat up a few girls and occasionally he got a one-night stand, but that was as far as it would go, because he didn't have what it takes to maintain a relationship. He would regularly approach the upper-class girls, but the knowledge of his insecurity would cause him to start stammering as soon as he did.

Devon used to coax him sometimes to call some of those girls when he saw them, but when he did and the girl stopped he would start sweating and he wouldn't know what to say to them. Devon would laugh and tell him that he didn't have any lyrics, but on one of those occasions, while he and Devon were living at their grandparents' house, Devon told him that he didn't need to have any money or any form of security to catch the girls.

Calvin asked him how he was supposed to do it, when he couldn't even invite a girl into the yard or take her out on a date. "You have to be ruthless in order to make money and get the girls," Devon told him. "Lying is the first element in the game, and you don't have to plan lies."

At the time Devon was going out with Dawn, a girl from Mount Carey, who used to work at one of the factories at Freeport, near the Montego Bay wharf.

Dawn and her best friend, Melissa, used to go to 10 Crichton's Drive to visit Devon, and eventually Calvin was introduced to Melissa.

The girls would have to hide each night when they turned up at the yard, because Aunty and Uncle didn't want any girls to visit either of the boys at their house.

The relationship between Devon and Dawn was similar to that of Percy and Ruby, because Devon would often beat up Dawn for the simplest reasons. Calvin on the other hand wanted to have that perfect relationship with Melissa, and he was doing well, until she broke his heart and went off with a policeman. Later she got married to one of Jamaica's National football goalkeepers and migrated to the United States of America.

During that same time, Devon introduced crack cocaine and cocaine powder to his little brother.

It occurred one Thursday, while Aunty was at St. Elizabeth and Uncle was out visiting the sick in the community.

It was in the mid-eighties, and at the time, crack cocaine were just getting prevalent on the island, and Devon used to hang out with some of the youths who used to push the drugs on the streets. He wasn't pushing at that time, but he would partake of the high life with his mates, who regularly took the drugs also.

That Thursday, Devon was smoking crack from a crystal toker pipe at home. Calvin was aware of crack cocaine and cocaine powder, but it was the first time he'd seen it or witnessed anybody using the drug. Curious, he asked his brother what he was doing, and Devon told him that he was chasing the devil, while he placed another piece of crack on the pipe.

"Run this," said Devon, as he stretched out his hand with the pipe to his brother.

Hesitantly Calvin took it, not knowing what to do with it, but Devon showed him how to smoke it.

When the piece of crack completely melted away Calvin handed back the pipe to his brother, who was looking at him strangely.

"How it mek yuh feel?" Devon asked.

"No better than how I was feeling earlier," Calvin replied quickly. The truth was that he did feel a buzz, but he wanted another go on the pipe. However, Devon didn't offer him anymore.

On another occasion, Devon had a plastic bag with some white powder, which he was snorting from the back of his hand, and he offered some to Calvin, who copied him and snorted it from the back of his hand too, but this time, Devon gave him a second and third line.

Later, Devon introduced his little brother to various paraphernalia and seasoned spliffs (a mixture of crack cocaine and ganja).

Calvin thought it was cool to chase the devil with his brother, and he also felt closer to him at that point, and at length he started to acquire the drug on his own, until he couldn't get enough of it.

CHAPTER THIRTEEN

HURRICANE GILBERT

It was now 1988, a year that many Jamaicans would never forget. Calvin was still living at his grandparents' house, and as usual, everything was unobjectionable for the first few months after his return from the streets. Soon, however, his grandparents started to curse him again.

It was nothing new to him, because it was the same mixture of emotions that he'd grown used to from childhood. One moment they acted like the perfect parents, who were leading him on the right track. Then in the blink of an eye they would switch and start to put him down, telling him that he was no good and wasn't going to turn out well in life.

On the whole, he was the perfect maid, who would wash their clothes, iron, cook, clean, and do the shopping. Nonetheless, whatever he did was never good enough. They never congratulated him for anything that he did for them either, but they were always quick to tell him off whenever he did something wrong.

The latter was a typical example of how most black parents, especially the underprivileged, treat their children, and that is one of the main reason why so many black youths ended up without any self-esteem, aspiration, or any belief in them own selves.

To make life easier for everybody, Calvin started to attend church with his grandparents on a regular basis. It gave Aunty and Uncle much joy, to dress up every Sunday morning and walk through the gates of the Burchell Memorial Baptist Church with Calvin by their side.

Instantly a bond was created between them. Ultimately, Calvin earned the title "Young Brother Riley" amongst the churchgoers, and the atmosphere around the house was better on the whole. Finally he was getting some long overdue respect; gone were the days of verbal abuse.

At length he began to attend the Youth Fellowship Group at the church, but initially he felt awkward mixing with the other youths, because they were from the other side of his bleak, insecure community. Still, he eventually blended with them comfortably. Although there were vast and visible dissimilarities between him and the other youths, nobody seemed to be bothered. After all, he was the precious Brother and Sister Riley's grandson.

Automatically his name got placed on the baptism list, even though he wasn't ready to get baptized, moreover, he still did not know much about religion. However, he didn't feel he was at liberty at the time to say he wasn't ready, because it was a do-or-die situation.

Eventually, he was forced to make a decision: either return to the streets with the daily struggles, or get baptized and continue to stay at home doing his grandparents' daily chores. He chose the latter.

On the whole, he was trying very hard to conform to the other youth's lifestyle at the church, and he was getting close to success, but the street life kept calling him.

Ultimately, the temptation of the street was too strong to resist, because he felt like he belonged there, even though he also needed the security at home. Thus he decided to rotate his time between the two communities, the religious and the nonreligious.

In the end he began to live a double life as a result, which was more sinister than living either lifestyle. However, on the whole, he believed most churchgoers lived much the same way he was living, because Aunty's and Uncle Roland's lifestyle was an example of many churchgoers.

During the weeks leading up to baptism day, Aunty sent Calvin to her friends' stores to get kitted out with new shoes, clothes, and a wristwatch. The overall vibe around the house was nice, and everybody was in a good mood.

Although Devon wasn't falling for Aunty's and Uncle's ideology, it still didn't make a big difference to them, because they thought he would eventually follow, once Calvin had been baptized.

On the whole, getting baptized in that particular church wasn't just for the sake of Christianity. To an extent, there was a greater value for Aunty and Uncle attached to the church. In a very special way, it was a great honour for them, as well as for all the other members, to be connected to the Burchell Baptist Church. After all, it was one of the most famous churches on the island, because one of the most beloved national heroes had preached in its pulpit. After he died, he was also buried underneath the same pulpit.

It all began with the late Reverend Thomas Burchell, who was born in 1799 and established the Burchell Memorial Baptist Church in 1824, situated at number One King Street, at the corner of Market Street, in Montego Bay.

Thomas Burchell was one of the leading Baptist missionaries and abolitionists in Jamaica in the early eighteenth century. He was a representative of the Baptist Missionary Society of London, England, who was sent to Jamaica with other missionaries to respond to requests from pioneer African Baptist. They were newly freed from slavery and needed support in establishing chapels and education on the island.

His time as a Baptist missionary spanned twenty-two years, between 1824 and 1846, which were the most notorious years in the history of slavery abolition.

Thomas narrowly escaped death during the slave rebellion known as the Christmas or Baptist War of 1831 in Jamaica. During the war, the Burchell Baptist Church was burnt down. It was rebuilt between 1833 and 1834, but Thomas and other Baptist missionaries were persecuted after the war.

On the other hand, Sam Sharpe, who was a preacher and deacon at the Burchell Baptist Church, was blamed for the initial slave rebellion.

Sam was born in Montego Bay in 1801 of African parentage. Although he was a slave throughout his life, he was allowed to become well educated. Because of his education, other slaves respected him, and eventually he spent most of his time travelling all over the island, educating other slaves about Christianity and freedom.

As time passed, he mistakenly came to believe that emancipation had already been granted by the British Parliament. He decided to organise a peaceful general strike across many estates in the western region. But it was a crucial time, because it was the harvest season for sugar cane.

The plantation owners started a reprisal, which led to the rebels burning the sugar cane crops. Ultimately, Sam Sharpe's peaceful protest turned into Jamaica's largest slave rebellion, and hundreds of lives were lost, including fourteen whites.

Two weeks after the rebellion was brought under control, the ringleaders were rounded up and subsequently hanged. Sam Sharpe, who was also rounded up, was executed on 23 May 1832.

He was initially buried in the sands of Montego Bay Harbour, but later was exhumed and given a hero's burial near the pulpit at the Burchell Memorial Baptist Church.

Just before Sam Sharpe was hanged for his role in the rebellion, he proudly said, "I would rather die upon yonder gallows, than live for a minute more in slavery."

The rebellion contributed to the 1833 abolition of slavery across the British Empire, and the centre of Montego Bay was also named after Sam Sharpe, who was made a national hero of Jamaica in 1975 and later appeared on the Jamaican $50.00 bill. A statue of him and other slaves was later erected at Sam Sharpe Square, and 23 May was dedicated to him as the official Labour Day in Jamaica.

*

Finally, the big day came for Calvin to take his stand and be baptized, which was meant to change his life forever.

It was Good Friday morning, Friday, the third of April, 1988. Such an act was supposed to wash him white as snow. Oh yes, his grandparents were expecting him to emerge from the holy pool white as snow. However, he emerged no better than before he'd been submerged, because his life was still crimson. Nonetheless, he always held God dearly to his heart – even though he wasn't upholding the rules.

As a Christian in Jamaica, one wasn't supposed to drink alcohol, smoke, gamble, steal, nor have unmarried sex, but eventually Calvin was indulging in them all.

A few months later he realised that he needed more than just the security of his grandparents' home, because he was twenty years old, and his life had no solid direction. Therefore he decided to make a choice; which was either to stay at home with nothing to look forward to in life or get out and find some work. Eventually he decided to choose the latter, which created a lot of animosity in the house.

Overall, there wasn't much that he could do at that stage, because his whole life seemed messed up and he considered himself as unintelligible to others, but he was adamant to move forward, regardless of his inability to read and write well.

In due course he decided to go to a security firm and apply for a job, because he thought it would be an easy task.

The security firm was owned and run by two ex-soldiers. It was said that one of them had earned his despicable reputation by leading a squad of corrupt police and soldiers in the atrocious killing of over fifty defenceless men in Jamaica, which is known as the Green Bay Massacre.

On the day of the test, he went with Chuck (one of Mass Vick's brothers), who also applied for a job.

When they placed the test papers in front of Calvin, it was an entirely different thing than he'd anticipated. Nonetheless, although his whole being started to turn inside out, he somehow found the courage to take the tests, because he was adamant to get what was rightly his.

From the outset, Calvin expected Chuck to pass the tests, because he'd been to school up until he was sixteen. Calvin had stopped when he was only eleven.

When the tests were completed, the clerk at the security office sent them away and told them to return the following day for the results.

Calvin left the office believing his dreams were once again being dashed, but on their return the next day, the result was quite the opposite.

Apparently he'd passed the tests with flying colours, while Chuck failed his. The following week he got stationed at the City Centre Shopping Mall in Mobay, with Patrick, another new recruit. They were sent to the shopping mall to guard the jewellery and boutique shops and ward off the street vendors.

Calvin wasn't really enthused with what he was required to do at the mall. In fact, from the outset he wanted to get a post at the airport, because a lot of ganja was being shipped out on the planes, and he wanted a piece of the action. He knew a lot of guys from the same firm who were working at the airport, and life was good for them. On the other hand, the idea of chasing away the street vendors, who were only getting the crumbs that fell off the rich man's table, didn't appeal to him – more so because he was feeling the same pain that they were feeling.

On a large scale, a lot of people chose vending on the island, because there weren't many options to make a living otherwise, and the majority of the population were experiencing hardship.

The tourist industry was the biggest money earner on the island (apart from the drug trade) but only the bigger business people and those who managed to gain employment by them normally benefited from tourism. For instance, when the cruise ships arrived at the ports, they would have transportation waiting to take all the tourists to the shops and restaurants that were owned and operated by the wealthy businesspeople. Those who came in by air were issued a map of the places that they should and shouldn't visit on their arrival.

Overall, most of the people who owned those establishments were foreigners, whose main goal was to make money, and when they collected the foreign currency, they normally sent it to overseas banks, which was one reason the Jamaican economy was plunging deeper into slowdown.

The politicians, on the other hand, didn't seem to care about the impact that the lack of foreign currencies was having on the island, because they were getting their cut of the profits. In fact, the businesspeople and the politicians wanted more than they were getting, and to achieve that, they used the police and the security firms to build a barrier between the locals and the tourists. The false excuse for their ridiculous actions was that the locals were harassing the tourists.

The vendors' only way of getting close to the tourists was to congregate at the tourist-designated shopping areas to braid their hair or sell them carvings, beads, and clothes. Some of them had nowhere else to sell their goods, because the police were always chasing them off the streets, and they couldn't afford to pay the hefty fees in the local markets. In fact, most of the tourists who visited the market that the government provided for the locals' were those taken there by the local hotel workers. On the other hand, the arrival of the tourists in the local's market always creates frenzy amongst the vendors. Frequently they would congregate around the tourists in numbers, as soon as they entered the market, wanting to sell them something. Some of the tourists misunderstood the vendor's eager attitude at times and called it harassment, and often times leave the market without buying anything at all. In this way, the vendors became the harasser, when they are actually the victims of circumstances.

Calvin knew most of the vendors who plied their trade at the mall, so he couldn't afford to be looked on as a sell-out; nor was he prepared to tarnish the reputation of his origin. As a result, he calculated how to do his job and keep his status as a street youth, because he couldn't risk losing his credibility at such a crucial stage in his life, even though his life was racing down a narrow slope. Therefore he told the vendors to scratch his back, and he would scratch theirs in return. In other words, he would ignore them and allow them to sell their beads and carvings to the tourists, but they would have to give him some of their earnings at the end of the day. This was done discreetly, because he couldn't risk divulging anything to his colleague.

It seemed the right thing to do at the time, because the vendors were people like him, not in general but literally speaking.

*

At that time, Uncle had resigned from the hardware store and begun to spend most of his days at home.

From the day Calvin started to work at the security firm, the atmosphere at his uncle's house changed dramatically, and it appeared his grandparents weren't happy that he was gaining independence, by earning his own money and having full control over it. Therefore, a few weeks later they told him to find somewhere else to live.

That didn't bother Calvin, because he was planning to leave their home soon. Still, getting a house in Jamaica to rent at the time was comparable to winning the lottery. On the other hand, he could not have afforded to furnish a room even if he did get one to rent, so he was fortunate to find refuge at Sister Clymis's house, one of his church sisters.

Occasionally, Sister Clymis would do the domestic work at Mount Salem for Aunty, and eventually a sort of family relationship developed between her and Calvin.

Sister Clymis was living at Green Pond, one of the rural districts around Mobay.

Green Pond was one of the toughest war zone ghettos, renowned for producing a lot of rude boys, and many youths lost their lives there as a result. Still, although the youths would fight amongst themselves and kill each other, in time of war it was always "all for one and one for all".

The elder residents were no way better than the youths, because they would shield them when the law came in to hunt them down.

There was more than one way to get into Green Pond on foot but only one road on which to drive into the district.

The community itself was surrounded by a number of other tough ghettos, but it was no exception, because they all had the same things in common, and although most of the ghettos around Montego Bay were close to each other, frequently the people would engage in bitter war, which resulted in many deaths.

Cyril Gully, the closest ghetto to Mobay City, joined with Canterbury, while Canterbury joined with Hendon, Paradise, and Clendevon.

Norwood joined with Clendevon and Paradise, but Flanker was on the outskirt, and close to the Donald Songster International Airport.

Green Pond was one of the smaller ghettos, surrounded by the districts of Farm Heights, Glendevon, Hendon, and Salt Spring.

Hendon, Farm Heights, and the Capture Lands were the closest ghettos to the community of Mount Salem.

Green Pond, like the rest of the ghettos, was politically motivated, and all the properties in Green Pond were once owned by the government. During election times, the party in power allowed its followers to go in and capture a piece of the land and build their homes on it.

An unpaved single-lane road ran through the middle of Green Pond, and on either side of the road were two mountains, where the people built their shops and houses.

There was always a feeling of apprehension on entering the community of Green Pond. Still, Calvin didn't mind living there, because by then he had grown used to living amongst the good, the bad, and the ugly. Sister Clymis, like majority of the residents in Green Pond, was poor, but she was well respected in the area, which was a bonus for him.

She was living on one of the hillsides in a three-bedroom house, with her son, Tony, her daughter, Sharon, and her daughter's son. The house also had a downstairs apartment that they sometimes rented out. Tony was on training at the Jamaica Constabulary Force (JCF), and as a result Sister Clymis let Calvin stay in his room. She was happy to oblige him, because she'd got to know him very well whilst she was working at Aunty's and Uncle's house as a helper. Oftentimes Calvin would sneak some of his grandparents' food and give it to her. She was no exception however, because he used to steal his grandparents' food and give it to the tenants too.

When Aunty and Uncle heard that Calvin was living at Sister Clymis's house, they were not impressed; in fact, they became very angry. On the whole, whenever Calvin had any differences with them, to them it felt like waging war. Yet he never used to hold any hard feelings against them. He only wondered why they had to behave in such a negative and uncivilised manor.

Eventually, Aunty started to spread rumours about Calvin and Sister Clymis. Aunty told everyone that she came in contact with that her church sister, who was even older than Calvin's mother, was having an affair with him.

Sister Clymis on the other hand ignored the false accusations and allowed Calvin to continue living at her house. For his part, Calvin was used to the false accusations by then, so anything people did or said couldn't really deter him. He was determined more than ever to move up in life by all means necessary.

*

A month after Calvin moved into his new home, he met and fell in love with a girl named Dawn (not the same one who had been close to Devon). She was four years older than Calvin, but he told her that he was twenty-three years old.

Dawn was of slim build, about six feet tall, and had a dark complexion with a straight baby face. She wasn't exactly his ideal kind of woman, but she had a lot of good qualities, and she was good-looking. She also had a single bedroom that she rented at an apartment house, about nine hundred yards from where he was living at Sister Clymis's.

Calvin was still naive at the age of twenty. Even though he was striving hard to achieve a lot of things for himself, when situations began to materialise, he just didn't know how to handle them.

He was like the man who bought himself a car and asked the car dealers to deliver it to his house, and although he was unable to drive the car, he wouldn't allow anybody else to drive it. In other words, Calvin was determined to change his aimless life by any cost, but he didn't have a clue about where he was going or exactly what he wanted out of life, and he was unable to stop and check himself at that time. On the whole, he was too involved with gambling and seasoned spliffs, which were taking over his life at a fast pace.

After he met Dawn and convinced her that he was the man of her dreams, he began to stay away from his new home. For a whole week sometimes he wouldn't go to Sister Clymis's house, because he couldn't get enough of Dawn. As they say, when the love is new, it makes you stick like glue.

*

It was now September 1988, and suddenly a lot of warnings began to be heard that a major storm by the name of Hurricane Gilbert was on its way to Jamaica.

A lot of Jamaicans were unbelievers when it came to such warnings. On the other hand, many of the locals would welcome a disaster any day, because that would give them reason to go out and loot.

On 12 September 1988, Calvin and his colleague were guarding the City Centre Mall, when Hurricane Gilbert struck the island.

It was the most intense hurricane and also one of the largest tropical cyclones ever observed in the Atlantic basin. It was the most destructive storm in the history of Jamaica.

The storm produced a nineteen-foot (5.8 m) storm surge and brought over twenty-seven inches (700 mm) of rain to the island, which caused inland flooding. Gilbert also destroyed crops, livestock, buildings, houses, and roads, even turning small aircraft into shambles. Close to fifty people were also killed, and in the aftermath, the storm left $4 billion in damage, a lot of devastation, homelessness, and death, vandalised business places, and an astounding rise in the cost of living, which has continued to rise ever since.

On the other hand, while the hurricane was in action, a lot of ghetto people were having a ball. Men were throwing big stones, logs, and iron bars through store windows to gain entry, while children were making trips from stores to their homes with small appliances, clothes, and food.

Calvin watched closely as a woman who was seven months pregnant or more struggled through the tempestuous wind and rain with a big refrigerator on top of her head.

Police were running around firing shots at the looters, but that wasn't enough to deter the poor people, who were taking advantage of the chance of a lifetime, to secure what some of them couldn't have got any other way.

While everybody was running around grabbing whatever he or she could lay hands on, Calvin was stuck on his location with his partner, watching and wishing he wasn't working, but it wasn't long before he decided to join the game.

He wasn't thinking about the after-effects. He was deafened and blinded by poverty. In fact, he didn't care if the looters vandalised the whole City Centre Mall, because to him, the whole establishment was controlled and run by a set of greedy people who didn't care about the well-being of the poor.

He knew for a fact that his partner didn't share his views, because a number of youths from Cyril Gully came to break into some of the stores, and he chased them away.

Eventually, Calvin told his partner that there was no way he was going to sit down and watch the rest of the people get rich, knowing that he could get a piece of the action too. His colleague wasn't interested in what was going on, but Calvin didn't care about the man's opinion of him, so he pulled the hood of his tall, yellow raincoat over his head to disguise himself, and off he went.

Initially, he made a quick patrol around the stores that he knew were most likely to get vandalised, and the first one his eyes caught was a large supermarket. As he arrived, a lot of people were going in and out of the supermarket with bags and boxes. He didn't hesitate, because he knew that the police would appear any moment. Therefore he went straight to where the cash registers were, but they were already smashed up. As he looked around the floor, he was surprised to find a hundred-dollar bill and two twenties that the earlier looters had left behind. He then ran around the back, where he found an old nylon bag. He picked it up and went straight to the liquor corner, where he began to fill it with expensive bottles of whisky, wine, rum, and champagne. Then he went to the cosmetics corner, where he helped himself to the most expensive things. Minutes later he left the supermarket and went in search of more loot, which he found in one of the City's leading garment stores.

As he got near the store, three men hurled an old car axle through one of the windows, and Calvin was one of the first people to get inside. He went straight to where the shoes were and picked up two lovely pair of shoes, for him and one for Dawn. (He couldn't afford to purchase one pair of those shoes in reality.) Next, he got two pair of jeans, two shirts, and a wicked frock for his girlfriend.

He folded the clothes into a bundle and placed it under his raincoat, but by then the store was full of unwelcome customers. There were lots of things that he would have liked to pick up, but he just couldn't carry anything more, so he decided to leave with what he had.

As he stepped through the broken window of the store, he saw a police jump-out jeep (a jeep with no top) coming down the one-way street. He was shocked at first, because guns were pointing in all directions. He thought about running, but he knew that he would only draw attention to himself. Luckily, a number of the looters were coming out of the store, while he was debating what to do, and when they saw the police jeep that was getting closer to the store, they split up in different directions and began to run. Calvin took advantage of the diversion and slipped away onto a side street, and off he went.

He didn't reach far before he heard gunshots firing and people beginning to scream, and as he was about to turn onto another side street, he heard when someone shout, "Nuh mek him got away." At that very moment a machine gun cut loose, and bullets ricocheted from a nearby wall. Some whistled over Calvin's head and in that same instant, he completed the turn by diving flat out on his stomach around the corner. Luckily the clothes he had under his coat cushioned the fall. However, he felt a burning sensation on his right thigh, but he didn't have time to look, because a thousand things were running through his mind at once.

He didn't hear the engine of the jeep or any footsteps coming towards him, so he picked up the bag and started to run again, and he didn't stop until he reached the safety of the mall.

When he returned to the mall his partner had a laugh at the sight of the bag and the smell of the liquor from the broken bottle. Calvin wasn't laughing, even if he wanted to, because he was convinced that his life had just been spared again.

He went into the little room that they shared as an office and sat down, and suddenly he felt the burning sensation on his thigh again, and he noticed a rip on his trouser leg, and all around it was soaking in blood. When he dropped his trousers and examined his thigh, he was surprised to see that it was a bullet wound, but it was only a graze, apparently caused by one of the ricocheted bullets.

He cleaned up and had a good drink, but he didn't give a drop to his partner, and later in the night the news was going around that two people had been shot outside the same store where he'd been. One died on the spot, and the other died in the hospital.

For the next two days he was stuck at the mall with his colleague. There was no way to communicate with Sister Clymis or Dawn, because they didn't have a telephone. When he finally got home, he received some good news.

Dawn was smiling from ear to ear when he turned up at her door, and he thought she was overjoyed to see him, but when she told him that she was pregnant with his baby, he felt like the luckiest man in the whole world.

"I was very excited, and the thought of having a baby activated a lot of consciousness in me and made me want to be a better father than Percy. Eventually we decided to name the child Gilbert."

A week later, Calvin and his partner got transferred to another location. This time it was at a family garment store in the middle of Mobay. Apparently the owners were being ripped off at the store, but they could not tell how or by whom.

At the briefing, Calvin and his colleague were ordered to go to the store and put a stop to what was really going on there. But the prospect of leaving the present location seemed daunting to Calvin. Although he wasn't happy with chasing the vendors away from the mall, he was getting more relaxed with each day's experiences.

CHAPTER FOURTEEN

Turning a Blind Eye

Duty at the store started at 8 a.m., but the store opened up for business at 9:00, from Monday to Saturday.

Calvin turned up for duty at 7:55 a.m. on a Monday, just as the store manager was about to open the door to let in the staff.

He stood back while the staff entered the store, but before he made his way in, Patrick turned up.

As the guards entered the store, the look of surprise was unmistakable on the faces of the staff, except for the manager, who knew the security was being posted there.

The manager was a young, beautiful unmarried girl of about twenty-two years old. She was of mixed race, and her attitude was that of the upper-class citizens.

Immediately she summoned all the staff to a meeting and introduced the guards, but a few of the staff began to mutter their displeasure at having to work under the watchful eyes of security guards. However, the manager responded firmly to the murmurings and told them that it was the owners' idea to employ security, and nothing could be done about it otherwise.

The manager's statement seemed to go down well. Everybody went their own way to start the day's duty. Meanwhile, the guards decided amongst themselves how they were going to carry out their instructions.

There was a baggage booth that needed someone there at all times. Although it wasn't the guard's duty to collect and issue bags, nonetheless, they decided that it would help to keep things under control.

Patrolling the floor was also of vital importance and most importantly watching the cash register. Patrick said he would start by patrolling the floor, while keeping an eye on the cashier.

The baggage booth was opposite the cashier at the front, close to the main entrance, and Calvin decided to station himself there, while observing the cashier and the customers. He didn't tell Patrick his initial feelings towards the staff's earlier attitude, but it was obvious to him that something off the record was really going on at the store. Nonetheless, he wanted to be sure before he started to point any fingers, so he began to conduct a secret investigation.

He always made it a point of his duty to be alert to his surroundings; because of the environment he'd grown up in, so it wasn't hard for him to detect what was really happening at the store.

Most of the store's staff were young people, his age and older. There were eight women and two men, and the youngest of the men was in his early twenties. He was of mixed race, like the manager, and he seemed to spend most of his time around her. However, Calvin perceived him to be a good guy who was still living at home with his parents. After a few days at the store, Calvin's earlier perception of him was confirmed.

The older man was a fireman, who would only go to the store to set up the clothes on display. He'd arrived after the store opened for business that morning. The way he dressed and his attitude showed that he was a down-to-earth person. In other words, he was a roots man.

Four of the women were wearing wedding bands, and later Calvin found out that one of them had three children and she was sending them to school single-handed, because her husband had been laid up sick in bed for a while. Two of the unmarried women were single mothers, who seemed worse off than the other women.

The two cashiers were married too, although one was on the verge of getting divorced. Still, it seemed like living was good for them, because they were always dressed immaculately.

Calvin knew that he would have to be a diplomat to deal with the present situation, and protecting his life was more important than securing his job. On the other hand, he was conscious of the hardships that most people were experiencing, because only those who had it all seemed to have a permanent smile on their faces, but the have-nots always seemed to have a streak of tears. He was mindful that there had been cases when security guards ended up in their graves, got hurt badly, or sometimes ended up in a mental institution. The latter was most common, thanks to the infamous obeah.

Now it is well known that most Jamaicans are being underpaid for the jobs that they do, and the staff at the store were no exception, even though the owners could doubtless afford to pay them more.

Later Calvin found out that the owners had a chain of other stores across the island and even elsewhere, such as America and the Bahamas, just to name a few.

Generally, poverty and greed play a vital role in how the poor make their decisions in life. Calvin was no exception. He was living in a world where most people were living on the breadline, and it was all about surviving by any means necessary. He was slightly different from the average struggler, though, because he was conscious of other people's suffering. As a result, he did what seemed right to him at the time and turned a blind eye to the stealing that was going on in the store. Along the way, he helped himself too. Consequently, he was helping the others rip off the owners of the store, because he was blinded by poverty and consumed by anger and suffering.

Before the first day ended, he made a breakthrough on one of the backdoor dealings. It was after 1 p.m., and some of the staff – including his partner, one of the cashiers, and the manager – was out getting their lunches. He was patrolling the floor, when a young female customer walked in and winked at the cashier, who nodded back to her.

Calvin went to one corner of the store and pretended to be busy picking up fallen items off the floor, but all the time he was watching the customer.

Hurriedly the young woman selected a number of items without checking the price tags, and in no time she was back at the cashier with her selection.

Calvin continued to play dumb and went to another section of the store where he could see the cash register. He noticed that the prices on the screen that the cashier was entering were less than the items' value. Suddenly he stood where the cashier could see him, if she should look up. When the sale was totalled, the customer handed over more money to the cashier than what registered on the till. At that precise moment the cashier looked around, and Calvin locked eyes with her for a moment.

The customer noticed the cashier's reaction and looked around, but by then Calvin was walking towards the checkout point. Without any delay, the young woman picked up her goods and marched out of the store.

Calvin stood beside the cashier and looked at her, but she avoided his gaze.

"Have you got your lunch already?" she asked him, but before he could say anything she spoke again. "I'll buy you lunch today."

As he was about to speak, she reached into her handbag and gave him two hundred dollars.

"You are a rich woman!" he told her sarcastically, as he took the money from her.

"Things are a bit slow right now, but if you are cool, we could all make some money," she declared.

"I'm cool," he replied, laughing, and then walked away.

For the rest of the day, he watched each move that she made, and he could always tell when she was cheating, because she would look in his direction.

As before, he didn't tell his partner what had happened. When the store closed and everybody was getting ready to go home, the cashier walked up to him and passed him another three hundred dollars. From that day on, he got regular money from her, which came in handy to support his drugs and gambling addictions.

Overall, Calvin used to show respect to all the staff and customers alike, and in return they all showed him a lot of respect too, far more than they showed Patrick. Even the old-school rude boys, (a group of retired gangsters) who used to sit on the pavement outside the store and asked passersby for money, showed him much respect.

Gradually, he used that respect to his own advantage, by starting up his own scheme.

It was early December 1988. Although the hurricane had shattered a lot of lives and put the economy on pause, people were still feeling the Christmas spirit, because more shoppers than usual were turning up to purchase clothes, as well as back to school uniform for their children. Covertly, Calvin calculated how to make some money on the side for himself. He did it boldly, so that nobody would recognise what he was doing.

Normally, when any customer entered the store with bags they would be asked to leave them at the baggage booth. On handing their bags over, they would then be issued a card with a number on it. A similar card would then be placed on the bags. On leaving the store, the customer would hand the card over to whoever was in the booth and retrieve their bags. Calvin decided to use the baggage booth to conduct his business. He held a selection of the numbered cards in his pocket and kept an eye out for the potential customers who were willing to make a deal. He could always tell when a customer wanted an item but couldn't afford to buy it because of the price tag. In the same way, he could recognise a customer who would make a deal.

He would simply watch their body language before walking over and say, "Dat nice, nuh true?"

If the customer was only looking but not interested, he could always tell, and when there was interest but not enough money to spend, the customer would say, "It's too expensive. I can't afford dat." That was when he would make his move.

He would then tell the customers that they could get the item at a discounted price, and if they were interested, he would issue them a card and tell them to select the items that they wanted and put it at a designated spot. Later he would pick up the merchandise, put it in carrier bags, and place the duplicate number on it. That way, even if he wasn't in the baggage booth, customers could always collect their goods from whoever might be there.

At length Patrick started to help himself to things from the store too, but he wasn't aware of Calvin's indulgence or that he was also being watched. However, one morning, the store had already been open for business, and most of the staff hung about chatting, while Calvin was seated in the baggage booth thinking about money.

Patrick, who was always late to report for duty, suddenly sauntered through the door, with a big smile on his face.

He was dressed to the teeth in his personal clothes instead of the security uniform that he was issued, which he hadn't worn since the day he'd realised that his feet were bigger than his boots.

As he made his entry, a few of the female staff applauded him sarcastically, but all that time the manager was scrutinising the shirt he was wearing with an incredulous look on her face. Calvin noticed the manager's reaction, as did the two other staff who was whispering, and instantly he knew that his partner was in big trouble.

Slowly, the manager strolled over to the baggage booth. Meanwhile, Calvin pretended he hadn't noticed what was going on.

"Come and see me in the office in a few minutes please," the manager whispered, when she got close to Calvin, and then continued to walk around the store.

Later when Calvin went into the office, the manager told him about the shirt that Patrick was wearing. "It was made exclusively for this store," she said angrily, and she was sure Patrick had nicked it from the shelves.

Calvin realised that it was a tricky situation, because if Patrick got exposed, everything could come out into the open. Therefore, he begged the manager to give him a chance and let him pay for the shirt instead.

Two weeks later, Calvin was summoned to the security office, and on his arrival, they told him that he was being transferred to another location at Freeport, near the wharf, while they sent another security guard to join Patrick at the store.

Calvin was sad when he received the news, but he pretended as if he was happy to be transferred to another location, and when he told the staff at the store that he was being replaced by another guard, they were not impressed. However, he told them that it was for the best, and he would visit them whenever he could.

*

At that stage, the novelty of Dawn's pregnancy had begun to fade, and she would only see her man every once in a while and when she did, he wouldn't have anything to offer her.

Eventually, it reached the stage when she could no longer work, so she couldn't afford to pay her rent. As a result, she had to give up her room and went to her mother's house to seek refuge.

Around that same time, one warm afternoon in downtown Mobay, Calvin popped into a rum bar to purchase a drink. The bartender was a pretty, slim, brown-complexioned lady, and although she was much older than him, he instantly took a fancy to her. He also offered to buy her a drink, which she gladly accepted, and he lingered longer than he intended, chatting her up.

This could be my lucky day, he thought after a while, or maybe this is just the way she deals with all the punters.

Later, when the bar began to get busy, he told her that he had to go, but he promised her that he would drop by another time. About a month later he was passing through the area and stopped at the bar, but the brown-skinned lady was no longer working there.

A few months later he went to visit his mother at Salt Spring, and out of the blue, Ruby told him that his sister Janet was working as a bartender in downtown Mobay.

The sudden, long-awaited information made him very happy, but when Ruby told him where the bar was located and began to describe Janet, he suddenly felt sick. However, he hid his feelings and told his mum that he was going to meet his sister and made his exit.

"If I'd lingered longer at Mama's house, I would've vomited on her veranda," Calvin exclaimed. "I left her house in a daze that afternoon and remained in a daze throughout the rest of the day, because I couldn't believe I'd almost asked my sister for sex.

"The mere thought of what could have happened between me and my sister made me very angry and sad, and even though I was eager to find Janet, Mama's revelation spoiled all the eagerness."

CHAPTER FIFTEEN

Living a Double Life

Calvin's next location was at a business complex at Freeport, but it was a boring place, because the buildings were isolated.

During the days there was more to contend with, because lots of people worked there, and people came in to purchase goods and do business, but at night it became a ghost town.

Two officers were required to be on duty during the days and two at night, which they did on twelve hours shifts.

One guard would sit at the back gate while the other would patrol the front of the shops.

Calvin and his fellow guards sometimes got a few jibes from some of the workers for being a security guard, but that was expected.

At night there wasn't much to do, apart from patrolling the premises, and when it reached midnight, the guards used to find a place to sleep.

Those who worked at night would take food with them, because food was only supplied during the days on pushcarts by a few vendors, apart from the cook shop that was situated on the field adjacent to the complex.

Calvin would mostly purchase his food from the cook shop, and eventually, he grew close to the family who ran the shop, and as time went by he would occasionally help out at the shop when he was off duty.

Mr and Mrs Williams, the owners of the cook shop, and their three children were very poor. Donovan, the eldest son, was a part time taxi driver, but he used to spend most of his days helping his parents at the shop.

Their daughter, Natalie, thirteen at the time, and her seven-year-old brother, Kian (Butty) were attending school.

Mr Williams had an older daughter from a previous relationship, but she was living in Kingston.

Calvin started a relationship with this family from the first day he went to the shop, and after he'd started to help out in the shop most people thought they were all blood relatives. However, nobody could tell if they weren't either, because all of them were of brown complexion, and Donavon and Calvin resembled each other. Eventually Calvin began to call the mother and father Mummy and Daddy, just as the children did.

The shop wasn't of much standard. It was built around a mango tree with bamboo, old signboards, and old zinc, and there was no flooring inside, or utilities of any kind attached. They usually used old car rims with charcoal to cook the food. Also, in one corner, they had an old refrigerator in which they kept the drinks.

Every morning without fail, they would purchase ice from the ice factory to keep the drinks cool throughout the days.

It was a struggling business, but they were surviving nonetheless, and all their customers were happy with the service that they were getting.

Mummy was the overall backbone of the family. She was the glue that held them together. With due respect, Daddy didn't have a clue about many things. He wasn't a lazy man, but he didn't possess the brains or the willpower in the enterprise, and he didn't have balls like Mummy. What she said was final, and she kept everybody and the business afloat.

*

Occasionally Calvin's superiors asked him to work on different locations around Freeport, such as the wharf, a garment factory, and a lumberyard. It was easy working at the lumberyard, because they had guard dogs patrolling the compound all night. All he had to do was to check up on the dogs occasionally, and the rest of the time he would stay inside and sleep.

At the wharf it was different, especially when the cruise ships came into port. Although it was Calvin's delight to see the tourists, he wasn't happy when they asked him to work there, because he was assigned to posts where he would have to stand on his feet for long hours. Overall, he was getting fed up with the job, because he wasn't making any money on the side, except when he helped out at the cook shop. He was also conscious of the way his life was going backwards, but he didn't know what to do to alleviate it.

Dawn would visit him at his workplace sometimes for money, but he was always broke. As a result, most of the time she would retreat empty-handed, with distress visible on her face. There was always that surging pain in her watery eyes when he told her that he didn't have any money.

One day Dawn went to visit him while he was guarding the business complex. He was seated in the guard's room with his colleague when she stepped through the gate. It was plain to see that she was hungry, because there was dried spittle at the corner of her mouth, and she could hardly walk on her tired, swollen legs.

He felt very embarrassed when he saw her, and if he had somehow been able to disappear without leaving a trace he certainly would have. On the whole, it wasn't because of her condition that he felt the way he did. It was merely because he didn't have a dollar in his pocket to offer her, and he'd only been paid the previous day. Also, if his colleague hadn't been present, it wouldn't have looked so bad either, because he would have told her one of his many lies. However, that fine day he could not find a single word to justify himself.

Ian, his colleague, who was also his good friend, knew about his gambling addiction, and he also knew that he smoked weed; in fact, most of the security guards smoked weed. But Ian didn't know that Calvin also smoked crack cocaine. Nonetheless, Calvin used to tell Ian lies sometimes when he got broke at the gambling house, or when he wanted a piece of crack, and Ian would lend him some money. He often used Dawn's pregnancy as an excuse too, but that day, the whole bucket of milk turned over.

Calvin started to speak, but the words were coming out in gibberish, and Ian started to laugh, because he knew that his friend was caught with his trousers at his knees. However, as a good friend would, Ian came to his aid and told Dawn that they hadn't been paid yet, and then he reached into his pocket and gave her a few hundred dollars.

Calvin's respect for Ian grew to the highest peak from that day.

The apparent distress on Dawn's face disappeared when she got the money from Ian, and all of a sudden she started to glow and seemed much stronger than when she first walked through the gate. However, that was the last time Calvin saw her until months later, after she'd given birth to a son.

A month or so later, Calvin thought his prayers were about to be answered, after they summoned him to the security head office, although, he didn't really like getting called to the office, because this was usually when they sent him to fill in at some location where he didn't like to work. Nonetheless, he thought that maybe they were planning on giving him a permanent transfer to another location, and the thought made him smile, because ever since he'd left the garment store, things had changed for him dramatically in the wrong way.

On the whole, he could no longer live the life that he had become accustomed to while he was working at the garment store, because he was now living solely off what he earned, and the little extra cash that he got from Mummy and Daddy was not even enough to support his addictions.

Later that day, when he reported to the office as requested, on his arrival, he was told that the company was losing contracts left and right; as a result they could not afford to keep on all the guards.

The news hit him like a ton of bricks, and he knew instantly that they were going to tell him that he was being made redundant.

After he received the news, he left the office on wobbly legs with a million things running through his mind at once.

He thought, I'm desperate for a change, but losing my job is absolutely not what I expected. On the contrary, even though I've been working steadily for nine months, I only have a few pieces of clothes to show for it, and I don't even possess a bank account. On the other hand, he'd established himself with a lot of different people and done a lot of crazy things too, but he'd achieved little in comparison.

Suddenly he felt embarrassed. The thought of going back to Uncle Roland's house at Mount Salem crossed his mind, because he could no longer reside at Miss Clymis's house if he didn't have any money to offer her on the weekends, but he dismissed the idea. Unlike in his early years, he was more determined to move forward at any cost, even though he didn't know where to get another job.

That afternoon he went to the free beach overlooking Mobay City and built a spliff. As he sat on a large rock smoking the joint and observing the miles of calm, blue sea in front of him, a thought suddenly came to him. With a smile, he convinced himself that he had found an answer to his present problem.

The following morning he got up early and headed for the cook shop at Freeport. Donovan was surprised when he turned up at the shop, and while they were preparing lunch, he told Donovan about his dilemma. Donovan assured him that he shouldn't worry, because a place was always there at the shop for him. Later that morning when Mummy and Daddy came to the shop, Donovan told them that Calvin would be working with them permanently, and Mummy and Daddy were very happy to have him by their side.

As time went by, the Williams family and Calvin got even closer, and eventually he started to sleep at their home sometimes.

They were living in a one-bedroom board house in Granville, one of the rural areas around Montego Bay. In the bedroom there were two old double beds and an old cabinet with not much in it. Donovan, Butty, and Calvin used to sleep on one bed, while Natalie slept with Mummy and Daddy on the other bed.

They also had an old kerosene stove in one corner, an old dining table, and an old refrigerator. The refrigerator stored all the provisions that they took to the shop for business each day. They would mostly cook a decent meal at the house on Sundays, but nonetheless they were all happy under the circumstances.

In due course, Donovan and Calvin became inseparable. They had a lot in common, because Donovan was a hard gambler too, and although they wouldn't participate in the same game, they usually lost their money. Also, they both liked to party, smoke weed with crack cocaine, and drink alcohol, even though neither of them could hold their liquor. Overall, Calvin and Donovan were both living a double life, which they concealed from Mummy, Daddy, Natalie, and Butty.

Donavon seemed to be more advanced than Calvin in many ways, and it was apparent that he'd taken a lot more risks too.

It's written in Proverbs (in the holy Bible) that "A man is known by the type of friends that he associates with." Calvin knew some of Donovan's friends, but he wasn't linked with them. He was also aware of some of the things that they regularly did, but they knew little about him. Nonetheless, as a street soldier, each man showed respect to the others. Whatever one did to survive was one's choice, because on the streets, each man does his own thing in his own way to survive – unless, of course, one tries to move in on someone else's turf or tries to stop someone from finding food to eat.

Ultimately, one day Donovan introduced Calvin to some of his dodgy friends, but from the outset he wasn't too keen on hanging out with those guys, knowing that they made a lot of enemies through their ruthless lifestyle. Nevertheless, gradually he became a part of the crew, even though he tried to deny his involvement with them. In fact, he wanted some action in his gloomy life, because he was already on the verge of plummeting into a terrible devastation. Gradually he came to think, *Why not take it to a higher level?*, but in the back of his mind there was also a voice that kept telling him not to get too close to those men.

If people would practice thinking twice before they act and listen to that voice in the back of their minds, many would elude a lot of mishaps in their lives. Conversely, many of the elder folks in Jamaica would phrase it like this: "When a horse is galloping, it doesn't hear the sound of its back foot." On the whole, many people are like that horse, because they move too fast and never stop to think twice or listen. As for Calvin, even though he wanted more in his empty life at the time, he wasn't really prepared for what was coming his way.

At the time he knew a few guys who had guns, but it wasn't his thing to use a gun. From childhood he had always carried a knife, but once he started to move around with his newfound acquaintances, he became the sole owner of an old .38 Smith and Wesson revolver. Gone were the days when he would only carry a knife. He was now carrying both gun and knife simultaneously. He wasn't a novice in handling a gun, because he used to clean them whilst working at the Anchovy police station. Before that, when he first beheld a real gun, he was in the company of Mass Percy. He was about eight years old at the time, when Mass Percy took him to visit Rasta John one day, and on their arrival at John's house they found him cleaning the guns in his backyard.

Curious, Calvin asked, "Ha wah dem deh fa, John?" but before John could answer he continued, "Mek mi see dem," while reaching out to pick up the handgun.

Translation: "What are these for, John? Let me see them."

"No, youth," John shouted, as he secured both guns out of the boy's reach.

It was the first time Calvin had noticed how menacing John looked. With the thick dreadlocks tumbling down his back, he almost resembled an angry lion.

For a tense moment Calvin shook with intimidation, but briskly John banished the troubled look in his big eyes, which were fire-red from the amount of ganja that he used to smoke. "Yout'," he said, "yuh mustn't play wid dem sinting yah yuh nuh. Dem dangerous. Yuh hear?"

Translation: "Youth, you mustn't play with these things. Them dangerous. You hear?"

But Mass Percy only laughed at the time, because he somehow managed to see the funny side of it all.

*

Eventually, Calvin was asked to embark on a mission with Donovan and his crew. His first impulse was to say no, but for him to back out at that crucial stage would simply mean losing face and all the respect he had built up. Now this is what they call peer pressure. A lot of youths find themselves in a similar situation, and the next thing you know, they end up in jail, peeping through the bars and endlessly repeating that they wish they had known, while the not-so-lucky ones find a permanent place six feet underground. On the contrary, Calvin didn't want to step back, because he felt he owed it to Donovan to throw in with him whenever possible – and the more so since money was involved.

Money was the pivotal factor, as it turned out. Poverty always played the major role in his daily struggles, but greed had a way of creeping in whenever money was involved, and when the two are mixed together, the formula has a tendency to blind you from reality and corrode your judgment.

At first, Calvin didn't tell Donovan that he didn't want to be a part of the scheme, nor did he say yes, he would come along. Instead, Donovan assumed that he was up for it, as was expected, that he would go along.

When the day of reckoning arrived, Calvin went to the free beach in Montego Bay to meditate. This time he brought a seasoned spliff and his pocket Bible. The latter can be found in most bad boys pockets in Jamaica.

After he was seated comfortably, with his back against a rock, he read a psalm, lit up the spliff, inhaled, and then exhaled the strong concoction of crack cocaine and high-grade weed, as he gazed at the beautiful magnificence of the blue Caribbean Sea. He sat in the same position, puffing the spliff; only moving occasionally to relight it while mulling over his situation.

At that stage he was very confused, because he didn't know what the outcome was going to be, if he should go on the robbery spree. He'd also thought about the price he would have to pay, if the worst scenario should unfold in the process. Losing his life wasn't absent from the list either.

The thought of getting killed on a robbery sent shivers down his spine, and he suddenly felt cold. Eventually he got up, flicked the last of his spliff into the sea, and walked away with an unwavering determination.

When the hour arrived for him to meet up with Donovan, Peter, and Paul, he didn't turn up. He knew they would call him the worst names when they next saw him, but he was prepared to take whatever they threw at him; after all, his conscience would set him free.

The following morning, he intentionally showed up late for work at the cook shop, expecting Donovan to be there, ready to give him a good cussing, but he was surprised to see only Mummy in the shop, cooking.

He enquired about Donovan's whereabouts, because he knew Daddy was in town buying drinks and getting ice at the ice factory, but Mummy replied somewhat angrily and said she didn't know where anybody was. Calvin on the other hand noticed how distressed she was, so he told her to sit down and let him take over the cooking, but she wasn't having any of it. She was being driven to get the lunch ready, thus she continued to put spices in the pots, while cursing Donovan for going out and not coming back in time to help her.

In the end Calvin managed to convince her to sit down, while he jumped into the driving seat. When Mummy was seated on the wooden bench in one corner of the shop and had calmed down, she asked Calvin if he knew where Donovan had been the previous day. Suddenly, a violent sweat broke out across his brow, and he was scared that something might have happened to Donovan. Nevertheless, he told Mummy that he hadn't seen her son after they parted at the shop the previous day. But he kept his back to her while he spoke.

Mummy was a very clever woman, and she knew Calvin wasn't telling her the truth, but she didn't put any pressure on him to tell her otherwise. She only folded her arms and tried to make herself comfortable on the bench, staring out the window with a dazed expression on her face. All of a sudden she spoke with a soft, motherly, caring voice. "I only hope Donovan all right, because me nuh know wah mi wuda duh widout him."

Translation: "I don't know what I would do without him."

"Him all right Mummy," Calvin assured her. "Maybe de gyal wah him deh wid nuh want to let him go," he concluded jokingly.

Translation: "Maybe the girl that he's with didn't want to let him go."

"Me hope it's only dat," Mummy said dreamily, as she continued to stare out the window.

Later that afternoon, Donovan turned up at the shop, looking tired and scared. On his arrival, he confessed that he'd gone to a party out of town with some friends, but the car broke down on their return. He also declared that they had to push the car for many miles until daybreak.

Everybody was convinced, except for Calvin, and later that same day, they went for a walk and Donovan filled him in on the real story. First, Donovan told him that he was very lucky not to have gone with them, because if he had, there was a possibility that he would have been killed. He told Calvin that they were planning on sending him inside the building for the cash, but because he backed out, Peter went instead – and he had been gunned down on entering the building.

Calvin was shocked and relieved at the same time, and he didn't know what to say to Donovan, who was shaking like a leaf at that point.

Calvin enquired about Paul, and Donovan told him that he'd run away to Kingston, because eyewitnesses had seen him lurking outside the building when the security shots went off. He also told Calvin that he'd parked the stolen getaway car in some bushes.

Back at the shop, a number of the regular customers were giving their own political opinion of how they think the country should run, while eating fried dumplings and fried salt fish, which was a normal occurrence.

As soon as Donovan and Calvin returned to the shop, Mummy was quick to notice the troubled expression on their faces, and instantly she enquired if everything was okay. Although they told her yes, she wasn't convinced.

Later that day, Donovan made a vow to Calvin that he wouldn't go out on any more robberies, and they both decided that it was best for them to stick with Mummy and Daddy at the shop.

On the whole, they shared the same purpose – to survive each day at any cost, because their hopes and dreams were somewhat shattered by misconception, and their destination in life was unsure. However, change was waiting patiently around the corner to reveal itself to Calvin, and it all began one Friday night, after he'd lost all his wages from the cook shop at the gambling house.

At the time, his only transportation was a pushbike that had no affix brakes or lights on it. That night, he got home about half past twelve, so he didn't bother to wake up the rest of occupants in the house, which he regularly did when he got home late, because Miss Clymis hadn't given him a set of keys to her house.

The downstairs apartment, which had no furniture inside, apart from an old armchair, was unoccupied at the time. Most nights, when Calvin got home late, he would use it as his late night suite, and the armchair used to be his four-poster bed. Tonight he couldn't sleep, thus he curled himself up in the chair thinking about the overdue rent he owed Miss Clymis and the money he also owed the drug dealer.

He was confused and he didn't know what to do, and although the night was cool, he'd begun to sweat profusely, and he was very agitated. Suddenly he got up, cautiously put his bike on his shoulder, and went through the gate.

When he reached some distance away from the house he jumped on the bike and started to pedal, even though he was going downhill.

At that time, the roads were almost impossible to drive on, let alone to ride a pushbike, because Hurricane Gilbert had struck the island viciously and left many huge craters in the roads. Nonetheless, while he was riding down the road, his thoughts were only on getting some money by any possible means. He had no idea how he was going to acquire this money that he needed so badly. He was also unaware of the car that was approaching him from the opposite direction, and the truck that was parked at the corner across the road. However, when he became conscious of the parked truck and the car with its blazing lights, it was far too late.

Using the bottom of his boots as break, he slammed on the back wheel, and at the same time trying to keep the bike to the side of the rough road, but he was moving too fast. Suddenly he was toppling over onto the approaching car.

Later he woke up on the back seat of a car. Strangely, he was still conscious of his mission, because when he regained consciousness he asked the two men in the front seats for his money. Then, as he became more aware, he suddenly realised that something good could come out of all that taken place that night. Hazily, he smiled to himself and decided that he had finally found the gateway to escape from paying his debts. Moments later he passed out again.

The next morning he found himself covered in blood on top of a bed, in the Cornwall Regional Hospital, and on close inspection of his injuries, he realised that he'd only got cuts and bruises all over his arms and a gash along his right eyebrow, but the most serious cut of all was the one underneath his right eye. To this day, the scar underneath his eye remains as a reminder of that night.

Later that morning, when the nurse finally dressed his cuts and bruises, and he was waiting to get discharged, the person he least expected to see appeared out of the blue.

Warily he smiled through his pain, and said, "Hello, Uncle," but Uncle didn't answer. Instead, he only stood where he was, looked at his nephew, and then shook his head, and Calvin decided to keep silent too.

When Uncle was ready, he spoke with a soft, soothing voice. "Son, what are you doing with yourself?" but Calvin didn't answer. Uncle spoke again, but this time with more anger in his tone. "What you really decided to do wid yuh life? Is this the way yuh intend to carry on for de rest ha yuh life?"

Calvin wanted to say no, this wasn't the way he wanted to live for the rest of his life; nor did he know exactly what he was really doing with himself at present, nor could he decide at that moment what to do with himself. Instead, he only remained silent, because he couldn't find anything convincing to tell his uncle. Furthermore, whatever he said wouldn't have made his life any better than what it was.

While he lay on the bed wallowing in shame and self-pity Uncle spoke again, but this time his voice was full of compassion. "Although you have to consider yourself fortunate, because a woman who knows you're related to me told me that she saw you in the hospital covered in blood."

Calvin was suddenly relieved by Uncle's last statement.

"I was on my way to have my hair cut at the barber," Uncle continued sympathetically to clear the air, "but I decided to stop by and see how serious you were."

Calvin was still bowled over, but he didn't know what to say. However, his silence made it seem like Uncle's speech had some effect on him.

"Do you have any money?" Uncle asked him.

"No sir," he replied, a bit too quick. However, that was the loophole he was waiting for, and ultimately he took the opportunity to tell Uncle Roland his side of the story, about what had happened the previous night.

Initially, he told Uncle that he was riding his bike home when the car hit him, and when he woke up everything had been taken from his pockets. Uncle knew right away that he was telling a lie, because he knew his nephew better than anybody did, and he could always tell when he was hiding the truth. Uncle spent his life trying to fathom why Calvin habitually lied. Nevertheless, he gave him some money before he left and told him to visit at 10 Crichton's Drive whenever he was able.

After Uncle left, Calvin lay on the bed thinking about the things that his uncle had said. He knew straight away that he would have to make some drastic changes in his life and fast. But as always, he didn't know exactly what he was going to do.

That afternoon when he got home, he told Miss Clymis the same story he'd told his great uncle earlier. A week later he moved out and went back to his grandparents' home, and he continued to work at the cook shop.

About two weeks after Calvin went back to his grandparents' house, Devon, who was living there at the time, went to visit him at the cook shop.

Initially, Devon told his little brother that he was only passing by and wanted to see what he was doing, but from the moment Calvin saw him, he knew straight away that he had been sent there by his grandparents to spy on him. Nonetheless, he didn't have anything to hide from anybody, because he was simply living the life that he had been able to live, up to that point. Conversely, he knew his grandparents weren't going to be happy with the report that Devon was going to take back to them, for the cook shop was shabby. But he didn't care what anybody thought. After all, he was making an honest living.

A few days after Devon visited him at the cook shop; his grandparents confronted him, and told him that it was clear to them that he was working for some low-class people.

Calvin was offended by his grandparents' remarks, because in reality, everybody had to survive, no matter how he or she looked or what they did.

At the time, the Williams were dearer to him than his own relatives, because they had taken him in when he was down, and he was grateful to them. Although he didn't have much cooking experience at the time, and the main thing that he possessed when he went to work at the shop was his personality, still, they accepted him wholeheartedly.

Ultimately, he pretended he didn't know that it was Devon who had given his grandparents the information. On the other hand, he didn't know that his Uncle and Aunty were planning to help him, until they summoned him to the veranda one evening in early January 1990, after he got home from the cook shop.

"I was terrified when they called me," said Calvin, "because of previous experiences. I thought they were about to give me another marching order out of number 10.

"There were all kinds of things running through my mind, and a sick, burning sensation was in my stomach. Nonetheless, gingerly I sat myself down on the leather lounge chair, while wondering what I must have done to earn myself another kicking out. I entwined my shaking fingers and held my hands in my lap, awaiting the verbal onslaught."

Aunty was seated at her table, stacking "Partner" money into thousand-dollar piles, while Uncle sat silently drinking a huge tumbler of Gordon's gin and Red Label wine. He noticed how uncomfortable Calvin was and told Aunty to break the news to him.

She said, "My good friend Mr Jump, who works as a room service manager at the Wyndham Rose Hall Hotel" – who was also a "Partner" member – "promised to get you a job there." Her tone of voice seemed less than happy, while she concentrated on the money in front of her. "But we don't know if you are interested. After all," she continued, with an edge, "you already have a big-time job, and maybe you don't want to leave it."

"Big-time job!" Uncle repeated. He kissed his teeth and then laughed at Calvin contemptuously.

"What kind of job is it?" Calvin asked happily, feeling relieved from his earlier apprehension.

"Yuh seem to like working in kitchens," replied Aunty, "therefore yuh uncle suggested that I ask my friend to get you a job in the kitchen, at the hotel. So if you are interested," she continued, "yuh can go there tomorrow morning and fill out an application form."

Calvin was shocked when his aunt told him about the job, because, in his wildest dreams, he'd never thought he could get a job at a hotel. On the other hand, he knew that he had to make some drastic changes in his reckless life, but he didn't know the changes would have come so soon. Alternatively, he didn't want to build up his hopes too soon, because he knew that the outcome could be different. Nonetheless, the following morning he scrubbed up nicely and went in to fill out the application form.

CHAPTER SIXTEEN

Rising for a Fall

The Wyndham Rose Hall Resort Hotel and Country Club was situated close to the house of Anne Palmer, the White Witch of Rose Hall, and about twelve miles outside of the city of Mobay. It had a capacity to serve twelve hundred guests, and it sat magnificently on a prime beach setting, on more than twenty acres of well-maintained land. Its facilities included a range of activities from volleyball to championship golf, entertainment every night of the week, four outstanding restaurants, and five bars. It also had meandering pools with a swim-up bar, its own water parks, and duty free shops.

On Calvin's initial arrival at the hotel, he was captivated by the size of the building and the expansive lawns. Many times he'd passed that particular hotel and many others around Mobay, but never once had he thought the day would come when he would finally set his feet inside one of them.

At the time of his interview, there were no guests at the hotel, because it had been badly damaged in Hurricane Gilbert, thus the whole building was being renovated. However, they sent him to the hotel's country club, situated about six hundred yards opposite the hotel, to fill out an application form.

After he filled out the form, Mr Jump came by and took it. Then he told Calvin to stay and have some lunch, which the hotel had provided for all of the workers.

"Even though I was very nervous, feeling out of place and uncertain about getting the job, I felt better after Mr Jump had spoken to me.

"When it was time for lunch, I was surprised to see the amount of food that they laid out on the tables, and I stuffed my belly before I went back home with no immediate expectation."

When Calvin got home that day he told his grandparents about the interview, but they didn't say much.

The following day, he went to the cook shop and told the Williams family that he was expecting a job at the hotel. Initially, he didn't know exactly how to break the news to them. However, when he finally told them about it, they were all happy for him.

A few days later, Mr Jump came by the house and told him to report for work the following day. He also briefed him about how he should conduct himself in order to keep the job that he had just been offered.

Calvin couldn't believe he was getting the privilege to work in a five-star hotel, and at the same time he felt as if he was letting the Williams family down.

That night he hardly got any sleep, because he felt like he was about to go into the land of the unknown. Nonetheless, the following morning he got up very early and prepared himself for the chance of a lifetime.

When the taxi pulled up at the hotel gate, he got out and sauntered awkwardly behind other employees towards the hotel.

Inside the hotel he was asked to sign in at the security office, and then he was told to go to the kitchen to see the head chef.

Inside the kitchen, he was amazed to see how huge it was. Minutes later, the chef ushered him and a few others into the staff cafeteria, where he briefed them about the job.

The chef was a tall, slim German, whose stern facial appearance resembled that of a soldier at war, and Calvin quivered in his presence.

He was given the position of a kitchen steward, and his job description consisted of washing pots and pans, sweeping and mapping floors, and emptying garbage bins.

At that point, there were no guests at the hotel, and all the staff, including the managers, were busy putting on the finishing touches, before the big reopening day, which was to be the twenty-fifth of January, just over a week away. The chef told all the stewards to go to the laundry and get used chef's clothes to wear.

That day, Calvin made friends with a number of the stewards, and before the first week had ended, he was settled in his new job.

Going into the day of the reopening, Calvin was overwhelmed to see the amount of food that was being arranged, and he wanted so much to participate in the preparation of the food. As a result, he would hurriedly do his job and then blend in with the cooks to help them prep.

The following week, after the hotel had been reopened, he was placed on the night shift, and by then all kitchen stewards were issued brown khaki suits, but he refused to wear his, instead he continued to wear the used chef's clothes.

During his second week at the hotel, he stole a twelve-inch chef's knife and brought it to the cook shop at Freeport. That day when he reached at the shop it was lunchtime and he helped to serve lunch.

"All of the customers were happy to see me, and everybody told me how I looked different.

"I was filled with elation by the things that they were saying to me, and at that same moment I realised that I'd changed for real, without noticing it. I also felt I no longer belonged in that circle, and eventually, the whole surrounding and the people around me seemed strange. I also knew that I could not totally give in to the transformation that I was going through. On the whole, because that family had been there for me when there was no one else, so I decided to keep my promise and stand by them."

*

One month into his new job, Calvin was ordered by his supervisor to stop wearing the chef's clothes. However, he wasn't surprised; sooner or later he knew he would have to stop wearing the uniform, because some of the other stewards were getting jealous of him, for the fact that he was chosen at times to help out on the range when it got busy.

Eventually he started to wear the khaki suit – and with pride, because he was one of the cleanest stewards on staff, but his pride was badly hurt when he got demoted from his self-assumed cook's position. However, before the end of the second month of his employment, he got posted in the staff cafeteria.

His job in the cafeteria was to keep it clean and help serve the staff meals, occasionally he also helped the staff cooks prepare the meals, but that was on his own accord.

His cooking skills and efficiency were always acceptable and appreciated by the cooks, who would often tell him that he had the wrong job. They told him to apply for a cook's position instead, but he didn't want to push his luck at that point, because he considered himself to be like one of the pawns in the game of chess.

There were over three hundred staffs at the hotel, and most of the managerial staff was white males from America, Germany, and Canada.

The hotel provided all the foreign managers and their families with living accommodation, and they got a monthly food allowance. Everybody except the head chef had breakfast, lunch, and dinner in the staff cafeteria.

Whenever Calvin was serving meals, he used to address everybody in the same manner, and he always smiled and treated everybody with courtesy and respect. His pleasant and courteous attitude didn't go unnoticed.

One evening, two months later, while he was in the process of tidying up the cafeteria, the head chef summoned him into his office.

"Initially, I thought I was in big trouble, because I used to flirt with some of the female staff. I also felt even worse when I arrived at chef's office and saw the food and beverage manager seated inside."

The kitchen was huge and everybody always looked towards the chef's office, when he was around. There was a big clear glass at the front of the office, and everybody could see what was going on inside.

Calvin felt all eyes on him as he knocked on the door and entered the office.

"Have a seat, Mr Riley," Chef commanded, without looking up from the pile of documents on his desk.

The food and beverage manager (the F&B) was on the phone by then. He was a chubby white American, and unlike Chef, he'd turned around and smiled at Calvin, as he continued to talk on the phone.

Calvin sat in the chair nervously for a few minutes, which seemed like an eternity, waiting for his judgment, but suddenly, the conversation on the phone ended, and the F&B manager swivelled around in his chair to face him.

"Have you had a good day, Mr Riley?" the F&B enquired.

Calvin told him, "Yes," he had a good day, and he was just in the process of completing his job in the cafeteria.

"Do you like working in the cafeteria?" the F&B asked.

At that point Calvin's heart sank in his chest, because he thought it was the initial move before the inevitable "you are fired"; thus he braced himself and said, "Yes sir, I like my job very much."

Chef swivelled around in his chair and said, "You also like to wear the chef's clothes, don't you, Mr Riley?"

Even though Calvin was nervous, he still managed to smile and said, "I always wanted to wear a chef's suit, sir."

The F&B manager and Chef looked at each other incredulously, and Chef asked, "Would you like to wear a chef's suit permanently then, Mr Riley?"

Instantly, Calvin knew that something good was about to happen, but he couldn't believe it was about to happen to him, and before he could answer, the F&B turned to him and said, "If you wanted so much to wear a chef's suit, Mr Riley, why don't you answer the chef?"

"Yes sir, I would very much love that, sir. Thank you very much, sir," he answered nervously.

"Don't thank me," Chef said. "Thank the F&B, because he was the one who recognised that you have a lot of potential."

The F&B joined in and said, "I've been observing how you conduct yourself in the cafeteria, Mr Riley. We need people like you to work out front with the guests so please continue in the same manner – and don't let us down," he concluded.

With that, he shook Calvin's hand, said goodbye to the chef, and left the office.

Chef immediately filled out an order form and gave it to Calvin, to take to the housekeeping department and collect three brand-new suits of chef's uniform.

Before he left the office, the chef told him that he was promoted to a third cook, and he would be working on the evening buffet, come the following evening!

Calvin couldn't stop smiling when he left the office, but he was happier not to have got fired than he was about the promotion.

Chef left the office, as Calvin walked out with his chest puffed up and his head held high.

He told the kitchen staff who had been observing the scene about his good news, and most of them were genuinely happy for him. There were also a few jealous faces, but on the other hand he didn't care. After all, he wasn't doing anything wrong.

His new job as a third cook was more interesting, and he felt proud to own his own chef's clothes, and he wore them with pride.

Initially, he was required to prepare the vegetables to be served on the evening buffet, and he helped set up the buffet and replenish the food during service.

"I had the most amazing experience the first evening I strolled down the length of the crowded terrace," Calvin declared enthusiastically. "It was a beautiful evening, and the sun had already set, but the golden glow was still reflecting on the sky, above the expanse of the blue sea.

"The cool sea breeze was welcoming on my warm face, as I stepped out of the hot kitchen, through the swinging doors and into the hallway that led onto the terrace. My tall white chef's hat was seated perfectly on my shaved head, and my clean, white apron was secured neatly around my crisp white jacket.

"The bar at the end of the hallway was in full swing, and bartenders were busy showing off their mixing skills while waiters and waitresses were moving swiftly around each other, balancing trays of drinks on one hand in the air.

"There was also a band on the stage opposite the poolside doing their thing, and all the guests seemed to be happy, because there was a lot of chatting and laughing all around.

"As I stepped onto the terrace I gently inhaled the fresh sea breeze, aftershave, perfume, alcohol and food as I boldly sauntered towards the food station. By the time I arrived at the buffet I'd felt like I was walking on air, and it was the first time in my life I'd experienced such a profound joy and attractiveness, which went straight to my head. I felt a bit dizzy, but I smiled as I nervously checked all the food, before I went back inside the kitchen.

"On the whole, I was totally captivated by the overall setting on the terrace that night and I'd made I silent vow, that one day, I would experience what it felt like to be a tourist, seated in a restaurant."

Two months later, Chef called him in the office again, but this time he wasn't nervous, because he was constantly on his best behaviour. Still, he was surprised when he entered the office and Chef smiled and said, "Have a seat, Mr Riley."

When he was seated, Chef replaced the ever-present stern look on his face before he spoke again. "How do you feel about working on the breakfast shift?" he asked, coming straight to the point.

"I don't have a problem with that, Chef," Calvin answered, without hesitating.

"That's what I like to hear," said Chef, as he busied himself moving piles of documents from one part of the desk to the other. A moment of silence ensued, apart from the sound of the documents Chef kept moving around on the desk and the humming of the walk-in refrigerator next to the office. "Okay, Mr Riley," Chef said finally, "take a day off tomorrow, and start working on the breakfast shift the following day. Your shift starts at 5 a.m., and make sure to be here on time."

Calvin thanked him and left the office with mixed feelings.

"After all that has been said and done throughout my aimless life, it was very moving for me at that point, to finally get recognised for doing something good and moving from one area to the other. It also showed that I was making progress on the job. On the other hand, I was about to embark on a new mission, and it secretly scared me.

"Conversely, at that stage, there weren't many changes in my life, regarding transforming myself into a better person. Instead, I was now walking totally in my father's and Devon's footsteps, by way of gambling, drinking a lot of alcohol, and smoking weed and crack cocaine.

"Aunty and Uncle were also having regrets for getting me the job at the hotel, because they couldn't see any progress in my life. I was only moving towards an ultimate self-destruction.

"Dawn wasn't getting any support from me towards the upbringing of the baby that I hadn't seen since he was born. It was only by chance one day I'd seen my child."

It was a beautiful mid-afternoon, and Calvin was walking towards Cyril Gully, downtown Mobay, when he saw Dawn standing proudly at the bus stop with her baby in her arms.

At first, he tried to conceal himself between the other pedestrians, but suddenly his eyes made contact with hers. Instantly he put on a broad smile and went over to greet her and the baby, as if it was his initial intention. But underneath his smile lay a bitter feeling of shame. It was one of those days when he felt very ashamed, more so for the way in which he was living his life without any meaningful desire. At that precise moment he was suddenly awakened, because deep down a part of him always wanted to be a good person in every aspect and forsake all bad habits. But on the contrary, another part of him only wanted to have a good time and make up for all the sad times that he'd had before. On the whole, he felt trapped and confused as he stood looking at his son, but he didn't ask when the child had been born; nor did he offer to hold him and Dawn didn't ask him if he wanted to. Still, she smiled and told him that she'd named him Kenique Brown and he was born on the twelfth of May, 1989.

When Dawn gave him the information, Calvin only smiled, but he didn't enquire why the child wasn't named after him. Nor did he ask after her health or the baby's.

Feeling guilty for the way he had treated Dawn, he took out his wallet and gave her a few hundred dollars. As she took the money, he told her not to worry, because he was going to take care of the baby. He also told her to meet him at the same place a week later, even though he had no intention of keeping his promise, and when the time came he didn't turn up.

However, about a month later, Dawn decided to take Kenique to his grandparents' house, but at the time, he and his grandparents weren't on good terms, because of the repulsive life he was living.

The day Dawn went to 10 Crichton's Drive, he was at work, but his grandparents told her what time she could find him there.

That night, he went home from work extremely late, as he always did. Aunty opened the door, let him in, and told him that a woman with a baby had been there to see him. She also told him the woman told her that the baby was his.

He felt ashamed when Aunty told him about Dawn and the baby and quickly went into denial. Aunty bluntly told him that she'd had a good look at the child, and he was the spit image of Calvin. Nevertheless, she didn't tell him that Dawn planned to return the next day.

The following morning while he lay in bed sleeping, Dawn returned. Initially, Aunty summoned him to the veranda without telling him the reason why. When he appeared at the front door, half asleep from the drugs and alcohol he'd consumed the previous night; he was shocked to see Dawn sitting there with the baby in her arms.

She looked at him questioningly, shook her head from side to side, smiled, and then looked at her baby in her arms as she rocked him gently.

Aunty and Uncle were seated quietly in their usual seats, observing the drama.

Calvin stood still at the door, half asleep, with his face covered in disbelief and shame looking at Dawn and his son, not knowing what to do or say, because he was caught with his pants down again.

Aunty broke the silence and asked Calvin if he wasn't going to hold his baby. Reluctantly he held his son, but even though he was earning lots of money at the hotel, that day he could not afford to purchase a box of orange juice to feed Kenique. Eventually he had to borrow some money from his aunt, to buy a pint of orange juice for his child.

Before Dawn left the house that morning, he promised her again that he would take care of the child, although he knew that he couldn't keep his promise, because he was being led by the influence of drugs, alcohol, and gambling.

The last time he saw the child was about three years later, when he entered the Hometown Supermarket, downtown Mobay.

That day, as he entered through the main entrance of the supermarket, his eyes met Dawn's and Kenique's. He froze in his tracks, but the child started to ran towards him with open arms.

Although the child didn't know that Calvin was his father, it was evident that there was a strong chemistry between father and son that could not be denied, and quickly he went down on his knees and allowed his son to run into his open arms. However, as father and son embraced, Dawn stormed over and pulled the boy away furiously, just as he was beginning to enjoy the beating of his son's heart against his chest.

He stayed on his knees and looked up at Dawn pleadingly, and the visible pain that he was feeling didn't go unnoticed, but she wasn't in the mood to show him any charity. Instead, softly but firmly, she said, "Please don't tell him that you are his father. I don't want to confuse him anymore, because he's calling another man Daddy already." With that said Dawn walked away with her son and left him kneeling there.

The hurt he felt, to know that his son was calling another man Daddy, was unexplainable, but that was the way he'd made his bed. He had no choice but to lie in it.

Ultimately, he made a vow: that the next time a woman got pregnant by him, he would stand by her and do whatever it took to support his child, because he didn't want any child of his to end up like him, or his dad Percy, for that matter.

A brief message to you, the reader of this book: don't ever neglect your children, because you will live to regret it somewhere down the line. It is something that will come back to haunt you one day.

CHAPTER SEVENTEEN

Drifting from Reality

The following day, after Calvin got transferred to the breakfast shift, he went to bed early that night, because he didn't want to be late the first morning.

At 3:00 a.m. he was wide awake, and by 4:00 he was leaving 10 Crichton's Drive.

He was fortunate to get a taxi when he reached the main road, and in less than ten minutes he was at the bus stop.

The staff bus, which was parked on Harbour Street, was waiting when he arrived.

As he got on the bus, Bennett, the breakfast supervisor, welcomed him, followed by Spanky, the lifeguard. Minutes later Junior Reid, another cook, boarded the bus, and the driver pulled away.

At the hotel, Calvin felt rather nervous and out of place. The other breakfast cooks didn't make it any easier for him either, because although they were professional cooks, neither of them was behaving professionally. Specifically, they made it known that they weren't there to teach anybody how to do the job.

Calvin knew they were throwing words at him, but he didn't let it affect his performance. Instead, he watched everything the rest of the cooks did and tried to do it better. Eventually, they realised that he was smart, and he wasn't the type of person that anybody or their words could keep down.

On his third morning, they put him on the breakfast buffet, because none of the other cooks wanted to work on the terrace. It was a job that most of them usually shied away from, because they considered it boring, but Calvin loved it from the first day he worked on it.

"I was very nervous that first morning on the terrace, but by eleven o'clock, when breakfast ended, I'd felt like that was where I belonged."

Unbeknown to him, the supervisors and the management team were observing his overall performance on the buffet and in the kitchen. In time, he became an integral part of the team, and they put him in charge of the breakfast buffet.

As the days turned into a week and the weeks turned into a month, he began to love every moment on the breakfast shift. In due course, he and the eight other breakfast cooks developed a close relationship that was like being blood brothers.

Everybody knew that the breakfast cooks were very good at their jobs and they were highly respected for that. On the other hand, all of them were angry, and they would at times act vile and uncontrollable. During the days some would smoke weed, while the rest, including the supervisor, while on the job, drank a lot of liquor, which they acquired from the bartenders. When they got intoxicated, they would swear and speak very loudly, and at times the atmosphere in the kitchen was like watching a series on the television. Gradually, Calvin started to adopt the rest of the cooks' bad attitude.

Overall, the worst thing about working on the breakfast shift was the time he had to get up in the mornings. It was all right on the weekends, because taxis ran all night, but on weekdays, most taxi drivers didn't start working until 5 a.m. so, he would have to walk nearly three miles to catch the staff bus. When he woke up late, he sometimes ran all the way to the bus stop.

One particular morning, while he was running to the bus stop, he got the fright of his life.

He'd decided to run on a back street to get to the bus stop on time. The back street in question was called Hart Street, which is one of the war-zone, ghetto areas in downtown Mobay. All who lived on that street, including women, men, and children, were known as gangsters. Lots of tribal wars were fought there, and a lot of people got killed on the streets.

The residents that lived on Hart Street got respect wherever they went, although sometimes other gangs would attack them outside of their turf, which often resulted in deaths.

From the time Calvin was growing up in Mobay, he often went wherever he wanted, and he knew a lot of people in most areas around town. Therefore he didn't have any fear when he decided to cut through Hart Street that morning. However, while he was running, he saw an unmarked car coming up the road towards him very slowly. He didn't take much notice of the car, even though he suspected the occupants to be police.

As the car got closer, it suddenly swerved on him and blocked his path, and the four doors flew open and four men jumped from the car.

Two were carrying M16 assault rifles, while the other two were packing automatic handguns.

"Tand up weh yuh deh, bwoy. Ha weh de bloodclaat yuh ting seh yuh deh guh?" one of the men barked at him.

Translation: "Stand up where you are, boy. Where do you think you are going?"

Humbly he stood still. Even his breathing stopped at that point.

There was no introduction to say, "We are the police." Instead, one of the handgun carriers stuck his gun under Calvin's chin, while the other three positioned themselves around him with their guns pointed at him.

Their initial approach and the way in which they posed the following questions were designed primarily to throw an individual off balance. Without breaking the sentence, the officer with his gun under Calvin's chin barked, "Wah yuh name weh yuh ha come from weh yuh live weh yuh ha guh, bwoy?"

Translation: "What's your name where you coming from where you live where are you going, boy?"

Calmly Calvin told them his name, where he lived, and that he was on his way to work at the Wyndham Rose Hall Hotel, where he was a cook. At the same time, he made a foolish attempt to reach for his ID in his pocket, but the gunman poked his gun further into his chin, pushing his head backwards in the process, and said, "One mo' move an' yuh dead, bwoy."

At that point, Calvin was standing on wobbly legs, and he began to sweat, even though the morning was unusually cold.

He had a chef's jacket and an apron in his hand, and wrapped in the clothes was his twelve-inch chef's knife.

One officer released him of the bundle and searched it.

"Bloodclaat! Ha who yuh ha guh kill wid dis, bwoy?" the officer asked when he behold the knife. Translation: "Who are you planning to kill with this, boy?"

"Mi did tell yuh seh ha work mi deh guh, officer," Calvin replied nervously. "Ha late mi late boss, dat's why mi have to run to catch de staff bus." Translation: "I did tell you that I was on my way to work, officer. I'm late boss, that's the reason why I was running to catch the staff bus."

At that stage, they allowed him to show them his ID, and after they inspected it, searched him thoroughly, and were satisfied, they returned the clothes and the knife and told him to go. But the one who'd held the gun under his chin told him not to run on the back streets, because he could have lost his life just like that.

Nervously, Calvin told them that he didn't have any choice if he was late. "Yuh cyan' seh we never warn yuh though," another officer told him, as he sat in the front passenger seat of the car. Translation: "You can't say we never warn you though."

Calvin was a bit rattled after the shakedown. Still, he continued to run again, and he didn't stop until he got to the bus stop. Unfortunately, the staff bus had already left, and he was late for work.

"Although I could have got killed that morning," Calvin exclaimed, "such an experience wasn't one that would normally get told to anyone, or cause any loss of sleep for that matter, because it was the normal way of life for every struggling youth on the streets. Over time one got used to the vicious, radical system and conditioned oneself to live with it."

*

Back at the hotel, soliciting the guests or other staff members in any way was strictly prohibited, and anybody caught breaking such rules, or any other rules outlined by the hotel, would have their employment terminated. But it was only a matter of time before Calvin started to participate and indulge in forbidden activities. Ultimately, he became one of "The Man".

It all started one morning, while he was busy flipping omelettes and pancakes behind the grill on the terrace. He noticed two young couples when they stopped at the cashier, but they didn't purchase breakfast tickets. Instead, a waiter appeared, spoke to them, and then escorted them to the buffet.

Calvin was amazed by the obvious intention of the waiter and the cashier, because it was the in thing for some of them to sell food to the guests and then pocket the money. Still, he pretended not to have noticed what was about to happen.

While the guests were admiring his beautiful fruit display, the waiter walked away, and then each guest started to select an assortment of the freshly baked breakfast pastries from the baskets and fresh tropical fruits from the brilliantly arranged fruit platters. Minutes later they arrived at the grill, and Calvin greeted them with warm courtesy and friendly enthusiasm. Then, the first guest was about to place an order for omelettes and pancakes, and Calvin politely ask for their receipts.

"The waiter and the cashier told us that it was okay to eat first and pay afterwards," one of the guests replied.

Calvin smiled and told them, "No problem, mon."

After the guests placed their orders, he told them that it was okay to take their seats, because he would send the orders over with the waiter.

When their orders were ready, he called the waiter he suspected of doing undercover dealings.

"How much mi deh get from de deal, blood?" Calvin enquired calmly, as the waiter arrived at the grill, but the waiter pretended to be taken aback by the question and asked Calvin incredulously what he was talking about. "Yuh done know what I'm talking about, blood, so stop behaving as if you want to take me for a fool," Calvin reacted quietly but angrily.

By now the waiter was acting jumpy. He knew that he had been caught red-handed, and the signs of guilt were evident in his eyes and in his tone of voice.

Calvin knew he had full control of the situation, and there were a number of things that he could do to resolve it. One, he could lodge a complaint to the management team about what had taken place, and the waiter and the cashier would be fired. On the other hand, most of the staff would've branded him as an informer, and that would definitely put him in danger, because informers were not tolerated anywhere on the island. They were public enemy number one.

Two, he could ignore the whole thing and walk away with his head held high, but at that point in his life, he couldn't afford to deny himself a little bit more, under the circumstances. Moreover, the earlier aspiration and self-discipline that he was generating, when he got the job, were almost forgotten. His reasons for living then were to stay stoned on seasoned spliffs, and to make his regular disappointed trips to the gambling house. Consequently, he decided to do what he thought was good for him.

"Mi want half of de money," Calvin told the waiter. "Yuh an' de cashier can share de rest of it, becah de both of you working together."

Ultimately, the waiter held up his hands and told Calvin to keep quiet, and later that same morning he got his first taste of tainted money.

The buzz he got from receiving the solicited money was a further enticement, and he wanted more. From that day on, he decided to observe every move that the waiters and cashiers made. It was easy to pinpoint all the participants in the scams, and he soon built up a strong clientele.

As he got deeper into the impure activities, his attitude also began to change. Eventually, selling the food undercover to the tourists was not enough. He wanted more, and he was prepared to get it by any means necessary.

"I'd made a silent vow to myself from the outset, that I wouldn't do anything foolish to embarrass Mr Jump or Aunty and Uncle, for the mere fact that they got me the job. Although at the time I wasn't living up to Aunty and Uncle's expectation, Mr Jump knew about my progress on the job, and he was very proud of me. Still, the temptation of making extra money to fuel my addictions was too great to ignore, thus I'd decided to risk it all by indulging in the corruptions."

The next step Calvin took towards self-destruction was to begin dealing in drugs on the job, without any thought of the consequences. Accordingly, his feet got bigger than his boots, and he began to fly without wings. At that stage he didn't have time to look back or think about anything positive (or anybody, for that matter), apart from how he was going to make the next dollar to satisfy his squalid needs. In sum, he was walking around with a big capital L on his forehead. He was still a loser, and his confused, messed-up life seemed meaningless. At a fast pace his self-destructive attitude was leading him into ever more shame and misery, and he didn't even realise it.

At the time he was earning over three thousand dollars a fortnight, not including tips or the ill-gotten money he made from the food and drugs that he sold to the guests undercover. Nevertheless, the more money he was earning the less ambitious he seemed to become, and eventually his life became an endless round of seasoned spliffs, alcohol, and gambling.

Because of his worthless attitude, he was unable to save his money, even though he'd reluctantly joined the compulsory saving scheme that the hotel had set up for the staff with the Jamaica Credit Union Bank.

He used to bank one thousand dollars every fortnight from his wages, but oftentimes he would withdraw most of it the following week after he squandered the rest on drugs and at the gambling house.

At that stage he was living a rather lonely life. Occasionally he would bump into Salomon, who was one of the top rude boys at Salt Spring, and Babs, who was living at Mount Salem. More frequently he saw Devon around town, although he was living at Carey Village. Marika, on the other hand, was living at Mount Carey. By then she had given birth to five children, while Van was doing twenty-five years in prison, before any chance of getting parole, which was recommended after the British High Court annulled his death sentence. Every once in a while he visited Ruby, who was also living at Salt Spring, but that was as far as it went, and in a strange way it felt normal to him, because he didn't know the value of family union. He was simply living his life the only way that he knew, on account of the teachings that he had acquired whilst growing up.

"The closest people around me by then were my co-workers and the men that I gambled with regularly. Conversely, I would often play the family guy at home, but it was done under pretence. I knew Aunty and Uncle had given up on me, because I wasn't making any progressive changes. I was only wasting my life away on drugs and alcohol – and gambling, which they didn't know about.

"As for my adopted family (the Williams family), especially my bona fide friend Donovan, they only saw me once in a while.

"As time went on I'd became someone that I myself did not recognise, but I didn't have time to stop and reassess my life, even though, consciously, I knew that I was wasting away at a fast pace. Ultimately, a part of me was desperate to change for the better, but I didn't know how to stop all the wrongdoings, or even how to slow down."

During that same period, Calvin experienced another disturbing event, this time at a family fun day that the hotel held for all the staff.

It was a beautiful day, and a cool breeze was blowing in off the blue sea. Everybody was in high spirits, because the hotel had poured on loads of fine foods and drinks for everyone to enjoy.

That day, while all the staff took part in various games, laughing and having fun with their families, Calvin suddenly looked around and realised that he was the only one present without a family member. Minutes later, without saying goodbye to anybody, he quietly walked away from the event unnoticed, feeling lonely, useless, and ashamed.

"While I was walking away from the event, I cursed my relatives silently and blamed them for all the bad times that I'd had throughout my life.

"Years later when I looked back, I realised that I was wrong to blame them, because I should've carved out a clean path for myself to walk on."

Calvin collecting a cash reward from Head Chef Michael Urban at Wyndham Rose Hall

CHAPTER EIGHTEEN

Standing on My Own Feet at Last

In early 1991, just over one year after he'd started working at the hotel, his grandparents asked him to leave their home again, because they could no longer tolerate his out-of-control lifestyle. On the whole, they'd hoped his life would change for the better when they got him the job, and maybe, just maybe he might one day start to go back to church with them again, but it was the absolute opposite. He'd managed to become a nuisance to them, instead of turning his life around as they had hoped.

As always, he didn't have any savings, because he was living for each day as it came. Worst of all, he didn't have anywhere to go or any friends he could ask to put him up for a few nights. As a result, he had to put up with a lot of disrespect from Aunty and Uncle. For instance, whenever he went anywhere and returned home after 10 p.m., they wouldn't even let him in the house. On those nights, he would sleep in the garage, underneath the house, where the yard dogs slept. Although the garage was infested with fleas, scorpions, and rats, it didn't bother him, because all he needed was somewhere to rest his tired head.

In the mornings, he used to get out of the garage very early, before anybody should pass on the road and see him in the dogs' bed. Neither did he want the neighbours or the tenants to know what was really going on in his life.

After a while, Calvin couldn't take any more of the constant put-downs from Aunty and Uncle or the restless nights in the infested garage. As a result, he started to search for a place to rent, and in less than a week one of his co-workers, Arnold Harris (aka Carrot) tipped him off about a furnished room that was up for rent at his house.

"Initially, lots of butterflies were dancing inside my stomach when Carrot told me about the room, and the prospect of having my own place and a set of keys seemed daunting to me, because I'd never had such privileges before.

"I was about to embark on a new mission, that could either make me or break me, and I was scared. Nonetheless, I built up the courage and told Carrot that I would come around to have a look at the room."

Carrot on the other hand was an all-round good man. He was much older than Calvin, and most people liked him because he was kind and friendly and genuinely down to earth. He was the type of man that would give a friend his bed while he slept on the floor. Granted, he was a heavy rum drinker, and a lot of people suspected him of smoking crack cocaine, but he was a straight rum drinker and a ganja smoker.

Carrot was living with his uncle and aunt and their daughter, Betty. They were all mixed race and majority of their other families were first class citizen on the island, but Carrot was the black sheep in the family, because his lifestyle didn't reflect his complexion.

The house they lived in was situated on Cottage Road, overlooking Jarrett Park, Montego Bay's number-one football stadium.

It was a massive two-story house, in good condition. Carrot and his family lived upstairs and they rented out the ground floor, which was used for living and commercial purposes. There was a medical doctor's office at the front of the building, and three small bedrooms, and a local West Indian restaurant and bar at the back.

Calvin was pleased with the location, if still apprehensive.

On the day he went to view the room, Carrot escorted him to the house and introduced him to Margo, the woman who leased the restaurant, bar, and bedrooms from his aunty.

Without any delay, Margo ushered Calvin through the half-lit, smoke-filled rum bar towards the back, and showed him the small dining room and the small kitchen. Next she took him through the kitchen back door and showed him the laundry room and the backyard, before she finally showed him the bedroom.

It was a small bedroom, furnished with a double bed, a small bedside table with a bedside light on top, and a single lounge chair. At the back, next to the room, was a small shower room with a toilet and no washbasin.

Calvin thought the place was ideal for him, and as a result he told Margo that he would take it. Margo, who had already decided that she liked him, rented him the room without hesitation.

He was ecstatic, because he was going to be the only live-in tenant on the premises, apart from Skiers, Margo's live-in caretaker.

Skiers were about twice Calvin's age, a very good carpenter and craftsman who could make anything out of wood, but he had a major weakness for the indulgence of ganja and the rum bottle. In some ways, he reminded Calvin of Percy, and not long after he moved in, they became best friends, often sharing weed and rum with each other.

"I was walking on cloud nine when I left Carrot's house that day, and it was one of the happiest times in my life, because I was about to own my first room at the age of twenty-three, and I had a job. It was exactly what I'd always dreamt of from a child, and the feeling I experienced was second to none.

"When I broke the news to my grandparents, they were shocked, because even though they couldn't tolerate my way of life, deep down I knew that they didn't really want me to go."

At Cottage Road, the double bed took up most of the small room, but anything was much better than the prospect of sleeping in the infested garage at his grandparents' house. He was now the sole holder of a key. It was also the first time in his life he'd owned a house key. Even though the place was rented, it still gave him a good feeling.

Finally he could do whatever he wanted to do without offending anybody. On the whole, it should have been a new start to turn his life around, but things didn't get any better when it came to making amendments to his reckless and aimless lifestyle. He was still losing his money at the gambling house, and he'd begun to drink more alcohol and smoke more than ever – and he didn't care what anybody thought of him.

At the time, Akroman and Bwoysie were his two favourite friends, and the both of them also worked at the hotel. Akroman was a fantastic range cook, and Bwoysie, initially employed as a kitchen steward, later got promoted to a butcher.

Akroman, who was older than Calvin, were living in the ghetto of Flanker with his girlfriend, while Bwoysie, who was single and older than the both of them lived in the ghetto of Canterbury, at his cousin's house.

Carrot, who was also single, became one of Calvin's favourite friends too, but that was only after he'd gone to live at Cottage Road.

Back at the hotel, the German head chef was replaced by an American, whose personality was the opposite of the German, and before long, Carrot had him eating drugs from the palm of his hands.

Sometimes when Carrot was too hung-over to go to work, he would gave Calvin the drugs to deliver to the chef, and in the process Calvin too became one of the new chef's favourite cooks.

After Calvin's shift finished at one o'clock, he sometimes went by the caddy shed to gamble with the caddies. Other times he would hang around the hotel until Akroman and Bwoysie completed their shift at three o'clock and clock out the same time with them. Oftentimes when the chef signed the time sheets, Calvin would get paid for the extra hours that he wasted waiting for his friends.

Later the three of them would go by the fisherman's village, close to the hotel, where they would hang out with the villagers and play dominoes, smoke weed, drink rum and Guinness stout until the 5:30 staff bus was ready to leave for Montego Bay.

Frequently he and Akroman went to Bwoysie's house at Canterbury to smoke more weed and drink Guinness stout while Bwoysie played his cousin's big sound system.

Bwoysie's cousin was a renowned don in the area, and he owned one of the biggest houses in the ghetto, with a shop attached. They held regular parties at his house, sometimes on an open lawn in the ghetto, where the people in the community often gathered to socialise. Sometimes they would take the sound system out of the area to hold parties elsewhere.

Calvin knew a few people who lived in Canterbury, before he met Bwoysie, but the first time he went into the ghetto, he was with Bwoysie and Akroman.

On leaving the main road to enter Canterbury, one has to cross a wooden bridge, and night and day a number of youths lurked on the bridge, or just on the other side, with a sinister motive.

Most people who entered the ghetto for the first time, unescorted, got searched thoroughly by the youths and routinely relieved of their personal possessions, and those who resisted normally got hurt in the process.

There was also another way into Canterbury from the notorious Cyril Gully ghetto, but one would have to be living in the area to contemplate taking that route.

Canterbury was considered one of the most feared ghetto areas around Mobay, and most of the men, women, boys, and girls who lived there had been through a run-in with the police at some stage in their lives.

On the whole, a lot of people feared the residents of Canterbury mainly because of their renowned riotous lifestyle. A lot of the youths were hotheads, and many notorious gunmen born and lived in the area. It didn't take much for a fight to develop amongst the residents, although they would stick together in time of war. The police, on the other hand, would not go after a wanted man in Canterbury. When a serious incident occurred – for instance, when someone was killed – the police would turn up in ridiculously large numbers to deal with the case, even being escorted by soldiers sometimes.

Incidentally, late 2003 marked the biggest war in Canterbury between police, soldiers, and gunmen, which lasted more than four days and nights. During the days, whilst people were attending their business around town, they could hear the police, soldiers, and gunmen exchanging gunfire, and at nights it was no different, because soldiers would hover above the ghetto in helicopters with the lights assisting those on the ground. Throughout the prolonged days, nobody could get out and nobody could get in.

Ultimately, four police officers were killed and a number of others were wounded. Six gunmen were also killed and many wounded, and many got arrested.

In the aftermath, the residents went back to their normal lives, and it was business as usual. After all, it was the way of life for them.

Sometimes Calvin would also hang out at Akroman's house, at Flanker.

The inhabitants of Flanker had a reputation for violence and resorting to obeah, and most of the residents were political activists. They were classed as squatters, who forcibly captured government and rich civilians' land and built their houses on it. Frequently the residents would fight amongst themselves, even killing each other in the process, but when there was a political affair, they would stick together and fight.

It was one of the most talked-about ghettos around Mobay, because often an incident in the area would fill the newspapers and the newscasts.

A lot of renowned gangsters emerged out of Flanker. Some died in the area, at their homes or on the streets, in police shoot-outs or in gang warfare elsewhere. Some of those infamous gangsters acquired their reputation solo, while some obtained theirs through the clique that they hung out with. Nonetheless, the majority lived and died the same way. A fortunate few migrated to America, Canada, or Europe.

On the whole, most of the youths who lived in Flanker didn't need to prove to anybody that they were rude boys, because the mere mention of Flanker as their home town would put fear into the minds of the natives.

It was also renowned that most of the women who lived in Flanker refused to date the local men in the ghetto, which caused the broken-hearted, disdained men to wage war against outsiders who entered the area to visit their women. The result was always the same; the visiting men usually got robbed and whipped. Those who secured free access to visit their women would have to be highly respected or have connections in the area.

Calvin had known a few people who lived at Flanker before he met Akroman. He'd also been to a few parties there before with Ian, his old security friend, who had relatives living in the area, and at one stage he had a short relationship with a girl he'd met on the beach, whose family was huge and well connected.

Akroman, whose hobby was fishing, was well respected in Flanker. He wasn't a gangster, neither was he involved in any political affairs. He was a complete family man. Nonetheless, he once had a cousin believed to have owned a Taurus automatic pistol, and he was one of the first and most feared gangsters to rise up in the community of Flanker.

The police and civilians alike were scared of Akroman's cousin, because he was considered very dangerous by the amount of crimes that he regularly committed, including a few lives he had taken along the way.

It took the police and soldiers a very long time to take this infamous, elusive outlaw out of existence, but after he was killed, the police were left with a crucial problem on their hands, because the gun he owned was never found on his dead body.

Akroman was very close to him whilst he was alive. Therefore, people in the area have long believed he inherited his cousin's gun. For that reason and because of his cool, respectable demeanour, a lot of people in the community would show him respect. Calvin used to enjoy chilling out at Akroman's yard, because it was relaxing and there was always a big pot of fish soup cooking. They would also drink liquor, smoked weed, and played dominoes.

On the whole, Calvin and his friends had different personalities. Akroman was determined and focused. On the other hand Bwoysie, who always broke his cigarettes and smoked half, wasn't an easy person to study. He was the quietest of all, and he had a tendency to laugh silently. At times you would have to be looking at him to know that he was laughing, because it only showed on his face.

Calvin was more open, yet he'd managed to keep his gambling addiction and crack smoking a secret from his friends.

Shortly after he moved into his room at Cottage Road, Calvin miraculously discontinued the crack smoking.

"I was fortunate to finally break the horrible drug spell that my brother Devon had placed on me.

"I decided to quit after it was clear that a large quantity of bad drugs were in circulation, which was making the users sick. At that precise moment, I also realised that the novelty of using crack cocaine had worn off, because I wasn't getting a better buzz from it than I got from smoking the pure weed."

Akroman and Bwoysie would sometimes accompany Calvin to Cottage Road after work to smoke weed and drink liquor. Carrot would sometimes join them too, and whenever there wasn't enough money to purchase the liquor, Calvin would get credit from the bar. However, when the time came to pay the bill, he was left on his own, but that didn't bother him, because he enjoyed being looked on as the main man. Percy used to have the same attitude towards life. As the elderly folks in Jamaica would say, "Chip nuh fly fur from de block," or "suh de father, suh de son."

Translation: "Chip never flew far from the cutting block, or a son will adapt his father's attitude."

There was no mistaking where Calvin was heading. At that crucial stage in his life he was totally walking into his relatives' footsteps.

Chapter Nineteen

Finding Love

A few weeks after Calvin moved into his new home, he met Carrot's cousin, Betty.

It was a warm night, and Carrot was sitting with him in front of the house, drinking rum and smoking weed, when Betty appeared on the balcony of the house and said, "Arnold, are you teaching the young man to drink rum like you?"

Carrot laughed and said, "Dem yah man yah a veteran in a dis, mon! A wah yuh a talk 'bout me, cousin?" Translation: "This guy is a veteran in this game. What are you talking about my cousin?"

Calvin's heart suddenly skipped a beat, when he looked in the direction of the voice and saw his friend's beautiful "browning" cousin, smiling down at him. Naturally, he smiled back at her, and he was convinced that an instant spark had ignited between them. He'd seen her a few times before, but they'd only said hello to each other in passing.

Carrot was a wise man, and he was always quick to spot a play. He noticed the attraction between his friend and his cousin and introduced them. Betty lingered awhile before she went back inside the house.

"Although I was attracted to my friend's cousin, the thought of getting together with her hadn't crossed my mind at that stage. However, the following day was my day off, and I decided to do my laundry. While I was hanging out my washing on the clothes line at the back of the house, someone began pelting me with gravel from upstairs. When I looked up, I saw Betty smiling down at me."

Instantly a conversation was started, and at one point, Betty mentioned that she was going to the local market, which was only a short walking distance, and he asked her if she wanted him to follow, and she immediately said yes.

Later, they both got changed, and off they went.

There was a slight tension between them as they walked and talked, but it was also plain to see that a connection had started to form.

During their trip to the market and back to the house, a relationship had developed, and they made a date to go to the cinema at the Strand Theatre that same night.

Calvin was very excited, and he was looking forward to his date, because it had been a while since he had taken a girl out, let alone to the cinema.

Late that same afternoon Eric (aka Chino) came to visit him at the house.

Chino was seventeen and in his final year at school. He was one out of many boys and girls who were on working experience at the hotel, and it was every staff member's duty to teach the youngsters while they were posted in their department.

Chino, with his witty attitude, reminded Calvin of himself, so he had taken him under his wing and was mentoring him on the job. He was also trying to get him a job at the hotel after he was graduated from school.

That evening Chino had gone to Cottage Road to collect some money that Calvin had promised him, and he lingered until Betty was ready and the three of them walked the mile and a half into town.

After Chino went his own way downtown, Calvin and Betty decided not to bother going to the cinema after all; instead, they walked back home and ended up in Calvin's room. The outcome was the beginning of an unbreakable union between them.

Betty kept her affair with Calvin a secret, because she didn't want her parents to know about it. Calvin on the other hand was happy with the way things were, because he wasn't really looking for a permanent relationship. Furthermore, he didn't know how to handle a steady relationship, because he was scared of having his heart broken, so he was running wild, even though he'd spent his life searching for love and affection.

However, he didn't know exactly what Betty wanted, because they didn't discuss any relationship issues. Still, the bond that was forming between them was getting stronger each time they met. Betty appeared to be the settling-down type of woman, who had a lot of love and respect to give, but it was also plain to see that she would require the same in return.

On the whole, she wasn't a bad woman. She was honest and kind, and when she smiled her brown eyes would light up any room. Nonetheless, although she was the best woman he'd ever met, he still wasn't ready to settle down.

She was eighteen years older than Calvin, but it didn't matter much to him; because he felt safe knowing that she was there for him. Then again, at twenty-three years old, his only aim was to have all the fun he possibly could.

In due course, it was brought to Betty's parents' attention that she was seeing the young man who lived downstairs, and a massive quarrel ensued.

Her dad was furious, because he expected his daughter to find a distinguished rich man, and he let his feelings show, but her mother's reaction was the contrary. In fact, her mother was a hypocrite like Aunty and Uncle. She was a member of the Seventh-Day Adventist Church, so she spoke to Calvin nicely when she saw him, as if everything was okay, but she often cursed him behind his back and showed Betty much disrespect and used foul language to her covertly. Betty on the other hand continued to deny having an affair with Calvin; after all, he was clearly much younger than she was and didn't fit the standard of her parents' requirements.

Calvin humbled himself and continued to act in the usual manner, but he always felt embarrassed and guilty whenever he came in contact with Betty's parents, knowing they didn't regard him as someone who was good enough to be with their daughter.

Gradually the truth revealed itself, and ultimately, Betty's parents' unwillingly accepted the revelation of the relationship, but they didn't accept Calvin as their son-in-law in any form.

Regardless of the unrelenting tension at the house, Betty was in love with Calvin, who was her best friend and confederate. Thus she continued her affair with him. Also, she was playing a significant role in his life, because she kept him on the straight and narrow. However, months later, he began to contemplate about moving on again.

Although Betty humbled him and he was enjoying what she had to offer him, the time had come for him to start running again, as he always did. But Betty was there to stay, whether he liked it or not.

It wasn't because he didn't like Betty anymore that he had decided to start running again. It was more to do with the fact that he couldn't take any other girls back to his room, because she was always present. Eventually, he felt suffocated and squeezed up into a tight bundle, and as a result it began to play on his mind, because he wasn't ready for any commitment at that stage in his life. Regardless of that, he took her to meet his grandparents one day. When he arrived with Betty at 10 Crichton's Drive and he made the initial introduction, he knew instantly that his grandparents weren't pleased. Still, they somehow managed to conceal their astonishment and their resentment of him having an older woman who wasn't a Christian, and they made a good impression on Betty.

Later Calvin left 10 Crichton's Drive feeling good, but he knew when he returned on his own again, he would have a lot to answer for.

A few weeks later he paid them another visit, and this time he went alone. While they were seated on the veranda talking, Aunty asked him why he had chosen a much older woman, but before he could answer; she began to lecture him about the church. Then she asked him why he didn't get one of the nice, young Christian girls from her church.

While she was lecturing him, Uncle kept silent, but Calvin knew he was only waiting for his turn to lecture him, but before

Uncle got the chance to speak, he revealed that he was leaving his present residence.

There was an immense silence, followed by the obvious question, and Calvin lied by telling them that he couldn't afford to pay his rent.

Even though Uncle and Aunty couldn't put up with his aimless lifestyle, it was still a pleasure for them to have him around the house. For that reason, they told him he was always welcome to come back and live with them any time he pleased.

Later that same day, he broke the news to Betty that he was moving back to Mount Salem, because he couldn't afford to pay the rent anymore. She was devastated and very sad, because he had become her closest friend, but his mind was already made up, and there was nothing she could do or say that could persuade him to stay.

"Less than a year after moving out of my grandparents' house and into a room of my own, I was preparing to return to the place where I knew there would be no freedom or happiness.

"I was jumping out of the frying pan and into the fire.

"At the time, my only possessions were some clothes and an eighteen-speed pushbike. The bike was my best possession. I'd purchased it with cash from the hotel, (an award) for an overall good performance."

Once more he was back underneath his grandparents' wing, but there were no changes in the way they liked things to be done in their home. Again they refused to give him a set of keys to the house, and the doors would be locked at ten o'clock each night.

It was hard coming down from his high horse and conforming to their way of living again, but he didn't have much choice.

On the whole, he missed the freedom that he'd acquired at Cottage Road, and he frequently felt lonely without Betty, who had become his closest pal. He visited her at the house a few times but gradually stopped.

Overall, he didn't need anyone to tell him how much Betty was in love with him, and he had strong feelings for her too. Still, he couldn't allow himself to fall in love, even though he was convinced that Betty was now the only person, who loved him unconditionally.

Although he'd got his freedom at last to be with other girls, he was left feeling empty and heartbroken.

*

Back at the hotel, Calvin was in his prime and on the surface his life seemed to be in order.

He had finally given up on the drugs dealing, and he would only participate in the food scam occasionally, when it presented itself to him.

Previously, the new head chef had given him the opportunity to show off his cooking skills, by way of doing cooking demonstrations for the guests at the poolside, every Wednesday and Saturday afternoon.

He would choose whatever food he wanted to demonstrate, cook a portion of it in the kitchen for the guests to sample, and bring a small gas stove and some uncooked food with all the ingredients to the poolside, to demonstrate how he cooked it.

"It was one of the best things that had happened for me, when I was chosen to do the cooking demonstration, because it brought out the real person that was always hiding inside of me, and it also transformed my cooking and social abilities in a major way."

By then Calvin had successfully acquired a job from the new head chef for Chino on the breakfast shift, and he was also teaching him how to run the buffet. At length, he also started to take Chino on the cooking demonstration, until eventually Chino got the position on the buffet and on the cooking demonstration.

Calvin was now cooking breakfast on the range and helping to prepare ahead for the following day, which he gradually found more interesting, but occasionally he still worked on the buffet.

At that point, his respect amongst most of the line staff and the management team was growing rapidly, because he showed much interest in his job and in the hotel on the whole.

For that reason, whenever some of the managers were having any private barbeque at their quarters, they would always choose him to run it.

Back at Mount Salem, the atmosphere was changing as usual. One evening he was at home when the phone rang. Aunty picked it up and spoke to the caller, and then told the caller that she would see if he was at home.

Calvin knew straight away that it was Betty, before his aunt asked him if he wanted the call. He asked her to tell the caller that he wasn't at home.

He felt foolish after Aunty hang up the phone, because he knew that he was betraying the only person who genuinely cared about him.

From that day, Betty regularly rang, and Aunty told her that Calvin wasn't at home, without even asking him if he wished to speak to her, until at length Aunty told her not to ring her phone again.

Uncle on the other hand was soft-hearted and wise. He had figured out that something must be wrong for Betty to keep on ringing the phone like she was doing. Uncle also knew Calvin better than anybody else, or so he thought, so he kept dropping hints regarding the phone calls.

But Calvin wouldn't budge. Conversely, he knew that Betty wouldn't tell his grandparents why she kept calling him. However, one day she rang the phone, and Uncle answered. They spoke for many minutes, but Betty didn't really tell Uncle the main reasons why she wanted to see Calvin, but she was crying on the phone. Later, Uncle persuaded Calvin to visit her.

At first he was a bit reluctant, but eventually he did go to visit Betty. Unfortunately, he got there too late. It seemed Betty had found out that she was pregnant with his baby and wanted him to know about it, but because he refused to take her calls or visit her, she had an abortion.

When Betty told him what had happened, he was breathless, and if he'd got a cut then, he wouldn't have bled.

"I'd never felt so hurt and ashamed in my life, and I wanted to cry, but I didn't know how, because I was muddled with both shame and grief. That night, I made yet another vow to change my reckless lifestyle, because deep down I knew that I wasn't living right, and other people were being made to face the consequences."

A few months later Betty decided to migrate to Bermuda, to stay with some of her relatives, and months later she went to the USA, to live with other relatives before eventually returning to England.

Before Betty made her initial exit, Calvin tried to make peace with her, because it suddenly dawned on him that he was about to lose his best friend, but there was nothing he could do or say that could justify the way he'd treated her.

The day before Betty departed, she told Calvin to grow up and be a responsible man, and he promised her that he would be a better person the next time they met.

That night, although he went to bed very early, he couldn't sleep, because musing on his past mistakes, the deep-rooted hurt that he bore, and the bad decisions that he had made throughout his life kept him awake.

The following day, he took the initial step by leaving work early without Akroman and Bwoysie, and during the months that followed, he met up with them only occasionally, until gradually the bond he had with them got broken.

"It was a very hard decision to make, because my friends were closer to me than my family, and ultimately I ended up feeling like a total loner, because Betty was gone and so were my friends."

At that point, Devon was in prison doing time for petty theft, while Marika was still living at Mount Carey. Ruby on the other hand was still living at Salt Spring with her lover. Salomon was still living there too and running a cook shop. Babs, who got married to Winston Angling, aka Twinny Bug, a famous Jamaican footballer (soccer player) was still living at Mount Salem. They had two children together, but Babs had two other daughters in a previous relationship. As for Van, he had been in prison for almost fifteen years, and Calvin wasn't hearing any news about him.

During that same time, Calvin found out that his sister Janet was teaching at a basic school, and although he felt apprehensive initially, nevertheless, without thinking twice, he decided to meet her officially.

The school was located on Railway Lane, one of the dilapidated, war-zone ghetto areas in Mobay, and the half-board, half-concrete school building appeared to have seen better days, when it served other purposes.

On his arrival, Calvin saw a brown-complexioned woman as he entered the front door, and he assumed she was one of the teachers.

There were about twenty little deprived children in the classroom, some of whom were seated around a few old, rundown chairs and old desks. Others stood screaming at each other, while some were crying.

When Calvin came in, the lady told the children to keep quiet, and the ones who were screaming stopped, but a few of the others were still crying.

He said a pleasant good afternoon to the lady and asked her if one Janet Beckford was working there. She looked at him in some confusion and said, "I am Janet Beckford."

For a tense moment his tongue stuck to the roof of his mouth, and his heart skipped beats. When he managed to snap out of his astonishment, he told Janet that he was her little brother Calvin, and suddenly, there was a magnificent silence everywhere, and he could see a mixture of feelings in his sister's eyes.

It was plain to see from where he was standing, that Janet didn't know what to make out of the sudden information. He didn't know exactly what to do either, because she was the woman he'd come close to asking out on a date once before. She was his sister, and for years he'd wanted to meet her. At the same time, he felt pity for her, because she didn't look anything like the lovely lady that he'd once met in the bar. He could also see that life wasn't treating her well, and it made him very sad and upset at the same time.

He wanted to embrace her, but instead he shook her hand.

There was so much that he wanted to say to her, but he didn't know where to start. Eventually, he told her that he'd heard about her and wanted to meet her, but Janet didn't reply, she only kept looking at her brother. From there on, neither of them could find words to say to each other. Finally, some of the kids began to behave unruly again, and he told her that he was leaving, so she could carry on with her class. He promised that he would return to visit her again, and made a quick exit.

"I was happy to meet my sister at last, but I felt relieved when I made my exit, because the whole experience, from the very day I heard about her existence, to the day I met her in the bar, to the information that I got from Mama, and the thought of repeating what my mother and father allegedly did, (being that they were brother and sister) and to finally meeting her was too much to bear at once.

"That day, I made a silent vow that I wouldn't let Janet disappear out of my life again."

Months later, Calvin decided to visit his sister again, and this time, joy had replaced the sadness in his heart, but on his arrival, his heart was broken when he saw another lady at the school teaching. When he enquired about his sister, the lady told him that she wasn't working there anymore.

"All of a sudden I felt sick and empty, because I didn't know if I would ever see my sister again.

"I walked away in a daze, and at that precise moment I wanted to hate my mother with a passion, for hiding my sister's existence for all those years, but I couldn't, because she was my mother and I loved her very much."

Seemingly, Calvin had largely given up on being a family man, because he felt he didn't belong to a family, even though he was living with his grandparents and had a lot of relatives all over the island. Finally, he convinced himself that he was a loner, but he was going to do whatever he had to do to survive, and maybe someday, start a family of his own.

Ultimately, he began to hang out with some of the breakfast cooks, who were sharing a rented house on Queen Street, in Montego Bay. Before long, he was spending most of his time there, when he wasn't at work. Most nights, instead of sleeping in his bed at Crichton's Drive, he would rather to hang out with his mates and slept on their floor. In the mornings they would get ready and go to work together. At length, he and his new crew made friends with Delroy, Tilly, Rupie, and some other youths, who were living on the same street.

Queen Street was also a ghetto area, but it wasn't notorious, unlike some of the other ghettos.

His new crewmembers were Slowly, Eric (Chino), Author, Shippy, and Shippy's brother Banton.

They were all working on the breakfast shift, except for Banton, who was self-employed. Later Renroy (Author's cousin) moved in too.

During that time Devon got released from a short stay in prison. He wanted to stay in Mobay, but he had nowhere to live. Calvin felt sorry for him and decided to help.

Initially he told Devon to find a room to rent and he would purchase a bed for him.

After Devon found the room, Calvin gave him money to pay the rent, bought him a double divan bed, and gave him some of his clothes, sheets, and some additional money.

"It was the very first bed I'd bought, but he was my brother, and I wanted him to know how much I loved him, regardless of the fact that he'd almost killed me when I was younger."

Nonetheless, not even that could stop Devon, because a few months later he held up an American black woman and robbed her of cash and jewels. He later hid the woman's handbag and his shirt that he was wearing at the same spot, but after a long and strenuous search, the police uncovered the bag with his shirt. His shirt was positively identified and his fingerprints were found on the bag. Ultimately, the police got fed up of his notorious behaviour and wanted him dead.

For many days the police were looking for him without success, but eventually, help came from an unlikely source.

The source who told the police Devon's whereabouts was none other than Ruby, who found out that he was hiding at Salomon's house. Somehow Devon found out what she had done, but he had little chance of escaping the brutal judgement of the police. Suddenly, he found himself with only one choice, and that was to hand himself in voluntarily. Although, knowing the reputation of the Jamaican police, he also realised that he would then be a dead man, even if he should walk into the police station with his hands high above his head. However, his survival techniques kicked in, and he decided to ask Uncle Roland for help.

At the time, Devon couldn't approach 10 Crichton's Drive, because he was like salt with no flavour to Uncle's taste. He was bringing pure shame and dishonour to himself and the rest of family with his notorious lifestyle, and Uncle was totally fed up with it. Therefore, Devon had to write a letter and give it to Mass Vick, to deliver to Uncle, but when the letter arrived at the house, Uncle showed no interest until Aunty started to cry.

Although Uncle was adamant not to help Devon, he was unable to say no to Aunty, who undoubtedly loved Devon with all her heart. As a result, Uncle decided to call his pastor and explain to him the problem at hand, and the pastor didn't lose any time in running to Uncle's aid.

Uncle and Aunty summoned Devon into the house, while they sat in silence waiting for the pastor. When the Reverend Doctor Leo Robinson finally arrived, Devon and Uncle got into the pastor's car and off they went to the Anchovy police station, where Devon was most wanted.

The police arrested Devon on arrival and slapped him with a charge of aggravated robbery. Later they allowed Uncle to bail him out, with a guarantee that he would turn up at court. The pastor also decided to stand as surety.

Before the police turned Devon loose, they told him that he owed his life to the pastor and his uncle, because if they hadn't brought him in, they were going to kill him.

When the day came for Devon's trial, which was held at a district called Cambridge, about seven miles from Mount Carey, Aunty went alone to the courthouse to support him.

Later it was clear to Calvin that one character was present at the courthouse whom Devon wasn't pleased to see, because of what she had done, and that person was Ruby.

As soon as Devon alighted from the car, Ruby started to hurl abuse at him, and she even went so far as to lift up her blouse and held her breasts up to the sky, asking God to let Devon get sent to prison. In the end her wishes were granted, because Devon received a three-year sentence.

Even though Ruby regularly hurried to Devon's rescue on previous occasions when he got into trouble, there was a big part of her that hated him with a passion, and she would often hint that she was keeping a big secret for him, but nobody knew what it really was.

The following week Aunty went to the Spanish Town District Prison, against Uncle's wishes, and paid an undisclosed amount of money to get Devon released and took him home with her. Even so, regardless of what Aunty had done for him, it didn't stop Devon from continually reoffending over the years.

"According to the popular phrase, a leopard can't change its spots, and once a person is a thief, he or she will always be a thief. Nonetheless, although the leopard cannot change its spots, on the contrary, it is possible for anybody to change their habits and lifestyle. But this, my friend, is up to you as an individual, to really want those changes in your life, and make the necessary move to achieve it."

As for Calvin, he was determined to change his lifestyle by all means necessary, because he was adamant not to end up like his brothers or other youths.

CHAPTER TWENTY

Finding More Love

Calvin thought hanging out on Queen Street with his friends was the way forward, to change his reckless lifestyle, but he was only drifting away from the path of reality.

His co-workers were moving forwards and making visible progress, but he was moving backwards, by consistently gambling his money away.

His only possessions were the same as before, a few suits of clothes and his pushbike, which all his friends would ride occasionally, but even so, he felt content.

"Queen Street was my home, and the rest of guys were like my blood brothers, because we looked out for each other and showed each other love and respect.

"A few of the guys in the crew were a bit older than me, but most were younger. Nonetheless, all of us were on a level with each other, and most of the time we used to cook and eat together, watch movies and cricket, play dominoes and football, and go fishing on the free beach at night.

"For me, it was the perfect way to live, and it was exactly the way I'd wanted to be with my siblings while growing up. I was simply living the life that I'd missed out on, but always wanted to live, and it felt good to finally be living my dreams.

"But even though I was experiencing the essence of brotherly love, there was still something special missing from my life. I didn't know what that special something was, until one fine day a woman who went by the name of Veron Brown walked into my reckless, disorderly life and changed it dramatically."

It all started after Veron rented the studio flat next door to Calvin and his friends on Queen Street.

At first sight, Veron appeared to be a decent, intelligent woman, and she was well aware of how attractive she was.

She was about six feet tall, with smooth dark brown skin and a distinctive long chin. Most of all she was perfectly shaped in all the right places. In fact, the Jamaican folks would describe her as having a Coca-Cola bottle shape.

Unquestionably everybody liked her, and the moment Calvin laid eyes on her, he fell head over heels in love. He didn't have the courage to approach her and tell her exactly how he felt. Instead, he only talked with his friends about his attraction, each time he saw her. His friends, on the other hand, only laughed and told him that he should go and express his feelings to her. However, one day Chino, the youngest crewmember, went up to Veron and told her that one of his friends was madly in love with her. Veron told Chino to tell his friend that he should come and tell her himself. Calvin took that as an invitation and boldly went over to introduce himself. After that, everything seemed to fall into place. Days later, he took her out on a date to watch a movie at the Strand Theatre.

"We sat in the back row at the theatre, and although I can't remember the movie that was showing, I'll never forget how proud and happy I felt, sitting next to the woman that I was physically attracted to, and from that night, I knew something special had happened in my life."

Finally, Calvin thought he'd found his dream woman, and although Betty was the first woman to love him unconditionally, Veron was the first to make his heart skip a beat, since he becomes a man. On the whole, she was a good conversationalist, and although she had Christian leanings, (because of her religious upbringing), she was also streetwise, with a broad knowledge of the ever-present struggle that the underprivileged were facing, and how the politicians were running the country.

When they initially met, Veron was going out with a minibus driver, she told Calvin that the relationship with the man was on the brink of collapsing, and shortly after they met she finally ended it.

She also asked Calvin if he was seeing anybody else. He told her that he had a girlfriend in America, although there was no confirmation of a relationship between Betty and him. Nonetheless, he and Betty were still in contact, but only by the occasionally letter. Still, although the feelings he had for Veron were second to none at the time, he still did not want to cut strings with Betty. Moreover, Devon had once told him, while he was training him, (how to get the girls), that he should always tell a woman that he had a girlfriend or that he'd just broken up with her. By doing this, Devon said, "You will be able to have more access to a wider range of women, without having to undergo much jealousy from them." Devon went on, "Some women are funny and will think something is wrong with you if you haven't got a girlfriend."

It wasn't a technique that Calvin would normally practice, but Betty and Veron were very special in his life, and he wanted to keep the both of them. Furthermore, he thought there was still enough time to play the field, before even considering settling down with one woman.

Unlike Betty, Veron didn't have any children, but she made it clear that she wanted to have some in the future, even though she was convinced, for some unknown reason, that she couldn't have any children.

Calvin was utterly moved by Veron's comment, and he promised her that he could get her pregnant, but she quickly changed the subject, and he let it go.

Overall, Calvin felt like a new man after he met Veron, and it was also clear to everybody that he had changed. Oftentimes his friends would tease him for spending too much time with her.

After the relationship started to blossom, he decided to cut down on the habitual gambling, and he was also trying to save some money. At the time, his relationship with his grandparents had begun to turn pear-shaped again, because he was frequently staying away from home. On the other hand, Aunty and Uncle were concluding that enough was enough, but before the inevitable happened and they kicked him out, he packed his bags and moved in with Veron.

"Living with Veron was one of my most passionate experiences, because it happened to be the very first time I cohabited with a partner who was there for me and I for her. Initially, it felt good living with her and having my friends living a few steps from my front door, and it seemed as if nothing could ever go wrong at that point in my life. Nonetheless, a few months later, that initial feeling changed, and I decided to find a place of my own, because I'd begun to feel insecure, and I also wanted to prove to Veron that I had ambition. Thus I bought a bed and rented a room in the ghetto of Paradise.

"The day I moved into my new room, Veron accompanied me and we both decided to sleep there that night, which happened to be the only time I'd ever spend in the room, because although my intensions were positive, I couldn't pull myself away from Queen Street.

"One month later, I got a letter from the Human Resource Department at the hotel, and after I read it I realised that I was being redundant, without any prior warning. Suddenly, I felt like I was cursed and my world had begun to turn upside down. I was also very embarrassed at that point, because the rest of my friends were still working at the hotel, and I was left stranded with no work and no money.

"After I got redundant I couldn't afford to pay the second month's rent and had to give up the room. Fortunately Veron allowed me to move back in with her."

Calvin, who had tried previously to prove to Veron that he was an ambitious man, was left feeling embarrassed and useless.

Veron worked on the night shift at the Half Moon Resort Hotel as a cashier, and before Calvin came into her life, she was surviving independently. Although it was obvious that he would put a strain on her pocket, nonetheless, she offered him a roof over his head, food on the table, and sometimes even money in his pocket.

While Calvin was out of work, he would mainly stay at home and do the housework, and although he was still feeling embarrassed for not having a job like his friends, he would hang out with them nevertheless, suffering silently from humiliation.

"At that point in my life there was no need for me to steal to survive, unlike the early years, when I was growing up in Mount Carey, but because of past experiences at 10 Crichton's Drive, and my ever-present insecurity, I was living each day in fear of getting kicked out by Veron, just because I wasn't in any position to support her or myself.

"Although Veron wasn't showing me any bad vibes (unlike what Aunty and Uncle used to show), eventually it reach the stage when I was getting tired of living each day in fear of getting kicked out. I was also getting weak psychologically, and I couldn't think straight. The worst fear of all was that of losing my self-control, and I was constantly scared of getting pulled back into a life of crime.

"During that time, I thought about my siblings a lot and spent numerous days looking back on the good and bad times I had growing up. Seeing where I was at that time. As I analysed some of the decisions I had made over the years in order to survive, my body would shiver with fear of what the future might bring if things didn't change for the better in my life.

"I used to also pray a lot, and each time when I prayed for changes in my life, I promised God that I wouldn't give in to temptation again, if he got me another job, and I even vowed that I would start attending church again.

"In due course, at the beginning of 1993, it seemed like my prayers were answered, because I was offered another job.

"Apparently, my friend Slowly used to work part-time at a small hotel, as well as having his permanent job at Wyndham, but he couldn't handle both jobs. So he decided to stick to his job at Wyndham and offered me the other, at the small hotel.

"I was very excited when he asked me if I want his part-time job. It came at a time when I was living on the edge of despair.

"After Slowly took me to the hotel and made the initial introduction, the manager gave me the job without requesting any further recommendation."

Chapter Twenty-One

Surrendering to Greed

The Grandiosa Hotel was only five minutes' drive from the city of Mobay, and three minutes from the Donald Sangster International Airport. The Ramparts Inn Guest House was only yards away from it, on the opposite side. Robert, one of Calvin's friends, worked there as a bartender.

The Grandiosa was a beautiful hotel, set elegantly atop a hill overlooking the vastness of the blue sea, Gloucester Avenue (the Hip Strip), and the airport.

The hotel wasn't surrounded by a huge manicured lawn, nor did it have the luxury of a golf course. Still, it had thirty-six rooms, a dining hall, and a bar with lounge area, a rectangular swimming poll, and banquet facilities upstairs with a view of the tranquil sea below.

Overall it was a wonderful place for those who worked there and for those who only wanted to relax.

The owner of the hotel, who was also the manager, was a good black man. He was one of the real sons of the island of Jamaica. He had migrated to the USA when he was a young man, but on his return he didn't go and build a mansion in the hills. Instead, he built a hotel and secured a working environment for his native people.

From the outset, the boss respected Calvin for his remarkable personality, for the way he cooked, and for his endless interest in the day-to-day running of the hotel. Ultimately, a relationship developed between them until they were more like brothers than employer and employee.

"On the whole, because of the relationship I had with the boss and his family, and the rest of staff, I genuinely felt like it was my destiny to be at that particular hotel. On the other hand, the twelve hundred Jamaican dollars a week wages that I was offered could only fill a little hole in the prolonged hardships. Nonetheless, I was grateful for the job, and the thought of ripping off my employer never once crossed my mind.

"Because I was the only chef, I had to cook breakfast, lunch, and dinner, but I didn't really have a problem fulfilling my requirements. In fact, I enjoyed every minute of it, and for once I felt free from corruption, because everybody around me was honest.

"I was also determined to keep that job by any means necessary, because I didn't want to revert to the experience I had when I got redundant from Wyndham."

Despite the fact that Calvin was happy for the opportunity to start living an honest life (not to mention the vows he had taken), eventually temptation appeared, and the lust of the flesh and the pangs of poverty propelled him to start mixing his boss's business with self-indulgence.

From the start, he knew that he would be treading on forbidden ground, because it was against the hotel rules to solicit the guests, let alone break the law by dealing in drugs.

He thought about the consequences if things should go wrong, but in the long run he convinced himself that the big risk was worth taking.

It all started after a group of black American men turned up at the hotel. Initially, Calvin was happy when they arrived that evening, because business was slow at the time and they ordered a lot of food. They also tipped him and the waitress, and they had a lot to drink at the bar before they went to bed that night. The following morning was the same: they ordered a lot of breakfast and during the day they also bought lots of drinks from the bar.

Later that afternoon, Calvin was hanging out at the bar while the men were gathered at the poolside chatting and laughing, drinking Red Stripe beers, and taking turns to see who could dive into the swimming pool and make the least splash.

After a while, two of the town's infamous drug dealers arrived and went to the poolside to join the Americans. After much laughter, one of the Americans walked away with the drug dealers.

At the time Calvin didn't think much of the drug dealers' visit. He was only interested in the Americans. He was hoping that they would get hungry and order jerk chicken and burgers.

That evening, Calvin did a massive preparation in the kitchen, ready for the Americans to start ordering dinner, but he was disappointed when they only ordered toast and juice.

That same night, just as he was leaving work, he met the two drug dealers at the hotel main door, one carrying a travelling bag.

As they walked by, Calvin nodded to them, and the strong scent of the weed that drifted behind them as they hurried up the stairs almost knocked him off his feet.

Calvin was well aware of people swallowing drugs to take out of the country with them. He also knew that men and women were being used as mules to smuggle the drugs. It was the latest way of smuggling drugs off the island. Frequently the news on the radio or in the newspapers told of tourists getting sick at the airports or on the plane with drugs inside of them. The biggest news was about a white woman who died on a plane when a parcel of cocaine burst inside her stomach. It was said that the drugs poisoned her body and turned it blue. On the whole, it was a risky business, but Calvin was tempted to get a piece of the action. He decided to carry out an undercover investigation, to find out if it was really drugs the Americans were smuggling and to see if he could work his way into the drug trade.

The following morning, the Americans got up early and ordered toast and juice. This time they were quieter than the previous day, and they spent most of the morning inside their rooms, only coming out occasionally to have a quick swim in the pool.

Late that same afternoon, the Americans checked out of the hotel. Instantly, Calvin began to put all the information together, that he had gathered so far. Ultimately, he concluded that the weed he had smelt on the dealers, when he was leaving the previous night, was that which the Americans had came to collect. He was also convinced that the reason why the men didn't ordered any dinner the previous night, or any breakfast that morning, was simply because they wanted to have an empty stomach to store the weed that they were smuggling. Also, the toast and juice that they ordered the previous night, and that which they ordered that morning, was what they use to help swallow the drug. Finally, when the men occasionally went for a swim in the pool, they were only trying to digest the weed inside their stomach.

Calvin smiled to himself, after he had put all the information together. From the look of things, he believes there was lots of money involved, money that he could not resist getting hold of.

One month later, the Americans arrived again, and the same procedure occurred, with the drinking and eating of lots of food on their arrival. The following day, the boss had his breakfast early before he went away on business. The Americans had their breakfast late, and just like before, they were hanging out at the poolside drinking Red Stripe beers, chatting and laughing and jumping off into the water.

Then, again out of the blue, the drug dealers suddenly appeared. This time around, the atmosphere at the poolside got intense after the dealers arrived, and you could almost hear a pin drop while they whispered.

All this time, Calvin was sitting at the bar, pretending he was watching the television, but secretly he was observing the scene at the poolside and wondering how he was going to get close to the Americans and get a piece of the action. Covertly, he was also scared of moving in on the drug dealers' turf, knowing what bloody outcome such an action could cause.

Minutes later, the drug dealers said their goodbyes and promised to come back the following day. Both Calvin and the bartender remained at the bar in silence as the drug dealers disappeared around the corner, and minutes later the Americans began to chat and laugh again. As Calvin watched the smugglers, a part of him became envious of the freedom that they seemed to have, and another part was desperate to get closer to them.

Suddenly, the biggest American, who seemed to be the leader of the pack, got up and sauntered towards the bar with a swagger. While he was walking over from the poolside, Calvin noticed how muscular he was and wondered what they really got up to in the States. He also wondered whether living in the States was just like what he'd seen in the movies.

"Yow, Chef," the smuggler greeted him, as he sat down at the bar.

"Yow, ma men, you cool?" Calvin replied, as he knocked fists with the smuggler.

"Yeah, man, I'm cool. Just chilling. You know what I'm saying, Bro?" The smuggler laughed as he ordered two Red Stripe beers from the bartender and offered Calvin one. *This could be the moment I've been waiting for,* Calvin thought to himself, as he thanked the smuggler and took a long swig from the cool beer and set the bottle on the bar.

Without thinking about the consequences, he took his chance and boldly asked the smuggler if he wanted to smoke a joint with him.

Quickly the big American said, "Yeah, Bro, I would love that. That's exactly what the doc ordered, you know what I'm saying, Bro?" He ordered a few more beers and told Calvin to meet him upstairs at his room.

Minutes later, Calvin was seated in the smuggler's room, drinking Red Stripe beer and smoking a joint of Lams Bread weed, which he had brought with him. This special type of weed, (lams bread) gives the user a good vibe and it doesn't makes you hungry,

After the initial pleasantries and small talk, Calvin gently took out a small branch of ganja from his pocket. It may have had the biggest and prettiest buds that the smuggler had ever seen on a branch, because his eyes nearly popped out of their sockets.

Calvin put the herb to his own nose and took a quick sniff, shook his head in disbelief at how good it smelt, and held it under the smuggler's nose so he could share the experience.

Wordlessly, the smuggler took the branch of herbs from Calvin's hand with care, inspected it thoroughly, and then took a long sniff. He rubbed his nose with the back of his hand and returned the buds to Calvin and bobbed his head in confirmation.

"I knew straight away that I'd made that important first impression. The only thing left was to choose the right moment to pose the question."

A moment of silence ensued, and Calvin broke it by giving the smuggler the big top bud from the branch of herbs. He then tore off a smaller bud and crushed it in his palm to build a spliff.

After the fresh joints were lit up, Calvin cautiously waited until the weed and beer were hard at work inside the man's brain before he began to discreetly quiz him.

Expertly, Calvin began to emulate the American's way of speaking and said, "Damn, this shit is really good, man. You know what I'm saying, Bro?"

At that point, the smuggler was sitting with his legs stretched out in the middle of the bed, eyes closed, and back resting on the headboard. His joint had gone out, dangling between his lips, while he bobbed his head to the tunes of Garnet Silk (a Jamaican reggae singer) playing on the stereo as he slowly drifted into another world.

It was evident to Calvin that the man had gone into a different world psychologically, with the blend of Garnet Silk's inspiring lyrics and the strong weed, not to mention the beer.

Lams Bread wasn't the type of weed to play with. When it hits you, it takes you to a higher level mentally.

Abruptly, the huge smuggler half opened his eyes that were fire red at this stage, laughed with a roar and then said, "Yeah, Bro. This is some damn good shit, man."

His eyes seemed to have closed without him attempting to close them, as he started to bob his head again, but much slower, and Calvin knew instantly that he had him exactly where he wanted him.

"Yow, Bro," Calvin began, but the smuggler didn't answer. He continued, "How much you paying for all the shit that you taking back with you?"

Just before he completed the sentence, the smuggler sat upright in the bed, with eyes wide opened and looked Calvin straight in the eyes. Calvin started to wonder if he'd made a big mistake, and sweat broke out across his forehead.

Again, the smuggler laughed, louder than before, and slapped his thigh with an open palm, and then suddenly went serious again and said to Calvin, "Damn, you're one smart motherfucker, man. You know what I'm saying, Bro? How the fuck did you manage to work out my business, man?"

Calvin wasn't sure at that point if he had made the right move, or if it was safe to prolong the conversation. Regardless, he confidently ploughed on. "Look, man, you done know how it goes, ma man. I've been around for a long time, done a lot a shit to survive too, so I get to know what's what. You know what I'm saying, Bro?"

The smuggler laughed again, even harder than he'd laughed earlier. Calvin didn't know whether the weed and beer had gone to his head and made him laugh or whether he was simply laughing at him, but he began to laugh too.

After a while, the smuggler abruptly stopped laughing and said, "You know, Bro, I don't really do business like this. You know what I'm saying? Anyway, why do you think I would want to tell you about my shit?"

In defence, Calvin replied, "Because I can give you a better deal."

After minutes of silence the smuggler declared, "You seem like a good brother, and I'm only hoping I can trust you, Bro, so I'm gonna let you in on how we do things. You know what I'm saying, Bro?"

At that point he was quite serious, and Calvin tried to look and sound serious too.

"We're paying seven hundred American dollars for a kilo of the weed," the smuggler told him.

In disbelief, Calvin replied, "What! Seven hundred bucks?" and paused. Then he said, "Damn, this is Jamaica, you know what I'm saying, Bro? The land where the weed grows bountifully! Tell you what, I'll do it for five hundred US, and I guarantee it will be much better weed than what you are getting for seven hundred."

It didn't take a lot more persuasion for the smuggler to tell Calvin that he would do some business with him. Calvin on the other hand couldn't believe what he had heard. Everything was moving in the right direction as he'd hoped it would. Maybe a bit too fast, but he didn't see it that way, because he was too eager to make some fast money. On the other hand, he didn't know where he was going to get the drug or how to prepare it.

The smuggler told him that he would take a kilo to start with, if he could have it prepared that same day.

"No problem, Bro," Calvin replied, not knowing whether it was even possible to accomplish the mission.

The smuggler then pointed to one part of his little finger and said that the pellets shouldn't be any bigger than that. Instantly Calvin was dumbfounded. He knew he looked confused, and he felt like a right fool, because he didn't have a clue about the pellets. However, he assured the smuggler, "No problem, Bro," and told him that he would like some money in order to get the show on the road.

The smuggler suddenly didn't seem to be in any hurry. "How do I know I can really trust you, Bro?" he suddenly asked, with a deadly expression on his face, one that Calvin hadn't noticed before.

"I love my job, Bro," he replied, a bit nervously. "I only hope I can trust you too, Bro, because it ain't easy to find a job on this island."

Calvin didn't feel intimidated in any way, but he suddenly realised the seriousness of what he was getting himself into. At that precise moment, the temperature on the air conditioner seemed to get cooler, and a chill went down his spine.

"Okay, Bro," the smuggler finally said, after a moment of deliberation, "I'm cool. You looked after me, and I'll look after you too. You know what I'm saying, Bro?" He got up and went into the bathroom.

He returned with $300 US and one of the pellets. "You'll get the rest of the cash upon your return with the merchandise, Bro."

Calvin took the pellet and carefully examined it, before returning it to the smuggler. Then he took the money and said, "Don't you worry your head now, Bro. I'll be back before you know it." He folded the money, stuffed it into his pocket, and left.

"I felt relief when I finally walked out of the smuggler's room. Suddenly a different feeling came over me, a sort of demonic feeling, and all my initial fear was gone."

Back downstairs, Calvin stopped at the reception and asked the receptionist if he could make a phone call. Minutes later he was on the phone to his friend Slowly and instinctively put on a sad face as he pleaded for his friend to come and stay at the hotel while he went to visit his aunty at Mount Salem, who had taken badly sick that morning.

The receptionist was listening, just as Calvin had hoped she would. When the call ended, she told him how sorry she was to hear about his aunt's misfortune.

He thanked her, rubbed his eyes, sniffled, and walked away sadly. Once out of sight, he smiled as he went into the restroom and splashed water into his eyes, to make it seem as if he was genuinely upset and crying.

"At that stage, I was progressively transforming into an evil person unconsciously, and I wasn't prepared to let anything or anybody stand in my way."

As soon as Slowly turned up at the hotel, Calvin was off like a bullet.

When he got downtown he went to Strand Street, where a number of youths would regularly gathered, to buy foreign currencies on the black market, and then sell it back to the highest bidder. It was a huge business, because they would exchange the currencies for far more than what the banks were offering.

After Calvin changed the American dollars into Jamaican currency, he went into the nearest pharmacy and purchased a few boxes of latex gloves. Then he went into a supermarket and bought two rolls of cling film, what Americans call plastic wrap. From there he headed to Church Street, where a Rasta man was selling weed under a shed, and purchased a kilo of the weed. Later he went to Mount Salem, to pay one of his old friends a visit. The friend in question knew every trick in the bad book of life. Calvin explained to the friend the size pellets he wanted and the urgency of having them made, and after a deal was sealed between them, the friend got a number of youths to prepare the pellets. During the process, Calvin watched every move they made. When the processing was done, he'd learnt every trick in the book where making pellets was concerned.

Back at the hotel, he boldly delivered the merchandise to the satisfied American, collected the remaining cash, and paid Slowly.

There wasn't much money left in his pocket at the end of the day, but he didn't care, because he was convinced that there was bigger money to be made, and that was only the beginning.

A month or so later the smugglers returned, and although the drug dealers visited them as before, the leader still requested double the amount that he purchased from Calvin initially.

"Although I was getting a piece of the action that I always wanted, I felt jealous when the drug dealers came to the hotel to visit the smugglers, but I humbly kept my distance, because the last thing I wanted was seemingly to become the rival of seasoned drug dealers."

This time around, Calvin didn't need to beat around the bush, because overnight he had become a professional pellet maker. Unconsciously, however, he was heading deeper and deeper into a dark world, which was full of deceitfulness.

Accordingly, he decided to get himself a right-hand man, to do the running around for him. His friend Delroy was living on his own at Queen Street, and Calvin chose him, with the intension to use his house as a base to do the packaging. Together they organised a group of youths from Queen Street to help them make the pellets.

It was no secret to the rest of staff, that some of the guests were smuggling drugs, but as a general rule, whatever the guests did was tolerable, so long as they weren't destroying any of the hotel's property. Ultimately, some of the staff began to get suspicious of Calvin's involvement with the Americans, because each time they arrived at the hotel, he used to find an excuse to go into town.

Although the boss used to go away often on business, some of the loyal staff would fill him in on whatever happened in his absence. One day, he called Calvin into his office and gave him a warning about his frequent absence from the hotel and his job. Calvin was very frightened, and he tried to pull the wool over his boss's eyes with various excuses, but the boss wasn't having any of it. Before they parted, he told Calvin that the conversation they had should be taken as a warning in itself.

"I felt very embarrassed when the boss confronted me, because consciously I knew that I was betraying him and myself, but like before, I'd allowed myself to be lead astray on account of poverty and greed. I just didn't have the will-power to resist temptation, and my self-worth was at an all-time low."

Around that time the group of Americans stopped coming to the hotel, but the dust hadn't settled before a different group of smugglers replaced them.

CHAPTER TWENTY-TWO

Mixing Business with Pleasure

The next group consisted of five burly white men and one pretty little white woman, who happened to be the boss.

By chance Calvin met them on their first visit. By then he could easily distinguish who was there to collect drugs from those who came to enjoy the usual four S's: the sun, sand, sea, and sex.

"At that point I wasn't praying, and all the vows I had taken while I was struggling without a job were forgotten, and it seemed like I was walking hand in hand with the devil unconsciously."

Apparently, he was getting off work early one evening, because there weren't many guests at the hotel, therefore his service wasn't needed, and the boss was away on business.

As he stepped out through the main door, a minibus pulled up into the parking lot, and a beautiful white woman was the first person to alight from the front passenger seat.

She was just over five feet tall and clad in black leather boots, a black leather miniskirt, a white blouse, and a black leather jacket. Her long black hair was tied in a ponytail, and she had the smallest feet he'd ever seen on a woman, with perfect legs to match. The only makeup that she seemed to be wearing was red lipstick, which was applied evenly on her half-full lips. Overall, she was one of the most attractive white women he'd ever seen.

She was struggling with a holdall bag, and he offered to help her. After he placed the bag on the ground, he introduced himself. "I am Calvin, the hotel chef."

When he took her hand to shake it and looked into her calm, clear, blue eyes, he was instantly mesmerised. Her hand was as soft as silk, and when she smiled the whole of her countenance brightened up.

"I am Lisa. Nice to meet you, Calvin. Thank you very much for your help; you're so sweet."

Her voice was like music to his ears, and her smile disclosed perfect white teeth.

He stood one side observing her while she waited on her companions to get out of the bus.

Suddenly, she turned around and said, "I saw you, Calvin. Why are you looking at me like that? You're only making me nervous."

Her words enticed him, and with his most seductive voice he told her, "I am sorry if I made you nervous, Lisa. That would be the last thing I would ever want to do. I just can't help but admire your loveliness. Would you feel better if I told you that you're the most beautiful woman I've ever seen?"

She laughed. "Should I take that as a compliment, Calvin?"

"Please do," he told her.

"Thank you," said Lisa, with a smile and a dreamy look in her eyes.

He enjoyed listening to her musical voice and was spellbound by her enchanting looks. At the same time, he didn't want to push his luck too far, but he was being driven by lust and the need to make some money out of the drug trade.

By then her companions were out of the bus and heading towards the reception area. Lisa lingered behind, rummaging through her handbag.

At that moment, Calvin decided to push his luck a bit further and said to her, "Your attractiveness has made me very nervous; look at me."

She turned to look at him, and at that precise moment he started to pretend his legs were trembling.

Lisa found it funny and laughed. In fact, she was laughing so hard that she had to hold on to his shoulder. Suddenly she stopped and looked straight into his eyes and said, "You're so funny, Calvin. I haven't had a good laugh all day. Thank you."

Instantly, Calvin felt a jolt of electricity fly through his body, and he told himself that he had to get a piece of this goddess.

He picked up her holdall bag and accompanied her to the reception. He wanted to linger awhile, but he didn't want to make it seem too obvious, nor did he want to end up back in the boss's office, for another warning of any kind. Therefore, he handed the bag to her and told her that it was nice to meet her and he would see her around.

"Do you have to go now?"

"No, I can stay a little longer if you want me to," he answered hastily.

"Great. I would love that."

"Okay," he said softly, with a nervous smile. "You'll find me chilling out at the bar when you're through," and he walked away briskly.

Half an hour later, while he was seated in the lounge area watching the television, Lisa appeared, and suddenly the place went silent. The only sound that could be heard was that of the television and the flowing of the clear water in the swimming pool outside.

Lisa sauntered over to him with a broad smile on her beautiful face, and at that point, everybody who was seated at the bar looked in her direction.

"I want to make sure that you're behaving yourself, Mr Chef," she whispered, when she got close to him. Before he could reply, she continued, "I won't be long now. I'm only going to my room to freshen up myself. Before you know it I'll be right back." She swivelled her hips as she went through the door.

After Lisa walked away Calvin glanced around, and to his surprise, the rest of the guests and the bartender were smiling at him.

The bartender laughed and said, "Go on Calvin. Ha you dat yuh nuh? How yuh manage fe get dat deh one deh, man?"

Calvin, feeling very proud, puffed up his chest and replied, "Yuh have to talk de talk and walk de walk, blood," and a few of the guests laughed.

In less than an hour Lisa reappeared and created a stir at the bar again. This time she was clad in white sneakers, white jeans shorts and a white T-shirt with a USA logo in red, white, and blue printed on the front, and it was obvious that she wasn't wearing any brassiere, because her nipples, which all the men at the bar noticed, were indenting the T-shirt material.

Her long black hair, now combed out, shimmered on her shoulders like water running over rocks and cascaded down her slender back.

She sauntered through the bar door, holding a purse in her left hand with a packet of cigarettes, and in her right hand she held a lit cigarette.

Her lustrous bearing captivated all those who were seated at the bar and caused Calvin's blood to rush through his veins. Instantly his body began to pine for her.

They had a drink at the bar before Calvin invited her to the poolside, away from the prying eyes and ears of the other guests and the bartender.

From where they stood at the poolside, they could view the grandeur of Gloucester Avenue, the lights on the airport runway, and the beauty of the shimmering lights across the span of sea. They could also see lots of people moving back and forth on Gloucester Avenue and clearly hear the music that was playing at the street dance at the Dead-End.

While they gazed into the night, Lisa kept rocking to the music while Calvin's heart continually raced rapidly against the wall of his chest.

Suddenly, he asked her if it was her first time on the island. She said no, she had been there a few times before. He also asked her if she wanted to go out for a while, and she said, "Yes, I'd love to go out and let my hair down."

Without hesitating, he called a taxi and off they went to the street dance at the Dead-End.

*

Gloucester Avenue (the Hip Strip) was the heart of the tourist zone in Montego Bay and the ideal place to be for anyone visiting or living in Jamaica.

There were about thirteen hotels, over sixty shops, and more than thirty-five bars and restaurants on the strip. There were also local beaches, including the world-renowned Doctor's Cave and Cornwall Beach, banks and car rental facilities.

The Hip Strip started from the edge of Mobay town and ran westward, where the road ended at the border of the airport property, known as the Dead-End. There you could watch the planes come and go, as the runway were only yards away.

There was also a beautiful free beach with white sand at the Dead-End, where the bar was situated on the beach, flanked by three hotels.

The Dead-End was a regular hot spot for tourists and locals alike. Frequently they would hold parties and carnivals on the street.

Calvin decided to take Lisa there, because he knew a lot of tourists would be there, and he wanted her to feel safe.

When the taxi arrived at their destination, she wouldn't allow him to pay the driver. "I like to be in control," she told him, and he didn't argue.

There were lots of locals at the Dead-End that Calvin knew, and each one told him how beautiful Lisa was. At length, the compliments spurred him on, and he revelled in the moment with pride.

After an hour or so mingling with the crowd, they moved on to the Sir Winston nightclub, where they danced to the beat of the live band that was playing.

"By then I'd begun to fall for this woman, and it felt like a spell had been cast on me, but I didn't care, because I was enjoying every moment.

"I stayed close to her all the time and when I wasn't holding her hand my arm would be around her shoulder or her slender waist. She on the other hand seemed to enjoy my affection and the closeness, because she reacted pleasingly to my every move.

"At one point, she pulled my head down to whisper in my ear, but the first thing she did was to thrust her tongue into my ear seductively. Then she whispered, 'I want you to take me back to the hotel and make love to me until morning comes.'

"I was looking forward to making love to her at some stage, but I wasn't expecting it to be so soon. My heart started to beat very fast and the realisation of what I was about to do gave me an instant arousal. On the other hand, I knew Veron was waiting for me to come home, and I was also risking the possibility of losing my job by going back to the hotel with Lisa. Regardless, nothing and nobody could have stopped me from having the time of my life with that goddess of a woman that night.

"I held her tight and told her, 'Your wish is my command, Lisa,' and she giggled and told me that she was ready to go, and I didn't need second telling."

Quickly Calvin made his departure from the club with Lisa. Outside they got into a waiting taxi and off they went.

Back at the hotel, the security guard on duty was shocked when Calvin turned up with Lisa. Although it was against the rules of the hotel for any staff to enter the guest rooms for any reason other than housekeeping and room service, the guard willingly turned a blind eye to Calvin.

As they sneaked into the bedroom, Lisa flicked the light on, pushed him against the door roughly, and then began to fumble with the zip of his trousers.

She looked deep into his eyes and pressed her breasts firmly against his chest, licked her lips and kissed him passionately. From there on, the rest of the night was magic.

"It was an experience of a lifetime for me, because no other woman had ever made me feel that way.

"At daybreak I reluctantly got out of Lisa's bed and showered, and then sneaked out of her room, and stealthily went downstairs before the rest of my colleagues turned up for work.

"The security guard was dozing off in the receptionist's chair at the front desk, and I asked him to open up the kitchen for me. After I got changed, I cooked up a huge breakfast and gave it to him, which was well appreciated, before the hotel receptionist and the waitress arrived."

There was a constant smile on Calvin's face during breakfast, and when an order came in for room service to be delivered to Lisa's room, he prepared it very special, under the watchful eyes of Pauline, one of the waitresses.

On Pauline's return from Lisa's room, she looked at Calvin and smile. Then she shook her head and said, in a mock-scolding voice, "Not a lane without a turning. Now I know why you were paying special attention to that specific breakfast."

Calvin pretended he didn't know what Pauline was talking about, but after the waitress reached into her pocket and took out a folded piece of paper and handed it to him; he knew instantly that his cover had been blown.

Sceptically he unfolded the piece of paper, which read, *Come and see me at my room when you are not busy*, with an X for a kiss at the end of the sentence and a neatly sketched, cheeky smiling face next to it.

He looked at Pauline and smiled sheepishly, but devotedly she told him to go and have fun and not to worry about her, because his secret was safe.

"I knew that I could trust Pauline to keep my secrets, unlike Daphne, the other waitress, who liked to gossip."

Later that morning, after the boss drove out of the hotel car park, Calvin, who was struggling to control his anticipation, cautiously headed towards Lisa's room and knocked on the door. She opened it in seconds to let him in.

By this time the five burly white men were chilling out at the poolside.

As Calvin entered Lisa's room, he asked her who the five men were and what was their purpose (as if he didn't know). She told him they were working for her.

"What? Are you a celebrity?" he asked. She laughed and told him that she was more than a celebrity. "Are you a princess?" he asked jokingly.

"Damn, you are asking a lot of questions today, Calvin. What's got into you?"

"I just wanted to know where I stand really, because I couldn't handle one of those men, if they decided to beat me up."

She laughed and hugged him as she began to plant kisses all over his face, again and again.

Half an hour or so later she allowed him to get back to work, but before he left the room, he told her that when he came back, he wanted to know exactly what was happening.

Half-heartedly she promised to tell him.

Calvin was busy throughout the rest of the day, thus he couldn't get back to her room, but that night, after he was through for the day, he met her at the bar.

This time she was attired in a tall, skin-tight black velvet dress, and on her little feet she had on white lace-up leather slippers. Her shiny black hair was tied in a bun, and as before, she had on minimal makeup.

By then, the chemistry that was flowing between them was much stronger. The fondness he felt for her was second to none, and even though he was well tired, all he wanted to do was to make love to her. Selling her drugs was no longer of much importance at that point.

They made an arrangement to meet up later that night, and Calvin went home to change clothes.

Back at Queen Street, he found the house deserted. Hurriedly he got showered and dressed, and before water could warm he was back at the hotel to be with his goddess.

On his return, Lisa was seated at the bar with the five men. She was delighted to see him, and gleefully she introduced the men to him, who accepted the introduction reluctantly, but although the reaction from the men left him feeling a little uneasy, it wasn't enough to deter his burning desire for Lisa, thus he sat himself down, but he didn't say much.

"Okay, lads," Lisa said half an hour later, "it's time for bed now!"

Calvin thought she had decided to forfeit their date, but she was actually telling the men that it was time for them to call it a night.

He was shocked when he realised what was really happening. On the whole, from past experience, he knew the smugglers needed to get a lot of rest before they began to swallow the drugs, but it was the first time he'd seen the leader giving the mules a direct order. He knew then that the little woman, with the pretty face and the sexy body, was much more than met the eye.

Ultimately the mules went to bed reluctantly, and Lisa and Calvin called a taxi and left the hotel.

"I would love to have a quiet night with you by the sea," Lisa told him, as they got into the taxi.

Calvin told the driver to take them by the Dead-End, and as soon as they arrived, Lisa went to the bar and ordered two bottles of Red Stripe beer. Calvin then took her to a secluded spot on the sandy beach, where they could relax in private.

He'd noticed a sudden stern look on her face, (maybe she was only trying to mask her fear) while they were in the taxi, but he decided not to enquire about it. Instead, he'd only squeezed her hand reassuringly. However, when they were seated on the beach, he asked her what was bothering her. She looked at him and smiled. Then she filled her lungs with the fresh sea breeze and replied, "I'm only wondering if I can really trust you, Calvin."

Her response didn't surprise him, because he wasn't expecting anything less from a drug dealer. He also knew she was being quizzed by the mules, possibly about her involvement with him, by the reaction that he got from them earlier, but he was prepared to use all his skill to control her, to his advantage.

"In what way are you wondering if you can trust me Lisa?"

"Concerning my line of work," she replied defensively, after a moment of silence.

"For the record," he confessed, "I often do your type of work. Not exactly the way how you do it, however, but I often provide the goods."

She looked at him as if she'd only seen him for the very first time. Finally, she asked, "How do you know what type of work I do?"

"For a lesser person than me, it wouldn't be so obvious," he replied, while caressing her hand reassuringly and looking at her face. "I've been in the game for a long time, so I know who is who," he concluded.

"I knew there was something about you that I couldn't really put my finger on. You're one clever boy, do you know that?"

"You have just told me, Lisa," he replied sarcastically, "but shall I take that as a compliment?"

She only laughed and leaned into his arms and kissed his cheek.

Now that he had wormed his way into her heart, he decided to pose the most important question of the night. "Are you running the business all by yourself?" he asked, half expecting her to tell him to mind his own business.

"I'm only the right-hand woman for a dealer in the States," she began, "and my main job is to take the carriers to the designated places and ensure that everything runs smoothly. All the carriers are in my care until they return to the States and deliver the merchandise."

"How are you planning to get the product? Do you have somebody preparing it for you already?" he asked.

"Why do you ask?"

"I would be more than happy to provide the goods and prepare it for a reasonable price," he replied, with a business-like tone to his voice.

Conversely, he'd initially thought they were there to collect a shipment of ganja, but they were more advanced in the business and out of his league. Therefore, when she told him that the goods were coming down from Colombia, he didn't need any further telling, because the mere mention of Colombia meant cocaine.

"You are too far out of my league. I only supply the weed," he told her sadly.

"Not to worry," she said and began to plant kisses all over his face.

"Why should I worry when I already have you?" he asked her jokingly, but deep down he was very disappointed.

"It would've been nice to do business with you nonetheless," he confessed, "but what can I do if your business is not my business? The fact still remains though," he continued, to soften the atmosphere, "that I'm happier just being with you than doing anything else."

Lisa hugged him and kissed him then said, "You are really a nice guy," but Calvin only chuckled, because no sweet talk was going to wipe away his disappointment.

Later that night, he took her back to the hotel and spent some time with her, before heading home to Veron.

Two days later, while he was in the kitchen preparing lunch, the bartender rang the phone and told him that his girlfriend was at the bar, wanting to speak to him.

Standing motionless with the phone in his hand, after the bartender hang up, Calvin thought of the consequences if

Veron should turn up unexpectedly to see him while Lisa was lounging at the poolside or, even worse, sitting at the bar having a drink, and out of the blue a sick feeling came over him. As he replaced the phone in its cradle, his body shivered with fear of the unknown.

He undid his soiled apron with trembling fingers, straightened his jacket, and took off his hat before he went downstairs towards the bar.

His heart was pounding, as he came into view of the swimming pool, but he was relieved when he found it deserted.

Still feeling nervous, Calvin boldly stepped through the bar door, half expecting to see Veron with a big smile on his face and a million stories spinning off at once in his brain, but instead he found Lisa standing on her own at the bar, dressed in a pinstripe suit.

As he entered, she smiled at him apologetically, held his hands, and then told him that she was about to depart. Suddenly a huge lump appeared in his throat, and he had to choke back the tears.

Unintentionally, he had developed strong feelings for Lisa over the few days since they had met, but the signal of her departure intensified his affection for her immensely.

As the odd couple held hands, Calvin noticed tears at the corners of Lisa's eyes, and he knew instantly that she too felt something for him, and the realisation of her adoration caused the lump in his throat to grow even bigger.

After standing in silence looking at each other, they hugged briefly and kissed, but it seemed like it lasted for an eternity.

Lisa pulled herself away from the embrace and gave him an envelope. As she turned and walked away, she told him not to miss her too much.

"I'll look you up the next time I return to your beautiful island," Lisa promised, as she left the bar.

Feeling sad and empty, Calvin returned to the kitchen and opened the envelope, expecting to find a love letter. Instead, he found three hundred American dollars and a bundle of Jamaican dollars.

Although he was disappointed not to have found a love letter, nonetheless he was more than happy for the money. After all, he hadn't had to risk going to jail to get it.

A month later, while he was lounging at the bar for a drink, Lisa sauntered through the door and kissed him on his cheek. Immediately they picked up from where they had left off the last time, but three days later they were saying their goodbyes again, and this time would be the last, even though Calvin didn't know.

"Although she didn't promise to return, every day I would hang around the bar, half expecting her to appear and kiss me like she did before, but that day never came. At one point, I eventually concluded that Lisa was only using me as a shield, against any possible threat from the mules or anybody else for that matter.

"In a big way, I was sad when she didn't return, but in an even bigger way I was happy, because word of my inexcusable behaviour had begun to pass amongst the staff. There was no doubt that the same words had reached the boss's ears too, so I decided to humble myself and look after my job. Nonetheless, temptation came my way again. This time around it was to be more sinister than I could ever have imagined.

CHAPTER TWENTY-THREE

Playing with Fire

It was late September 1993, and business was slow at the hotel. Most of the rooms were empty, and the majority of the staff was put on shorter hours.

Calvin was in a better position than most of the others, for the mere fact that he was the only chef, although Daphne, one of the hotel waitresses, would occasionally run the kitchen when Calvin was off work.

On the whole, most days, after breakfast ended, Calvin would only prepare a small portion of lunch and then spent the rest of his time at the bar, watching television or reading a book. However, one day he was standing at the poolside watching Henry, the handyman, cleaning the swimming pool, while on the far corner of the poolside an elderly white American couple were seated, smoking a joint.

The weed smelt good, and Calvin went over to compliment the couple, without any intention to solicit them.

He introduced himself and then told the guests how good the weed smelt.

Trudy, the woman, replied and said, "We wish we could get some to take back to the States with us." At the same time Johnny, her partner, joined in by emulating the Jamaican accent and said, "Yah, Mon, we want some of this ting yah to bring back to we yard, Mon."

By then Henry was close to where they were seated and he giggled. Calvin laughed too, but instantly his brain switched into survival mode, and he replied in his native language, "No problem, Mon. Our first priority is to make sure dat all our visitors get what deir (their) hearts' desire."

The couple laughed in unison. Either they were amused by the way in which he had spoken his native language or by his boldness. At the same time, Calvin kept a solemn face, and like a well-trained soldier, Trudy scrutinised him, to see if he was serious or only joking.

By then Henry was out of earshot, so Calvin lowered his voice and said, "I could meet you guys at your room to discuss the matter, if you are serious."

As soon as he completed the sentence, Trudy whispered, "Yes, meet us at our room in fifteen minutes or so," and hastily gathered her things.

Calvin excused himself and went towards the kitchen with a happy feeling in his heart, as he thought of the big difference a few thousand dollars would make at that point in his life.

Twenty minutes later he knocked on the couple's door, and Johnny opened it and told him to come in.

As he entered, Johnny offered him a seat and at the same time Trudy appeared from the bathroom, with a bath towel hanging loose around her neck.

Calvin told Johnny thanks and sat down in the offered chair, and the couple sat down on the bed. All of a sudden, a tense silence descended upon the three people, as they sat in the hotel room looking at one another, not knowing what to say.

A funny feeling came over Calvin, and he thought, *something's definitely not right*, but quickly he shook off the thought and told himself that it was only his nerves. *It has been a while since I've done any dealing. I'm getting soft,* he told himself, *but this is a chance to make another step out of the never-ending struggle.*

As soon as he overrode his earlier intuition, he broke the silence and got straight to the point. "What amount of de herbs you guys talking about?" he asked them both.

"Can we get about half of a kilo?" Trudy asked abruptly.

"Yah, mon, can we get half a kilo," Johnny anxiously repeated what his partner had said.

Instantly, Calvin realised that it was the woman who was calling the shots. He wished it were the man, because he seemed much easier to convince. However, he told them how much it was going to cost to get the supply.

Surprisingly, Trudy agreed to pay the asking price without any fuss, and Johnny decided to stay quiet during the money talk.

"There is one problem though," Calvin said.

But before he told them the problem, Trudy asked instantly, "And what could that be?" with a not-so-happy tone of voice.

"Well," Calvin began, still feeling a bit uneasy, "I will need some of the money upfront, to sort out the merchandise."

Johnny wanted to give him the money, but Trudy would not have any of it. She was one determined woman. With a stern voice she told Calvin, "My money will not part with me until I receive the buds. It's deal or no deal, young man."

All of a sudden, Calvin realised that he was faced with a complex situation, which could swing many ways, but he didn't want to end up at the wrong end. The worst thing that could happen, he thought, would be the couple telling him that he was under arrest for drug trafficking when he came back with the weed. He also thought about walking away, but he was already deep into it. Ultimately, he decided to go along and deal with the situation as it presented itself to him. On the other hand, he was being driven by a will to survive by any means necessary. Therefore he agreed to the terms and informed the couple that he would get the weed, said his goodbyes, and walked out of the room.

Back downstairs Daphne was sitting in the lounge, watching the television on her own.

Calvin, who was already on a verbal warning for neglecting his job, boldly went over to Daphne and told her that he was going into town briefly to collect some money and promised her that he would give her some on his return if she would run the restaurant while he was away.

Daphne, like many other single women on the island, couldn't say no if someone offered to give her some money, because she was raising her three children single-handed, and every dollar went a long way. She told Calvin that it was okay for him to go, and he hurriedly got changed and slipped out the back gate, unseen by the rest of staff, and into a waiting taxi.

When the taxi reached town, he got out and headed off to Church Street, where he persuaded the Rasta dealer to give him the weed on credit.

After he got the weed and gave his word as surety, he quickly brought the weed to Queen Street and gathered his crew to help him process the pellets.

The guys were happy when Calvin turned up with the weed for processing, because most of them were living on the breadline, and not even the crumbs from the last loaf of bread were left in the bottom of their bread pans.

Although the youths didn't tell Calvin up front that they too would love some money from the deal to buy food to eat, he already knew, by the conversations that some of them were having, about their situation and the obvious expectation.

Calvin couldn't tell them at that point that there was no certainty of making any money from the deal. Instead he built up their hopes, in order to get the job done, but only he knew the dilemma that he was in. Ultimately, if the deal didn't work out right, he would have to answer a lot of questions.

As Bob Marley stated in one of his songs, "Belly full but we hungry. Rain a fall but the dutty tough. A pot a cook, but the food nuh nuff." Meaning: although there is life there is no hope, and even when the people are working, whatever they earn is not enough to make much difference in their lives. Finally, there were more mouths to be fed than the amount of food in the pot to go around.

Eventually the processing of the pellets was completed, and Calvin was relieved to be seated somewhat nervously on the backseat of a taxi, going back to the hotel.

From the moment he entered the taxi, the other passengers could smell the herb that he was carrying, but it was normal for people to travel with drugs in public transportation. After all, everybody was trying to make a living, one way or the other.

The police on the other hand knew that a lot of people regularly travelled with drugs and weapons on public transport. The corrupt policemen usually licked their lips and rubbed their hands in anticipation when they caught someone with drugs, but it was a totally different story when the incorrupt officers caught a culprit in the act.

Unfortunately, the taxi that Calvin was travelling in was only two minutes away from the hotel, when it suddenly drove into a roadblock.

Nobody was allowed to leave the vehicles. Police with loaded machine and handguns were checking each vehicle with caution, and anybody who looked suspicious was being pulled out of cars or buses and lined up at the roadside, with guns aimed at them.

When the police eventually got to Calvin's taxi, one officer told the occupants in the car that they were looking for an armed and dangerous gunman, while pointing his M16 assault rifle in the car. Another policeman, standing on the other side of the car, aimed his handgun through the window and shouted, "Raasclaat, ah who got dat deh weed deh pan dem? It strong nuh raas," he concluded, as he opened the door. Translation: "Which one of you have the weed in your position?"

The two other passengers in the backseat looked at Calvin, as each person was ordered out of the taxi.

The policemen didn't need to ask who had the weed again, because Calvin instantly told them that he was the one who had it.

The officers searched the rest of the passengers, ordered them back into the taxi, and told the driver that he could go. Fortunately for Calvin, the policemen in question were two corrupt cops.

Calvin thought he had finally got caught by the police with his pants at his knees, and for a split second, he visualised himself in prison, but his vision was short-lived. The two policemen pulled him to one side and told him that they wanted ten thousand Jamaican dollars each, or he was going to jail.

Although he'd already started to imagine being in prison, he didn't really want to risk going to jail at that point in his life. So he told the officers to hold on to the weed and allow him to get the money.

Without any further ado, the officers took his details, told him where to contact them, and said to hurry, or else they might change their minds and lock him up instead.

Calvin felt relieved when he was allowed to walk away, but he didn't know exactly where or from whom he was going to get that sort of money. Furthermore, the money that he was going to get from the deal didn't amount to twenty grand, and the Rasta dealer was waiting to get paid for his herb, as well as the pellet makers, who were also waiting patiently at Queen Street to get some money to buy food.

"Suddenly, everything seemed to be going wrong for me all at once. The food truck turned over, I was getting deeper and deeper into trouble, and the clock was ticking away.

"One of the corrupt policemen slowly walked over to an unmarked car, opened the boot (trunk), looked at me from behind his sunglasses, chucked the shopping bag with the pellets inside the car boot, and walked away, after patting the top of the boot reassuringly.

"I felt sick at that point, and I was also determined to get back the pellets, even though I knew it was going to be a bigger risk than I'd taken to prepare them in the first place. But too much was at stake and a lot of questions were going to be asked that could only be answered by the pellets."

While Calvin was contemplating what to do, a taxi with only two passengers inside suddenly pulled up, and after the occupants got searched, he jumped into it and went back to the hotel.

On his arrival, he found out that the boss was still out and the hotel was still deserted. He went to the front desk and asked the receptionist for an international collect call to England.

"Hello," said his undisputed lover girl Betty, on the third ring, and all of a sudden Calvin felt like a weight had been lifted from off his shoulders. He didn't bother to beat around the bush but got straight to the point and spilled his guts to Betty about his predicament with the pellets and police.

Betty panicked and told Calvin to calm down and tell her exactly what had happened to him. He tried to explain his situation to her again, but his frustration triggered off a surge of stuttering, and Betty asked him what he wanted her to do.

He asked her if she could send him the money to pay the policemen. Even though he'd treated her badly and she was still hurting, Betty sent him thirteen thousand dollars through the Western Union money transfer.

"I was relieved when I collected the money, but another strange feeling came over me when I thought about meeting the policemen. For a tense moment I thought about more than one reason why I shouldn't go back for the pellets. One, the policemen could be leading me into a trap, to frame me for a crime that I did not commit, possibly killing me in the process. Two, they could take away my money and the pellets when I met up with them, and I couldn't do anything about it, or they might even decide to kill me and plant a gun and the pellets on my dead body.

"I didn't prolong the thoughts, because there were also reasons why I had to get back the pellets. One, the thirteen thousand Jamaican dollars that Betty sent me could pay the Rasta dealer and offer the pellet makers a few dollars. Two, because I hadn't been arrested for the pellets, I would have to come up with an excuse, other than my initial problem with the police, to explain to Delroy and the pellet makers why the food was so little, when there should be more.

"To top it all off, making excuses on a drug deal to cover oneself was not and never will be accepted. On the whole, most Jamaicans will stick together when they are hungry, but no matter how they struggle together or how close the friendship may be, when money comes into play, disloyalty, bad mind, and mistrust always surface.

"On the whole, I didn't want to create any unnecessary bad vibes amongst my friends. After all, they were almost living in my yard, so I did what I had to do to make life easy for myself."

Calvin went to the rum bar where the policemen had told him to meet them.

On his arrival, he saw one of them standing at the bar counter, caressing a cold bottle of Red Stripe beer, in deep conversation with an infamous drug dealer.

He froze in his tracks, and the policeman who chucked the pellets in the car boot appeared from behind the tinted glass of the rum bar and indicated to Calvin by a motion of his head, that he should follow him.

Calvin looked around to see if anybody was observing him, because he didn't want to be seen with a policeman. As a general rule, only three types of civilians held secret conversation with the police, apart from their family: rich businesspeople, drug dealers, and police Peggys (informers).

Calvin was not any of those; he was only doing what he must to survive.

The policeman who signalled Calvin went and sat in the front passenger seat of the unmarked car. Calvin gingerly walked towards the car, and the officer told him to sit on the backseat.

"As I entered the car I slumped down, so nobody could see me from outside, unless they got close to the car. At that same moment the second policeman appeared and sat in the driver's seat. Instantly a huge lump welled up in my throat, and I was finding it hard to breathe."

"Weh de money deh, yout'?" Translation: "Where is the money youth?" the first policeman asked, as the other lit a cigarette and blew the smoke ferociously in Calvin's direction.

"Mi couldn't get all of it, you know, boss," Calvin stammered in reply.

"How you mean seh yuh couldn't get all ah it, bwoy?" the officer with the cigarette asked angrily. "A fool yuh tek we fa, bwoy? Mek we lock up de raasclaat bwoy," he suggested to his accomplice. Translation: "How you mean to say that you couldn't get all of it, boy? A fool you take us for, boy? Let's lock up the raasclaat boy."

"How much money yuh have, yout'?" asked the first officer, who seemed to be in charge. Calvin told him ten thousand dollars, while totally ignoring the feisty policeman.

"We cyan' (can't) tek dat, yout'," the first police told Calvin. "Do you know how much years you can get in prison for attempting to export ganja?" the officer continued. "Man, mek we just lock up de bwoy, mi sey," the other police interjected.

"Tell you what," the first officer began, totally ignoring his accomplice, "Because you are a humble yout', mi ah guh let you off dis time, but de next time mi catch you, yuh better have whole heap of money, or else you going straight to jail."

With that said, he told Calvin to hand the money over, and reluctantly he did so.

After the officer checked the money, he put his hand under his seat, pulled out the shopping bag containing the pellets, and handed it to Calvin.

He took it, thanked the officer, looked around, stepped out of the car, and made his getaway quickly.

He was shaking like a leaf when he got into another taxi, and he was relieved when he got out at the hotel gate. He was even more relieved when he realised that the boss was still out, after he went in and got changed into his chef's clothes.

Later that same evening, he stealthily went to deliver the weed to Trudy and Johnny, half-expecting the worst to happen. However, when Johnny opened the door and he went inside, he felt at ease when he realised that there were no police waiting on him.

Trudy accepted the parcel and expertly weighed it with her bare hands, with a frown on her face, before nodding her head to confirm that she was pleased, and without uttering a single word, she took the money from her pocket and handed it to Calvin.

He took the money, thanked them, and left the room, but in his heart he wanted to say, *Thank you for not being the police.*

That very day Calvin made a silent vow to discontinue the drug trade, because it was costing him more than what he was earning. He was also convinced that it was a sign for him to stop, regardless of how sweet the money was or how tough the times might be.

"It would be so easy to say, 'If I'd known that things would turn out the way they did, I wouldn't have got involved with drugs,' but I won't say that, because like what Mama often said, 'If you lie with dogs you will rise up with fleas, and if you don't go to the fowl roost the fowl can't shit on you.'

"I knew exactly what I was getting into, and I also knew that there was a price to pay if I should get caught, but at the end of the day, it was a price worth paying to survive on the island.

"Yes, I had a job that I was thankful for, but if I wasn't working in the kitchen (where I was getting three meals a day), it would have been impossible to live off what I was being paid, because two hundred dollars from my twelve hundred a week wages was going towards taxi fare. On the other hand, one thousand dollars could hardly fill a few carrier bags with the most essential groceries from the shops, and utility bills and rent weren't included. In conclusion, surviving on the island was a dirty game, if you were not in an advantageous position."

CHAPTER TWENTY-FOUR

GETTING BURN

Every now and again Calvin used to confess to Veron about his wheeling and dealing at the hotel, but he never once told her about his infidelity.

Veron (like most Jamaican women) didn't have a problem with her man dealing in drugs. After all, most people on the island were involved in wrongdoings, one way or another. Calvin didn't know if Veron suspected him of cheating on her. Maybe he would've gotten away with it, but he pushed his luck too far after he met one particular white Canadian girl.

It was the middle of December 1993. About 50 per cent of the rooms were occupied, and as usual, he was constantly on the lookout for an opportunity to elevate him out of poverty.

That morning, the waitress didn't turn up for work. Therefore he had to cook and serve the breakfast. On the whole, he didn't have a problem with that, because after all was said and done, he was a showman, and he always liked to interact with the guests on a one-to-one basis.

He could see the guests through the glass at the front of the kitchen as they entered the dining hall. There was also a sliding window where the guests could go and speak to him at the kitchen.

There weren't many people in the dining hall that morning, because most of them had room service, and the last couple who had come to eat in the dining hall were almost through. All of a sudden, the dining hall door flew open, and a white middle-aged woman and a younger white girl, in her early twenties, walked in, went towards a table, and seated themselves. In that instant, the couple who were eating in the dining hall got up from their table, stopped at the kitchen window to pay for their breakfast, and left.

Calvin picked up the order pad and a jug of water and went out to take the ladies' orders.

He looked over the younger woman as he got closer to their table, but she didn't look in his direction. "Good morning, ladies how are you today?" he addressed them professionally, with the sound of music in his tone. Before they could reply, he filled their glasses with water and continued, "My name is Calvin, and I'm your chef and waiter for today."

"Fine," the elder woman said, "thank you very much. And yourself?"

"I'm fine, thank you, too," Calvin replied.

"This is my daughter Sarah," the woman continued, "and you can call me Caroline."

Sarah didn't acknowledge him but kept gazing at an invisible spot on the white tablecloth while chewing on a fingernail. It appeared as if she would rather be in her bed than sit at the breakfast table with her mum.

Calvin turned his attention to Sarah and asked, "How about you, my lovely lady?"

Slowly, Sarah raised her long eyelashes, without moving her head from the position that it was in, and then smiled mischievously as she stared deeply into Calvin's brown eyes. When he looked into her huge emerald eyes, he was instantly smitten.

It was the very first time Calvin had beheld such beautiful eyes, and suddenly he was captivated. Sarah on the other hand noticed his reaction and giggled with pleasure, before replying, "I'm okay, too. Thank you very much, Chef."

Her charming voice was like a symphony to his ears. To him, it sounded as if she was simply saying, *Come and get me if you can.*

Unsteadily Calvin took the women's orders, while unsuccessfully trying to avoid looking into Sarah's direction. She knew she had him under her spell and was enjoying every moment watching his discomfiture.

"Where are you from?" he enquired, aiming the question at Caroline, as he struggled to look in her direction.

"We're from Canada," replied Caroline joyfully. "We are only here for one week, but we're planning on enjoying every moment of it."

"Have you been here before?" he asked, still trying not to look in Sarah's direction.

"No, it's our first time," Caroline replied. "But it definitely won't be our last," Sarah interjected with a giggle.

By now Calvin was feeling uncomfortable around the women, and he felt relieved after he took the orders and went back into the kitchen. On the other hand, he was pleased to know that they were on their own.

Sarah was a bit on the big side, close to six feet tall, and weighed close to two hundred pounds, but apart from her immense, firm structure, she was beautiful on the outside. Her face was round like the moon, and her skin was pale, flawless, smooth and exquisite. When she'd giggled earlier, Calvin was pleased to see how white and even her teeth were. He'd managed to force a smile, because he was utterly enchanted by her green eyes. He also knew instantly that he had to find out exactly what lay beneath that shy, unyielding countenance of hers.

Twenty minutes or so later breakfast was ready, and he loaded up his tray and went through the swinging door, balancing the tray skilfully on one hand in the air, as he made his way towards his guests.

The mum clapped her hands as he skilfully spun the tray on its way down and placed it on another table.

After the omelettes, bacon, toast, coffee, and juice were served, he told them to enjoy and set about clearing the rest of the used tables.

During the process of clearing the tables, he overheard Sarah telling her mother that she would like to have her hair braided.

Before he went back into the kitchen, he stopped at their table, apologised for listening to their conversation, and told them that he knew someone who could braid hair.

Sarah was more talkative by now, and her mum kept silent as she quizzed Calvin about the hairdresser. When he told her that the hairdresser was on the hotel compound, she was delighted.

Suddenly, the mum wiped her mouth with her napkin and said, "There you go, my darling. You don't need to worry anymore about being stuck with me all the time on holiday. I'm sure Chef won't mind showing you around. Is that right, Chef?" Caroline asked and winked an eye at him.

He was shocked out of his skin, because Caroline was actually handing her daughter to him on a platter.

"No problem at all, madam," he replied. "So long as I'm free from work, I can always show her around or show her anything that she may need to see in the process," he concluded with a mischievous grin on his face.

The mum laughed and said, "You will do, Chef. You seem like the type of guy that I would happily take home and introduce to my parents."

By then Sarah was fully awakened, with a naughty smile running from ear to ear. Minutes later, he excused himself and went back into the kitchen, with a broad smile on his own face.

When Sarah and her mum finished their breakfast, they went to the window and paid their bill. After Calvin handed them the receipt, he told Sarah to meet him at the bar around midday, and she told him that she would be at the poolside sunbathing.

Just before they left the restaurant, Caroline looked at Calvin with admiration and laughed, winked at him, and nodded reassuringly, as she passed through the dining room door behind her daughter.

Later that morning, Calvin called Ivadnie at the laundry and told her to pick up her breakfast at the kitchen.

She was a housekeeping attendant and one of the longest-serving members of staff, who was his favourite friend at the hotel.

The first time they laid eyes on each other, there was an instant attraction, and he'd tried on numerous occasions to get her in bed, but she wouldn't have any of it, and whenever he made a pass at her, she would always laugh and show him her wedding band. "I like you a lot, Calvin," she would tell him most often when he flirted with her, "but I'm happily married, and I love my family and husband very much."

That morning, when she came to collect her breakfast at the kitchen, he told her about Sarah, and she promised to do her hair later that afternoon for a fee.

Calvin was delighted, because he wanted to impress Sarah – and possibly put her on his list, because at the time, there was a secret competition going on between him and two other male staff to see who could get it on with the most female guests. On the other hand, he was still hoping to find the ideal woman who would smuggle some drugs for him.

A few minutes past midday, Calvin went to the bar and pretended he was there to get a drink, when all that time he was on a mission, to pursue Sarah.

On his arrival at the bar, he saw the bartender walking towards a guest at the poolside, carrying a cold bottle of Red Stripe beer on a tray.

Seated comfortably on a deck chair at the poolside, in washed-out blue jeans shorts, a white T-shirt, and sunglasses, rubbing sun cream seductively on her smooth white legs, was Sarah.

Standing in the shade at the bar, Calvin watched her with a burning desire, while she flicked her long, thick blond hair backwards and let it cascade down her back. She collected the bottle of Red Stripe beer from the bartender and took a big swig, as he turned and walked away.

"I suddenly felt nervous at that point, because I knew she was waiting for me, but I didn't want anybody else to know about my mission. Furthermore, the boss was on the property, and I didn't want him to see me cajoling his guests."

Unexpectedly, Ivadnie was passing by the bar, and Calvin stopped her and took her over to meet Sarah.

"Hello again," he greeted Sarah, with the broadest smile on his face as he sauntered towards her.

"Hello," said Sarah, pretending to be startled by the visit.

Boldly Calvin introduced the women to each other, and suddenly Ivadnie noticed the spark bouncing between her colleague and the guest. Her eyes were darting from Calvin to Sarah as they spoke, with a surprised look on her face, and a few minutes later she'd promised Sarah that she would braid her hair, before excusing herself.

Calvin lingered at the poolside after Ivadnie walked away and nervously asked Sarah, "Are you having fun?"

"I like sitting in the sunshine," she replied, as she picked up a pack of cigarettes from the deck, offered him one, and then placed another between her lips.

Quickly Calvin produced his lighter, got close to Sarah, and flicked the flame in the same movement. But a gust of wind blew the flame out, and he went closer to her and bent down, to shield the wind. His hands trembled as strands of her freshly shampooed hair wafted up in his face.

As she cupped her hands to help guard the flame, her fingers touched his, and a jolt of electricity flew between their bodies.

Nervously she dragged on her fag, as he successfully lit his on the first attempt, caressing her voluptuous body with his wandering eyes at the same time.

She caught the movement of his eyes and giggled. "Do you like what you see?"

Feeling a bit embarrassed, he asked, "What are you talking about?"

She laughed again. "You are a bad boy, Calvin, but I like you."

He looked around to see if anybody was in earshot. Then he lowered his voice and said, "I like you too, and I would love to get to know you better."

"So you really were checking me out then, weren't you?" she asked and then giggled.

"Yes," he confessed, "I was admiring your loveliness, and I do like what I see. For the record, you are a very beautiful girl."

"Thanks. You are very cute yourself, Mr Chef," Sarah acknowledged, while gazing into his eyes over the tops of her sunglasses.

He glanced around again. This time he noticed the bartender and Ivadnie observing them at the poolside, through an open window at the bar. All of a sudden he got cold feet, said his goodbye, and walked away.

Back at the bar, Ivadnie said, "There you go Calvin. You can leave me alone now, because you find yourself a pretty white girl," with a bit of jealousy in her voice.

"You will always be my favourite girl, even though you don't want me," he replied.

The bartender shook his head and said, "Me nuh know how yuh suh lucky. How come you always get de pretty gyal dem?"

"Look and learn," Calvin told him, as he wandered off towards the kitchen, with a big smile running from ear to ear.

He was in the kitchen preparing dinner that same evening, when someone knocked on the window. To his surprise, it was Sarah, wanting to show him her new hairstyle.

"How do I look?" she asked, as she flung her long golden locks backwards and smiled at him wickedly.

"Very nice," he replied joyfully and smiled with her.

"What are you doing later?" Sarah enquired happily.

"I haven't got anything planned really. Why do you ask?"

"I was wondering if you would like to chill out with me and have a drink later."

By then her presence was causing his trousers zip to burst at the seam. "I would love dat very much," he replied, as his eyes darted from her eyes to her lips and back to her eyes.

"Behave yourself, Calvin," she told him with a commanding voice. "If you are a good boy later you might get some of this," she concluded, as she pushed out her massive chest towards the window, giggled and gyrate her body as she walked away.

He pushed his head through the window and asked, "Is dat a promise?" as she was walking away.

"See you later at the bar," she replied as she shook her golden locks and sashayed through the dining hall door.

That night, dinner took forever to be completed.

Normally, Calvin would hang around the kitchen until half past ten or so, but at exactly ten o'clock he was on his way through the kitchen door. As he approached the bar, he noticed Sarah seated at a table in the lounge with her mum.

He stopped and spoke to a few of the other guests, who were drinking at the bar, before he sauntered over to mum and daughter.

"Hello, lover boy," the mum greeted him cheerfully, when he got to their table.

"Stop it, mum," Sarah pleaded and giggled. "You are making him blush." She told Calvin to sit down in the chair next to her. "I got you a bottle of Red Stripe beer," she told him politely, as he pulled out the chair and sat down nervously beside her.

"At that moment, I was feeling rather anxious, because things were moving a bit too fast, and it felt like I was being watched constantly. On the other hand, I wasn't looking for an intimate relationship with Sarah, even though I was under her spell. I was only playing the game that I'd grown used to, with the possibility of making some money in the process, but at that point it felt like I was playing the role of her boyfriend."

Minutes later, Caroline downed the rest of her drink in one go and then got up and kissed her daughter goodnight. She then rested both hands on Calvin's shoulders and whispered in his ear, "She's a good girl, my Sarah is. Please take good care of her for me," and then she walked away.

The both of them sat in silence sipping on their drinks after Caroline left, and after a moment of silence Sarah suddenly rested an open palm on his thigh, underneath the table, squeezed it gently and asked, "Do you have any buds?"

He looked at her incredulously and asked, "What?"

"I mean," she began to explain, but he stopped her in midsentence and told her that he knew exactly what she meant. He then stroked the back of her hand under the table tenderly, looked into her eyes, and told her, "Let's go outside," and then got up with his beer and lead the way.

Outside, he led her towards the darkened corner of the poolside, took out the spliff he had in his pocket, and lit it.

Sarah inhaled the sweet smell of the sinsemilla herb, as he puffed on the joint.

"I've been waiting a long time for this," Sarah confessed, as she accepted the joint and took a big drag.

"Be careful wid dat. It will blow your brains," he warned her, as she coughed and handed the spliff back to him.

"I feel much better now," she told him, as she moved closer to him and kissed his lips passionately. "You are a swell guy, Calvin, and I'm glad that I met you," she said as their lips parted.

He was lost for words.

When he got up that morning he'd only had some weed and a few cigarettes, and enough money in his pocket for his taxi fare. *The day turned out fine,* he thought as he puffed on the spliff vigorously.

"What are you thinking about?" Sarah enquired, as she gently stroked his cheeks with the palm of her hands.

"I was just thinking how lucky I am to meet a beautiful girl like you," he replied, as he held one of her soft hands to his cheek, not wanting her to let go.

"My mum likes you a lot," she confessed. "She thinks you are a fantastic guy."

"It's nice of her to tink of me dat way," he replied, as he handed the spliff to her.

By then the night was quickly coming to an end. Over on the other side, the bartender was closing the windows and turning off some of the lights, while Sarah and her man locked in a tight embrace as their lips and tongues entwined together, again and again.

Eventually, he told her that he had to go soon, because he didn't have enough money to pay double fare on the taxi. She pleaded desperately for him to stay and promised him money for the taxi, but although the temptation was strong, he followed his heart and said no, he had to go home.

Ultimately they kissed and said goodbye, and then he went home to Veron.

Back at Queen Street, Veron was lying in bed, pretending to be fast asleep, when he got home.

He was conscious of Sarah's perfume, as it lingered in his nostrils, so he stealthily headed to the bathroom and had a shower.

"That night, I didn't hug Veron in bed like I always did," Calvin confessed. "I also turned my back to her in the bed, because I felt too guilty to look at her in the shadows of the room or even to breathe in the smell of her hair, and after a short while I pretended to fell asleep, but sleep was impossible."

The following morning, Veron got up early and turned on the television. Although he was also awake, neither of them made any conversation. Minutes later he got out of bed and went straight into the shower.

While he was getting dressed, a little conversation ensued, and before long he was telling Veron that he would be home early that night, as he walked out the door.

Back at the hotel, things began to get a bit heated, as the revelation of Sarah's and Calvin's relationship began to unfold as the topic of the day.

Ivadnie's attitude towards him was also rather different, and the staff members were all voicing their own opinion and passing their own verdicts. On the other hand, Calvin was getting worried sick, because he didn't want the news to reach his boss's ears.

That morning, Sarah and her mother had room service, and for the better part of the day Calvin was like a recluse in the kitchen.

Before dinner was ready to be served, he was putting a tray of chicken in the oven when someone suddenly knocked on the window. He turned around, and to his surprise, Sarah was standing at the window smiling at him.

The tray of chicken wobbled in his hands and almost fell to the floor. She giggled like a little girl and asked, "How come I haven't seen you all day, Mr Chef?"

"Sorry, babes, I've been tinking about you all day, but I couldn't get away," he stuttered in reply, "but I was hoping to meet up with you later and continue where you and I ended last night."

"I've been thinking about you too," Sarah replied genuinely, with the evident look of infatuation in her bright green eyes.

He suddenly realised that he had surely got more than he had bargained for. Sarah, on the other hand, knew exactly what she wanted, and she was determined to get it.

"I think I'm falling in love with you," she confessed abruptly, after he'd successfully put the tray of chicken into the oven and went over to her.

Nobody had ever told him outright that they loved him before, and it was absolutely the first time he was being told by a girl, that she falling in love with him.

Nervously he looked into her eyes, and a surge of lust immediately consumed him. Nonetheless, he didn't tell her that he was falling for her too. Instead, he only leaned forward to the window, caressed her soft, cool cheek, and kissed her lips tenderly. At the same time, the door to the dining hall swung open, and Daphne, the waitress, walked in and cleared her throat.

Sarah pulled away from Calvin shyly, but he remained in the same position and smiled at the waitress.

"Don't worry about me," said Daphne. "You guys can carry on doing what you are doing. I'll just mind my own business." With that, she headed towards the other end of the dining hall.

"It's okay," Calvin whispered to Sarah, "everybody knows about us already." But she only smiled nervously, pecked him on the lips, and told him, as she walked away, to meet her at the bar later.

Instantly he realised that he could no longer hide the truth regarding his relationship with Sarah, because the waitress (the hotel news carrier) had caught him red-handed kissing her. Thus, there was only one way to redeem himself, and that was to take the information directly to the boss.

He suspected his boss already knew about some of the things that he was getting up to, including having sex with his female guests occasionally. Nonetheless, where Sarah was concerned, it was totally different. It was more like a real relationship to her than a casual fling, and he didn't know if the boss would tolerate such a thing on his premises.

Later that evening, after dinner was completed, Calvin rang the boss and asked him if he could visit him at his quarters.

The boss told him yes, he should come. Minutes later he was knocking on the boss's door.

The door opened, and the boss waved him inside and offered him a seat.

"What's the matter now Calvin?" he asked, as he went to sit down in his comfy chair.

Calvin sat in silence, entwining his fingers like a child, not knowing where to start. Suddenly he blurted, "Can I go out with one of the guests?"

"One of my guests?" the boss enquired incredulously and laughed, but Calvin didn't reply, because he was waiting for the worst to happen, when the boss said, "Yuh nuh easy, Calvin? You come in here telling me that you want to go out with one of my guests. Who is this guest?" he asked, "Is she the young white girl that you were kissing at the poolside last night?" he concluded, before Calvin could answer.

The air conditioner was on full blast, but Calvin suddenly felt hot. Unconsciously he'd also begun to twist his fingers faster, and he couldn't look his boss in the eye.

"What's the matter, Calvin?" the boss asked, "Cat got your tongue now, but last night you were pushing it down Sarah's throat." He laughed out loud.

"Sorry about dat, boss, it just happened. I didn't –" "Didn't what?" the boss interrupted. "Didn't know that I was watching you?"

Calvin cupped his face with both hands and leaned forward, not wanting the boss to see how embarrassed he was.

"Calvin, you can go and have your fun with Sarah, but don't forget your responsibilities, or where your priorities lie," the boss warned, as he got up out of his seat.

Calvin was shocked; after all, when he went to see the boss, he was expecting a telling off, for his actions, because he thought the boss had already heard about his affair with Sarah. He definitely wasn't expecting to get the go-ahead.

"Thank you very much. I won't let you down," he assured his boss and got up too.

"One more thing," said the boss. "Try and be a bit more discreet. I don't want the rest of staff to start thinking you are the only one who is getting all the special treatment. It's not good for business either," he concluded, as he showed Calvin the door.

Downstairs, Sarah was seated in one corner of the lounge on her own, sipping a Red Stripe beer while waiting for her man to join her.

As Calvin walked through the bar door, she beckoned him over.

He went over and sat beside her, with a big smile on his face.

"What's so funny?" Sarah asked, and pushed a bottle of beer towards him.

"I'm just happy to see you, my darling."

"I thought you weren't coming to see me tonight," she confessed.

"I wouldn't miss this moment for anything," he replied, and she took his hand and squeezed it.

"Are we going to make love tonight?" Sarah asked suddenly, with lust ringing in her voice.

At that precise moment Calvin took a sudden swig from the beer and coughed, as the alcohol went down the wrong throat, and Sarah laughed, as he tried to stifle the cough.

When the coughing was under control, he told her, "I've been yearning for you all day. I can't wait to explore your beautiful body."

Sarah giggled and said, "You make me feel so special. I can't wait to feel your strong, naked body next to mine. Shall we go outside now, because I'm getting very, very hot in here."

As they got up and headed towards the door they bumped into the boss.

"Hello Sarah," he hugged and greeted her with a peck on the cheek, while watching Calvin over her shoulder. "What are you guys getting up to now?"

"Not a lot," replied Sarah and giggled. "Calvin taking me for a walk. It's a bit hot tonight, isn't it?"

"A walk?" the boss asked disbelievingly, as he let go of Sarah. "At this time of night? Anyway, you guys be careful, and don't do anything that I wouldn't do." He slapped Calvin on the back reassuringly on his way past.

"Do you have any more buds?" Sarah whispered, when they got outside.

"In that case, I think we should definitely take a walk," Calvin replied and led her towards the hotel gate.

At the gate, he flagged down a taxi, opened the back passenger door, and ushered Sarah inside, and then climbed in beside her. "To de Dead-End, driver," he ordered the cabbie, as he closed the door.

"Where are we going?" Sarah asked, as she made herself comfortable in the car.

"I'm taking you to a very special place, where we can smoke freely and watch the moon and the stars shining in the sky above us," he declared, as he snuggled up beside her.

Feeling safe in the company of her man, Sarah rested her head on his shoulder, and he hugged her as the taxi sped away.

Minutes later the taxi pulled up outside the bar at the Dead-End.

As they alighted from the car, he began to search himself, and then turned to Sarah and told her that he'd left his wallet at the hotel – which was a blatant lie; he simply had no money. However, Sarah gave him a hundred-dollar bill to pay the driver, but he pocketed the fifty dollars change, as he walked towards the bar with her on his arm.

At the bar, Sarah gave him a five-hundred dollar note to purchase the drinks as she walked out onto the sand.

He ordered two Red Stripe beers and blatantly pocketed the change, before joining Sarah on the beach.

"Let's go and sit over in dat secluded corner," he suggested and led the way towards a cluster of trees and rocks.

When they were both seated comfortably, he lit up a spliff, dragged hard on it, inhaled and exhaled the mixture of weed and fresh sea breeze, and then passed it to Sarah.

Leisurely she took a few big puffs and coughed as she handed it back to him, and as the coughing subsided she put an arm around his waist, rested her head on his shoulder, and whispered softly, "This is very beautiful. I could live like this all the time."

"Same here, darling," he replied, with passion oozing from the resonance of his voice. "It gives me so much pleasure being here with you," he continued, as he cuddled her and squeezed her gently but firmly. "If this is only a fantasy dream, then I definitely don't want to wake up."

"Me either," Sarah confessed with an affectionate kiss on his cheek.

He took another drag from the spliff and passed it to her, but she declined.

He gently released her and leaned back on the big rock behind them, while Sarah did the same and made herself comfortable beside her man. She nestled her head in the cleft of his strong arm, as they gazed out into the sea, each having their own thoughts.

Lights from the airport, the hotels, and the bar were dancing softly on the expanse of the water, as the waves gently flowed onto the sandy beach and back. Suddenly, Calvin pointed towards a group of stars in the clear night sky and said, "Look, the stars are dancing to the beat of our hearts."

Sarah giggled, snuggled up even closer to him, and held her lips for him to kiss.

They were kissing and touching each other everywhere possible, and then suddenly Sarah whispered, "Let's make love right here on the beach."

Calvin didn't need any more prompting. Quickly he began to fumble with his belt and trousers zip, but Sarah got up pushed his hands away playfully, and completed the task.

Later, after they were finally spent, they collapsed into each other's arms, kissing and caressing until they heard voices coming towards them.

Hurriedly they pulled on their clothes, lit up fags, and sat smoking in silence while looking out into the dreamy waters of the sea.

All of a sudden Sarah broke the silence and said, "That was fantastic. I've never had it so good before."

"I've never had it so good before myself," he replied, but to him, Lisa was second to none.

Sarah snuggled up closely beside him and said, "I'm in love with you, Calvin, but I'm scared, because I have to go back soon, and I don't want what we have to ever end."

He smiled to himself, because he knew he'd won her heart, but where it would go next he couldn't tell. She was going back to Canada soon, and that could be the end of them. In fact, from past experiences, he knew that it was not written in the game book to fall in love, because it only ever led to a broken heart.

"Say something to me, please," Sarah begged, interrupting his thoughts.

"I'm in love with you too, baby,(he finally admit) from the first time I laid eyes on you, but I don't want to think about what is going to happen in the next few days, because it will only break my heart."

Sarah tried to snuggle up even closer to him and said, "Let's face reality, Calvin. We both know that I have to go soon, but I promise you that it won't be the end. You will see. Mark my words. I'll prove it to you."

Sarah's speech touched him deeply, that he could not deny, but until he got a call from her or a letter on her return to Canada, he wasn't prepared to let his guard down. After all, he was only in it for sheer pleasure and the possibility of making some money.

"I believe you, my darling. I'll be right here waiting for you. For as long as you want me to," he told her and began to plant kisses all over her face.

Later he took her back to the hotel and subsequently went home to Veron, feeling much worse than he'd felt the previous night.

When he arrived at Queen Street, none of the guys were hanging out in front like they normally did. Veron was at home. He'd noticed the light from the television flicking through her window. Suddenly he thought: i*t's going to be hell to tell the captain tonight*, as he approached the door. On the other hand, he also knew that it was always better to face the music when you're in the wrong than to allow the situation to fester and persist. He had no excuse for not coming home early as planned, but he was prepared to lie his way through, on the spur of the moment.

Quietly he opened the door, went inside the house, and locked it. He heaved a sigh of relief, as he sat down on the sofa.

"Me just get away," he complained to Veron, who responded with a grumble, as if she was lost in the film she was watching.

He sat in silence until the adverts came on, and then Veron asked him, "Wah yuh deh say now?"

Translation: "What are you saying now?"

He paused for a bit before he replied, "I said I just got away. Some people came in unexpectedly and asked me to cater for dem tomorrow, so I was busy preparing de stuff."

He couldn't tell if Veron had bought the story or not, but he was sticking firmly to it nonetheless.

"If you get work to do, you nuh have no choice!" Veron pointed out. "After all, a dat dem deh pay yuh fi duh," she concluded.

Translation: "After all, that's what they're paying you to do."

Instantly he switched the topic from himself and asked, "How was your day? Were you busy?"

"Nuh more dan suh," (not really) she replied without interest, as the movie restarted.

Calvin kicked off his shoes and lay on the sofa, but before the movie Veron was watching ended, he was fast asleep, and after what seemed like only a short while, the neighbour's chickens suddenly awakened him.

Hurriedly he jumped up and looked out the window to behold the sun ascending over the treetops. Before long he was in and out of the shower, dressed and whispering goodbye to Veron, as he went out the door.

Twenty minutes or so later he was walking on cloud nine with a big smile and an extra spring in his steps, as he arrived at work.

The story of him and Sarah, which covered the hotel's front page the previous day, was now stale news. He'd been handed the license to be with her, and that was all that mattered.

Sarah and her mother had room service again, but she paid Calvin a visit at the kitchen, after breakfast was ended.

On her arrival at the kitchen, she was beaming like a bright light. Her long golden locks were tied in a ponytail, and she was clad in matching shorts and T-shirt that leave little to the imagination. Even her eyes were looking greener.

Calvin smiled as he admired his sexy white girl, but in the back of his head he wished that she wouldn't visit him at the kitchen. The last thing he wanted was to ruin the respect between him and his boss, because although the truth about the relationship came out, he didn't want to abuse the trust by rubbing it in everybody's face. Sarah on the other hand didn't give a damn; she was having the time of her life, and that was all that mattered to her.

"I'm going in town to rent a dirt bike later today," she announced with a happy giggle.

Calvin was pleased to hear that, because at least they could go out of town. Suddenly the waitress returned to the kitchen, and Sarah pecked his lips, said goodbye, and made her departure through the door.

Later that afternoon, he was standing outside smoking a cigarette, when Sarah blazed past on the road, on a silver and black Harley Davidson dirt bike. He smiled to himself and thought, the next few days are going to be crazy.

Later that same evening, after his shift was completed, he and Sarah went for a joyride on some of the back streets. Frankly, he didn't want to be seen around town, sitting behind a white girl on a bike. That would probably reach the front page of the local newspapers. In addition, the last thing he wanted to do was to disrespect and embarrass Veron.

Earlier that same day, after the boss announced that he was going to be away on business for a couple of days, Calvin decided to abuse the boss's trust in his absence, by making arrangements to sleep in one of the rooms with Sarah that night.

Valda was the receptionist on duty that day, and she was doing a double shift, because the other receptionist called in sick. Apart from that, she had to work the following morning too, so she'd decided to stay over in one of the unoccupied rooms.

From past experience, Calvin knew Valda would be calling on him for some dinner. On the whole, the staffs weren't entitled to meals, but he would always look after his chosen colleagues.

Valda was a tall, full-bodied girl who liked to eat regularly. Often times she would order a meal from the menu, but sometimes Calvin would give her freebies. Lobster was her favourite, but it was way out of her price range. She'd once vowed that she would do anything for a lobster. As a result, she quickly handed

Calvin a room key when he approached her and promised her a lobster dinner. Without a doubt, he'd made her the happiest girl on the island that day.

"I'll ring the phone once if the boss returns early, and I'll also wake you up in the morning," Valda promised him delightedly, as she handed him the key to one of the downstairs bedrooms, close to the swimming pool.

Later that night, after the rest of staff went home and the other guests went to bed, Calvin and Sarah moved stealthily towards the swimming pool, and noiselessly they stripped and went into the water, although after a while Sarah started to giggle.

Not wanting to attract any unnecessary attention, Calvin ushered her out of the pool and cautiously led her into the bedroom, where they pleasured and explored each other's body until they were both spent.

The following morning, they were suddenly aroused by the ringing of the bedside telephone. Minutes later Calvin got showered and dressed, before commanding Sarah to get up out of the bed.

When she finally got up, he remade the bed and escorted her furtively through the door, the same way they'd got in the previous night.

That morning, he started to prepare the lunch while he was serving breakfast, and by noon he'd completed the lunch. He left Daphne, the waitress, in charge of the kitchen and the dining hall while he went off with Sarah on the motorbike.

Together they frolicked on the north coast that afternoon, while eating jerk chicken, drinking beer, and smoking weed, but the day was short, because he had to return to the hotel to serve dinner.

That night after his work on dinner was completed, he went to the bedroom to visit Sarah.

He knocked on the door, and she opened it in seconds, but she didn't seem happy. Before he could enquire about her sadness, he heard the voice of a man speaking in the room. He looked over her shoulder and beheld a huge white man, sitting on one of the beds.

"Come on in," Sarah whispered, "he's only a friend from back in Canada."

Calvin accepted the invitation, went in, and closed the door behind him.

"This is Big Al," said Caroline, as he ambled towards them. "He's our friend from Canada. He's staying next door at the Ramparts Inn."

Unbeknownst to Sarah and Caroline, Calvin already knew about Big Al. It wasn't his first or second time on the island. He was a regular, and a lot of people around town knew him well and respected him.

You could always find Big Al on Cornwall Beach, the Doctor's Cave Beach, at the Dead-End, or at the Sir Winston nightclub, with an audience around him at the bar, listening attentively while he told them some of his many stories.

Feeling privileged to eventually meet Big Al, Calvin gladly stretched out his right hand as a gesture, and Big Al returned the gesture and they shook hands, but mischievously Big Al prolonged the handshake. Calvin on the other hand didn't make much of it, because he thought Big Al was either feeling tipsy from the after-effect of the sunshine and rum, or he was merely being overly courteous.

Suddenly Caroline and Sarah began to laugh as they looked on. All of a sudden, Calvin realised that Big Al wasn't tipsy, nor was he being overly courteous. The joke was all about the size of his hands.

Calvin suddenly felt inadequate, when he noticed how huge Big Al's hands were against his. It was the biggest pair of hands he'd ever beheld, but regardless of his hugeness, Big Al possessed a good heart. He was simply a happy man who only wanted to have fun – and fun he certainly had in Jamaica.

After listening to some of Big Al's many stories, Calvin finally decided that he had enough. He said his goodbyes to the folks, and Sarah followed him outside.

While they were walking down the corridor, it suddenly dawned on Sarah that the following day was going to be her last on the island. Abruptly she broke down in tears and he hugged and consoled her as they walked along the corridor. On the other hand, he'd secretly arranged to have the following day off work, in order to spend it with her. When he broke the news to her, she was delighted.

Eventually, before he went home, they decided to spend the following day on the north coast. At the gate they kissed and said goodbye, and he made his way home to Veron.

Later that night, as he made his way home, out of the blue he realised that he wasn't experiencing much guilt, regardless of the fact that he'd stayed out the previous night.

When he got to Queen Street, he found it deserted. None of the guys were hanging out front, and there were no lights inside Veron's house.

Stealthily Calvin sauntered towards the house, opened the door, went inside, and gently shut it.

Normally, Veron would be home at that time of night, watching television or sleeping, but she was not at home. A sudden tinge of jealousy made his heart skip a beat, and he wondered where she could be and with whom at that time of the night. Still feeling pent-up jealousy, he showered and lay in bed watching television, until eventually he fell asleep.

Later in the night, he was suddenly awakened by the sound of Veron, fumbling with her key in the door.

He pretended he was still asleep when she got inside the house. She in turn ignored his presence, headed straight to the bathroom and went under the shower. Minutes later she reappeared and sat on the tail of the bed watching the television, and he stirred in the bed, and pretending he was just waking up.

"How long have you been home?" he demanded, while rubbing imaginary sleep from his eyes.

"Me come long time, but you was sleeping like a baby, suh me nuh badder (bother) interfere wid yuh," Veron replied calmly.

He didn't prolong the conversation, and he thought Veron would, but she didn't either.

In another world, another woman would probably have told him to go back to where he was the previous night or at least asked after his whereabouts, but Veron did not. She wasn't the type of woman who likes to argue. She was the type of woman who kept everything to her bosom. It was up to you, as an individual, to work out what she thought or how she felt, and it was hard to do, because she didn't give many clues, unless, of course, it's a matter that offended her deeply.

"Looking back in hindsight, it was that same night the cracks started to appear in our relationship. Consciously I knew I wasn't that special man with the full package. I'd also strongly believe that she was having an affair too, although I couldn't prove it, and even if I could, I couldn't point a single finger at her, because I was just as bad. On the other hand, unconsciously I was only destroying the love that existed between us, by way of chasing sex and money, but I didn't have the willpower to stop myself. Still, the situation could've been different if there was any intervention coming from Veron."

The following morning bright and early, Calvin hopped out of his warm bed and into the shower. Twenty minutes or so later he was saying goodbye to Veron, and before he closed the door behind him he looked back at her and smiled. She in turn flashed him a half-hearted smile and quickly wiped it off her face. A little guilt surfaced as he walked towards the gate, but it was gone by the time he stepped onto the road.

Later that morning, he and Sarah mounted the Harley Davidson and off they went.

It was the first time they were having a whole day by themselves, without the distraction of work or anybody else. As a result, nothing seemed to matter to them as they frolicked at the Dunn's River Falls, amongst the locals and tourists, checking out the history and climbing six hundred feet to the top of the falls.

It was one of the best days he'd ever had on the island, but as with everything else in his life, it eventually came to an end, and they headed back to the hotel.

Caroline had made plans to spend her last night at the Sir Winston with Big Al. She also told Sarah, on her return that afternoon, that she shouldn't wait up for her, because she was going to crash out with Big Al at the Ramparts Inn.

That was music to Sarah's ears, and she suggested to Calvin that they spend the night together. Calvin on the other hand found himself with the biggest decision to make.

He was conscious of the fragility of his relationship with Veron. It was always on his mind, and he didn't want her to kick him out at that stage, because he didn't have anywhere else to lay his head. He planned to make things right with her, but it was difficult while Sarah was still on the island. Conversely, even though he was incessantly denying his feelings towards Sarah, unconsciously he was falling in love with her. He'd only realised the depth of his feelings for her while they were at the Dunn's River Falls, but there was no guarantee that he was going to ever see her again after she left. On the whole, his heart told him to concentrate on what little he had with Veron, but Sarah's spell on him was too strong, and eventually he decided to spend the last night with her.

That night, they pleasured each other as if it was going to be the end of the world.

At daybreak Calvin showered, dressed and went to work, and by the time breakfast was completed, he was back at the room.

While they were in the middle of making love, the door suddenly flew open, and in walked Caroline and Big Al.

Instead of apologizing and retreating through the door, they decided to stand in the middle of the room.

Instantly Calvin made an attempt to jump out of the bed, but Sarah wrapped her legs around him and whispered, "Don't stop. Let them watch; I don't care," but at that precise moment he had a flashback of that sad night, when Ruby had sex beside him in the same bed. Suddenly his erection went, and he looked at Sarah sorrowfully and got up, grabbed his clothes, and went into the bathroom.

"While I was in the bathroom I heard Sarah giving her mum and Big Al a good telling off for the way they'd behaved, but at that point tears were running down my cheeks, because I was hurting all over again. True, Caroline and Big Al had chosen to stick around and watch, but as for me, I was forced to lie in bed and endure the whole act."

That same evening he got permission to close the kitchen early, in order to accompany Sarah and Caroline to the airport.

As with most nice guests, it was hard for everybody at the hotel to see them go. The boss also met them at the reception and said his farewell. He told them that he was looking forward to welcoming them back at the hotel the next time they visited the island.

Sarah held on to Calvin in the taxi and cried all the way to the airport.

"I was deeply moved when we got to the airport, because it was the first time ever I'd experienced that kind of immense affection, and I found myself not wanting her to go either. However, I swallowed the huge lump that was forming in my throat, consoled her, and said goodbye."

As Sarah and Caroline went towards the departure lounge, Calvin looked on while stifling his tears.

Sarah suddenly looked back, stopped and waved goodbye again, before she turned the corner towards the departure lounge, and the lump was back in Calvin's throat as his lover disappeared from sight.

There is nothing I can do now but wait, he thought as he turned and made for the taxi stand.

Back at Queen Street, the house was deserted on his arrival. As a result, he decided to join his friends, who were sitting in Delroy's front yard opposite his house, playing dominoes.

He continued to played dominoes with his friends until late in the night, when a car suddenly pulled up at the gate and the driver killed the engine. Seated in the front passenger seat was Veron, and she lingered in the car for about half an hour, chatting with the driver.

While she was seated in the car, Calvin's mates decided to take the opportunity to tease him. At one point Delroy said loudly so the occupants in the car could hear, "Yuh tink sey my woman can sit down with a man in his car, at my gate, for so long, and me nuh know de man?"

An echo of laughter suddenly erupted from the rest of the guys, and Delroy answered himself by saying, "Yuh must be crazy, blood. My woman ha fe showed me nuff (much) respect."

"Calvin can't do anything about it," Renroy interjected, "because Veron will kick him out of her house." Again they all laughed out loud.

Moments later, Veron alighted from the car slowly and said goodbye to the driver, as he sped away.

"Yu a bun (cheat on) me friend, Ver," Delroy whispered, loud enough for Veron to hear him from across the deserted road, and together the guys laughed some more.

"Me never hear dat one?" Veron replied, and an even bigger roar of laughter immediately exploded from the guys.

One youth from out of the group said, "Nuh pay dem no mind yaah, Ver, dem just trying to wind you up." Translation: "Don't pay them any mind Ver, they are only trying to wind you up."

"Wind me up?" asked Veron. "You lot nuh have nothing to worry about, suh you can say whatever you want to say, because dat can't hurt me," she concluded, as she walked through the gate.

Throughout the exchange, Calvin kept silent. There was nothing he could say or do, because if he had opened his mouth, it would only fuel the bantering.

It didn't bother Calvin at first when Veron pulled up in the car, because he knew that she had a lot of friends, but after Delroy's remarks his better judgement suddenly got weak and ultimately he thought his friend was right, because Veron wasn't showing him any respect, by sitting in the man's car for so long. Uncle once told him, "A good friend will always tell you the truth and say if you are right or wrong." On the other hand, he was already at fault in many ways, so he didn't want to rock the boat by confronting Veron about the driver of the car, because that could start a big argument. As Renroy stated earlier, Veron would probably kick him out of her house if he said anything about her actions.

While the guys were doing their bantering, Veron didn't even look his way. He knew straight away that he was in big trouble, but it was nothing new in his miserable life.

The above is one of the instances how a lot of youths jump to unnecessary conclusion, over a simple matter (because of peer pressure) which eventually turn nasty most of the times.

CHAPTER TWENTY-FIVE

The Transition

The compromised relationship between Calvin and Veron got a little bit better after Sarah and Caroline went back to Canada.

Daphne had started to help out with the cooking at the hotel, which enabled him to spend more time on Queen Street.

The bantering from his friends regarding Veron became frequent, and at length it began to take its toll on him and drained his resistance immensely. But he had to endure it, in order to keep a roof over his head.

On one occasion, he decided to invite Veron to the hotel for a sleep over. The boss was away on business, and Valda, the lobster-loving receptionist, was on duty. Therefore he'd take the opportunity to impress his woman.

That night they had a few drinks at the bar, and later he led her into the same room where he and Sarah had made love.

It was one of the few times he'd taken Veron out on a date, since the beginning of the relationship.

"I must admit, that was a very bad insult to Veron, and she didn't deserve to be treated like that. She was worth far much more than I've given her,"

Two weeks after Sarah's departure he received a letter from her.

He was shocked when the landlord came and handed him the letter. He stretched out on the sofa in Veron's flat and read it with pleasure, deeply moved by the way she expressed her love for him and her feeling of loss, living each day without seeing him. He was delighted to know that he'd made such an impact on her. It also gave him a good feeling to know that she was still interested in him, and it wasn't just a holiday fling.

He smiled and thought of the good times that they had together and wondered, just wondered, if there was a possibility for him to visit her in Canada one day.

The thought of going to Canada thrilled him, and he laughed aloud. He also thought that going to Canada would be the chance of his lifetime. It would be the ideal move, to enable him to start living a decent life and secure something for the future. All of a sudden he began to reflect on all the hardships that he had experienced throughout his life, as far back as he can remembered, and suddenly a huge lump welled up in his throat, and tears started to flow, warm, effortless, uncontrollable tears, and his body shuddered as he hugged the letter and cried silently until he fell into a deep, peaceful sleep. Moments later he was awakened by Renroy, who knocked on the door, wanting to know if he was interested in playing dominoes.

He told nobody on Queen Street about Sarah. She was his secret weapon for the time being, and while his friends were giving him the banter, he would smile, because only he knew that things were going to change for the better one day.

After corresponding with Sarah for a month, he received a special letter one day with a fake gold chain enclosed, as a token of her undying love for him. A few weeks later she sent him another letter, stating that she was planning on returning to the island for two weeks.

This sudden news filled him with joy and left him walking on cloud nine. At the end of February 1994, Sarah was by his side again in Jamaica.

Initially, when she told him about her plans to return to the island, he was excited, but he was also dreading her arrival, because he knew that a lot of things would change once she was on the island. On the whole, his relationship with the boss was getting better, and things were going well at Queen Street, but his life was still empty and he didn't know exactly where he was heading.

He was excited that day when he went to meet her at the airport, but he was left with a troubled feeling after she told him in the taxi that she'd booked a room at the Ramparts Inn. Instantly he knew that her visit was going to create a lot of animosity and end up a total catastrophe.

At the time, there weren't many tourists coming to the hotel, and as with every other business, his boss and the owner of the Ramparts Inn were rivals. To make matters even worse, he'd requested the two weeks off work to spend time with Sarah.

Although the boss wasn't happy, nonetheless he'd told him to go ahead and have the time off.

On top of that, Calvin had to lie to Veron constantly during the time Sarah was on the island. For starters, Veron didn't know that he was off work, and every other day he went home with a mouth full of lies to cover his deceitfulness.

As for Sarah, the initial attraction that he had for her was gradually losing some of its vigour. She'd lost that thrilling appeal, the one that captivated him initially and placed him under her spell. He finally realised that he wasn't really in love with her as he'd thought. However, although the few months apart had changed things dramatically, he was planning on carving out the chance of a lifetime for himself, and he wasn't prepared to let anything or anybody stand in his way, especially feelings. He was on a mission, and nothing else mattered.

A few days after Sarah's arrival, she decided to rent another Harley Davidson dirt bike. This time around, Calvin decided to take her on a tour of his hometown in Mount Carey.

On the night that they went, there was a street dance in progress. For that night only, the members of the community treated him like a celebrity. Everybody who knew him was hanging around, checking out the bike and his white girlfriend.

It was the best experience he'd ever had in his hometown. He felt like he'd already made it in life, and he didn't want the night to end, because the feeling was tangible.

Eventually they headed back to Mobay and went to the Dead-End, where they spent some time smoking weed and enjoying the tranquillity of the night, before going back to the Ramparts Inn.

Sarah returned the bike halfway through the second week, because the money she'd brought to Jamaica with her had run out. As a result, Calvin had to support her for the remainder of the time. However, that gave him more reason to pose the long-awaited question to her.

At first, when he asked her if she would risk taking back some weed, she was hesitant, but it didn't take much persuasion for her to say yes.

"How will I manage to smuggle the drugs through Customs," Sarah asked him, and he told her that she would have to swallow it. Suddenly she seemed terrified and told him that she wasn't going to do it, but after he swallowed two of the pellets in front her as an example, eventually she changed her mind.

On the day of Sarah's departure, Veron was out visiting friends. Therefore, Calvin decided to take her to Queen Street, where the weed was being prepared, in order for her to consume the pellets.

On their arrival at Queen Street, the news of Sarah's presence spread like a wildfire up and down the street, more so because she was a white girl. Some of the residents even gathered outside the gate to have a look at her. Conversely, Calvin felt very proud for the attention that he'd got. He was "the man" of the moment, and he didn't care what anybody thought about him.

Most people around the vicinity respected Veron a great deal, so it was inevitable that the news would get to her at bird speed. But Calvin was so preoccupied with making money that he wasn't thinking about the consequences of his despicable action.

Sarah struggled from the outset to swallow the pellets, but ultimately she managed to consume half of a kilo. When she was done, Calvin gave her two tablets to take on her arrival in Canada, which would allow her to pass the pellets easily.

"Unlike the first occasion, Sarah was in high spirits when I took her to the airport later that afternoon. This time around there was no tears, and she definitely didn't act suspiciously.

"For me, there were no lumps in my throat. There was only one question in my mind, and that was "what if?", but I didn't fuss over the thought. Nonetheless, I requested half of the money upon the sale of the weed and wished her luck. She in turn accepted the deal and gave me her house phone number, and told me to ring her the following day, as we kissed and said goodbye."

Back at Queen Street, the news of Sarah's appearance reached Veron's ears, while Calvin was at the airport. She was upset because of the embarrassment it caused her. He, on the other hand, had next to no concern about his earlier actions or their after-effect. He was only doing what he could to make living more tolerable under the circumstances. Furthermore, he thought he had gotten away with it, as he always did.

That night, Veron went home very early, unexpectedly. Calvin was hanging out with his mates when she pulled up at the gate in a taxi.

"Calvin," she called, with a rather edgy sound to her tone, as soon as the taxi sped away.

"Wah yuh a sey, V?" he replied cheerfully, as if everything was all right.

"Me waan chat to yuh inside, right now if yuh nuh mind," she demanded.

Translation: "I want to chat to you inside, right now if you don't mind."

"Ver a guh kill him tonight," one of the guys suddenly whispered, loud enough for Veron to hear.

"When mi finish talking to him you can tek up dat deh responsibility deh, becah me nuh want nobody blood on my hands," Translation: "When I'm through talking to him you can take up that responsibility, because I don't want nobody blood on my hands." Veron interjected, before strolling off towards her house. Suddenly Calvin got up and followed behind, while his friends laughed and teased him.

As soon as Veron got inside the house she asked him about Sarah, and instantly he denied having an affair with her. "I only brought her on de base to swallow some weed," he told Veron. "You know how it guh, Ver," he pleaded, "I'm only trying to make some money."

Veron, on the other hand, like every other underachieved women on the island, understand the daily struggles and risks that most people, especially men, have to undertake to survive, so she didn't argue with him. Nonetheless, deep down he knew that she was still hurting, regardless of what had been said.

The following morning bright and early he got up, showered, and dressed, and then said goodbye to Veron and left for work.

On the whole, he knew that the boss was going to be very upset with him, because he'd allowed Sarah to stay at the Ramparts Inn, instead of the Grandiosa, but he wasn't to be blamed, after all he didn't have any control of the situation. Conversely, the boss had pulled him up before about his negligence. He'd got away with only a warning, so he thought he could talk his way out of trouble if it developed again, and so he continued to abuse the boss's trust. On top of that, the boss was continuing to hear rumours of him indulging in drug dealing at the hotel, something that was strictly against the hotel rules. From experience, Calvin knew that whatever is in the dark always comes out in the light, but he wasn't prepared for the repercussions thereafter.

Although he was feeling rather apprehensive, he thought everything would get back to normality, after a few days. He thought the damaged was already done; therefore the only thing he had to do was to get back to work and put on his best performance.

As he got close to the hotel, a funny feeling descended upon him. *It's only the after-effect of the past weeks,* he thought, and shrugged off the feeling, as he continued towards the gate.

On reaching the gate, the first thing he noticed was the light in the kitchen. The extractor was also running and he could smell bacon cooking.

"Daphne came in early to prepare breakfast, to show me up more like," he thought, and smile as he sauntered through the gate,

Valda was on her own at the front desk. He said his usual polite good morning to her, but she greeted him with a rather strange vibe, while pretending to be busy by shifting documents from one place to the other.

Maybe she's doing a double shift, or even a triple, Calvin thought as he made his way towards the kitchen to surprise Daphne.

As he sneaked into the kitchen, he was surprised to see an elderly man cooking breakfast. Abruptly his belly felt weak. Instantly he knew that he'd lost his job. Still, he introduced himself and tried to hide his feelings, as he set about helping the man get breakfast ready, but he wasn't there for long before the boss appeared in the kitchen.

The boss didn't greet him with that total brotherly love as he always did. Instead, he only said, "Calvin, meet me in my office, please," with a tone in his voice that said it all.

Immediately Calvin felt the blow deep within his soul, and his already weak stomach felt weaker with each step that he took towards the office. He was certain of what he was about to hear from his boss, and there were no ifs or buts about it.

He stepped into the office gingerly with a smile on his face and slowly closed the door behind him.

The boss was seated at his desk, reading a piece of paper, and he tried to keep a straight face when Calvin walked into the office, but eventually he ended up laughing. It was clear to see that he was struggling to make a decision. On the whole, the relationship the two men shared had been more like genuine brothers than worker and employer, but Calvin had destroyed it all, just as he did with most things he touched.

He knew deep down that his boss was feeling let down, because he had betrayed him big-time. He'd also convinced himself that he deserved what was coming anyway, but ultimately he tried to put on a sorrowful face, as if he was feeling remorse for his actions.

When he was seated, the boss put on his business face and gave him a sound lecturing about his conduct on the job since he'd started to indulge in the drug ring and the relationship he had with Sarah, which happened to be the nail in his coffin.

Ultimately the boss gave him an envelope with some cash, wished him well, and promised he would always be his friend.

Calvin thanked him and left the hotel feeling ashamed and very empty.

He didn't know how he was going to break the news to Veron, because he already had a mountain to climb to win back her respect and trust, let alone tell her he was out of a job. Silently, he wished he hadn't met Sarah, because although he had the time of his life with her on many occasions, she'd caused nothing but problems since the day she decided to return to the island.

That day, he stayed away from Queen Street until he knew Veron was at work, and when she returned from work he didn't tell her about his misfortune until the following morning.

That morning, he was still in bed when he should be getting ready for work.

Veron asked him if he wasn't going to work and he told her no, he'd got laid off because business was slow at the hotel.

She didn't prolong the conversation, but there was an instant change in the atmosphere.

Later that day he rang Sarah's house from a phone booth, and Caroline answered the call. They chatted for a while before Sarah came to the phone.

Sarah sounded tired on the other end of the line, and he asked her if everything had gone well, and she told him yes.

He was happy to know that she'd got past the immigration, and he told her to have a good rest and he would call her in a few days' time.

Two days later when he tried to call her again, the phone was dead. For a whole week he tried calling, but the phone remained dead. There was nothing left to do but wait for her call or a letter – which didn't come.

Eventually, he found himself at a dead end again, and like always, he didn't have any money in his bank account or any assets.

"I felt like a fool, and I was hurting badly at this point too, but I couldn't blame anyone, after all, I was my own enemy. I was destroying my own life and didn't even realise.

"I tried to appear happy amongst the guys on Queen Street, but deep down I was embarrass. The vibes around the house also got a bit intense, and I decided to spend some of my jobless days with Robert, my friend who worked at the Ramparts Inn, and two of our other friends, Dundee and Sixteen."

From the outset, Dundee and Sixteen were two of Robert's best friends. While Calvin was working at the Grandiosa he met them, after he went to the guesthouse to have a drink with Robert one day. Before long the four of them were best friends.

After losing his job, Calvin would sometimes meet Robert and the other guys at the guesthouse, and often times drink and smoke with Robert and some of his guests. Later, at the end of Robert's shift, they would head for a bar in town to continue their drinking spree. At times they would head for the Dead-End to party. Overall, in a big way, Robert, Dundee, and Sixteen enabled Calvin to stay clean, and although most of the time he had no money to buy drinks, they always dragged him along. In truth, they were some of the best friends he had ever had.

Back at Queen Street, his living situation had begun to head closer to a stalemate. He was now wholly dependent on Veron for almost everything again. She on the other hand was struggling more than ever to provide all the necessities in the house and sort out the bills, nonetheless, she did it without complaint, and she didn't let on to him that she was getting tired of the living conditions. As for him, secretly he'd begun to form his own jealous opinions, regarding Veron having an affair. As a result, he would have regular mood swings. Ultimately he'd also begun to feel insecure, because he was at her mercy.

At one point he contemplated moving out of her house, but he didn't have anywhere to go, on the other hand, he didn't want to give up what he had: because his friends and Veron were the closest people in his life. Although in some ways he'd felt trapped in an uncompromising situation, nonetheless he was determined to hold his head up and stay clean.

By mid April, Calvin's self-confidence had begun to fall at an alarming rate, and eventually he began to feel less of a man, because he was living in Veron's house and couldn't help make ends meet. His lack of confidence also had adverse effects on him psychologically.

Although Veron would sometimes show him some affection, at length they were like an old couple. They hardly ever talked and sex was almost off the menu.

Undetectable to Veron and his friends, he was living in a lonely world, the same world that he'd grown up in and the only world he'd ever truly known – the world he'd spent his life struggling to break free from, a world full of tears, unkindness, sadness, and corruption.

"I couldn't express my feelings to Veron. I didn't think she would understand. Well, it was a world where everybody had to carry their own burden, so it was pointless to tell someone how heavy your burden was, when that person already struggling to carry theirs. As for my friends, they were the last people I would want to express my feelings to.

"Through it all, I stood firm and resist temptation. More than ever I was determined to rid myself of corruption, because it was only making my life miserable. Above all, I felt guilty for the way I'd disrespect Veron, and I didn't want to let her down again, regardless of my needs, insecurity and lack of self-confidence. She was the first woman to touch my heart deeply, even if I didn't know whether because of the security I'd found with her or because I was truly in love with her. But whatever it was, my only intention was to prove to her that I was a responsible man and not a total loser. I was also prepared to do anything possible to warrant my position under her roof."

At the beginning of May he finally woke up and decided to go in search for work. For days he searched incessantly, but everywhere he went there was no vacancy. Oftentimes he would sulk and wallow in self-pity, but like many a times throughout his life, when it seemed like there was no way out of the hardships, a Good Samaritan always appeared to him. This time the Samaritan happened to be Knish, one of his neighbours, who worked on Gloucester Avenue (the Hip Strip) at the renowned Margaritaville.

When Knish told him about a cook's position at the restaurant, immediately he went in for the interview.

With his neighbour's recommendation and the one that he got from the Wyndham Rose Hall Hotel, they gave him the job and placed him on two weeks' trial.

The first evening he went to work with Knish, who was also working in the kitchen.

As they arrived at the restaurant, he was suddenly filled with apprehension, but Knish noticed his uneasiness and told him not to worry, because all the staff was good people. He also gave him a tour of the dining hall before they headed towards the kitchen.

On the whole, the outside of the building and the dining hall was in excellent condition, but Calvin was surprised to see the squalid condition inside and outside the kitchen, which was infested with rats and cockroaches.

The food that they had on the menu was very good. They were supplying a wide range of dishes, from Chinese and Italian cuisine to gourmet dishes. Although most of the dishes were new to him, after two days he could prepare almost all of them.

His quick learning of the menu and his calm demeanour amazed both the management and staff. Before the end of the first week, he was told that the job was his, but he didn't return to work the second week.

"Even though I was desperately in need of the job, to alleviate my present crisis, I couldn't cope with working in such a deplorable environment."

CHAPTER TWENTY-SIX

Breaking Away

It was now early June 1994, and Calvin's future was dangling uncertainly on a slender string. The daily struggles were prevailing, and the chances to deviate from it were relatively slim. At that point, he was getting very angry, waking up to the same situation each day. The only relief was to hang out on Queen Street with his crew, but even that was beginning to lose its flavour. Eventually, he felt trapped in a dark bubble, with no way of escaping. Then, finally, a glimmer of light appeared from out of the blue.

It was a warm afternoon, and he was hanging out with his mates on Queen Street, when Carrot turned up unexpectedly, accompanied by a strange young man.

Although Carrot knew Slowly, Davis, Chino, and Shippy well, he would only mingle with them at the hotel, so the guys were shocked when they saw him walking up the road.

"A yah suh de man dem deh hide out?" Carrot asked when he was in earshot. Translation: "Is this where you guys are hiding out?"

"Bloodclaat, a wah yuh a duh roun' yah suh, mon? A lost yuh lost, mon?" enquired Slowly in disbelief. Translation: "Bloodclaat, what are you doing around here, mon? Are you lost, mon?"

There was something familiar about the young man, but Calvin couldn't distinguish what it was until Carrot said, "Yow, Calvin, a mi blood dis from England yuh nuh. A Betty son, Steve. She and him deh 'bout. Me just drop by to tell de I, seen!" he concluded.

Wholeheartedly Calvin and Steve shook hands, but neither of them could find many words to say to the other. Suddenly the rest of guys began to quiz Steve about England's status in the World Cup.

The conversation about football continued for a while, until Carrot announced that he had to go.

Calvin told them thanks for dropping by and told Carrot to tell Betty that he would pop around some time. Minutes later Carrot and Steve said their goodbyes and left.

The news of Betty's presence on the island sent a lot of different signals to Calvin's brain. He'd spoken to her over the phone a few times, after she sent him the money to pay the corrupt policemen, and every now and again they exchanged letters, but the last time he'd seen her was in late 1992. So much had changed since then, but his lifestyle was almost the same. Overall, he had been to hell and back many times, and he was now living with a woman. Suddenly, the embarrassing feeling he'd felt the last time he saw her returned in a flash. One of the guys noticed the vacant look in his eyes and announced it within the crew. (It was fun for everybody within the crew to look out for the least chance to banter their one another.) That warm afternoon was no exception. They laid into Calvin until he made an excuse to leave.

He went inside Veron's house and sat down, while warm sweat trickled down his face. Nervously he took the flannel from his pocket and wiped it away. By then he was in a state of shock and confusion. It was a familiar feeling, but he figured the outcome was more likely to turn out well, if he played his cards right. On the other hand, he didn't want to hurt Veron's feelings anymore, than he already had, even though he wasn't sure how much he meant to her, because she'd kept her feelings hidden. Still, although he was going through a bad patch, the feelings he had for her remained strong. For all that, he was confident that he could reignite the love that Betty had once held for him; after all, true love never dies.

A week previously, he was seriously thinking about joining an agency to get another job. The agency in question was situated close to Betty's house, on Cottage Road. *"I could kill two birds with the same stone,"* he suddenly thought, as he weighed up the situation.

That night, when Veron returned home from work, she was surprised to found him wide awake in bed, watching television.

He didn't try to hide the obvious, remote look that was evident in his eyes. Veron noticed it too, but she didn't comment about it.

A conversation ensued, more than usual, but he didn't divulge the news of Betty's presence on the island. However, during the course of the conversation, he told Veron that he was serious about signing up with the agency. She was very pleased to know that he was finally going to get off his black backside and find a job. On the whole, she didn't need to tell him how hard things were, because hardships were the order of the day. Overall, it was hard getting by with the little contribution he made when he was working, let alone doing it single-handedly, now that he wasn't working.

The following day, he got dressed and told Veron that he was going to signed up with the agency, but instead of going to the agency, he went straight to Betty's house.

Betty's mum greeted him when he knocked on the door, giving him a warm welcome as before, but deep down he knew that it wasn't real.

Eventually Betty came to the door and greeted him happily, and instantly they both realised that nothing had changed between them, after all that time, as they looked each other over and smiled without saying anything.

As for Betty, she experienced the same magnitude of affection when he looked into her eyes and smiled. For him, it was the same Betty. The same kind, honest, and loving look was still evident in her eyes.

Without uttering a single word, Betty moved closer to hug and kiss him, and instantly the fire of love was rekindled between them.

There weren't enough words to express the passion that flowed between their lips. Only they knew what was going on deep within their souls. There was so much that they wanted to say to each other, but it wasn't convenient.

When they released each other, he stood looking at Betty; suddenly struck by how mistaken he'd been when he walked out on her. He knew that his life would have probably been better if he'd humbled himself with her. Immediately, he felt like a fool and looked away, shame faced.

"What's the matter?" Betty enquired, as the palpable sign of distress appeared on his face.

"Nothing," he lied. "Guess what?" he asked instantly, to change the subject. "I have to go and sign up wid an agency to get a job."

"That's good," Betty replied happily.

"I haven't got the hundred dollars though," he told her in embarrassment and hung his head.

As always, Betty didn't let him down. Instantly she went inside the house, returned with the hundred dollars, and handed it to him. Then she wished him luck and told him to visit her soon.

Steve and Carrot walked through the gate as Calvin was leaving. He chatted with them for a few moments, and an instant bond was formed between him and Steve. He promised to visit soon and continued towards the agency, feeling better than he had in months.

At the agency, he was guaranteed an interview for a job within the first two weeks of signing up. It was good news, and he felt like his lucky days were about to reappear. He couldn't wait to tell Veron about his good fortune either, but he told her only half the story when he returned to Queen Street. The reconnection he'd made with Betty was never divulged.

He thought it was best to keep Betty's presence a secret, but nobody could miss the astonishing changes in his attitude. Veron knew something had happened, but she couldn't distinguish whether it was to do with the agency or another woman. The guys also noticed the changes in him, but they too could not discern the reasons behind it. They eventually came to their own vague conclusion that Veron was giving him more sex than she normally did.

Later that same evening, Calvin jumped on his pushbike after Veron went to work, and within minutes he was at Betty's house.

On his arrival, he found Betty serving drinks behind her mother's rum bar. She was delighted to see him. She told him that Steve and Carrot were out partying, and he made himself comfortable at the bar with the other punters. She served him a drink of rum, and he lingered in the bar until all the punters went.

After Betty locked the door, they sat in the bar and decided to catch up on what happened over the past year or so. Betty filled him in on the experiences that she'd had before returning to England. As for him, he was embarrassed about the riotous life that he'd lived from childhood, and the past year and a half was no exception. If anything, his life was getting worse since the day he decided to move out of the room at Cottage Road.

"I was too embarrassed to tell Betty the whole truth, because at that point, the only dignity I had left was to lie and paint a false picture about my life. On the contrary, Betty already knew that I wasn't being upfront with her, but the love that she had for me blinded her better judgement, and she willingly accepted whatever I told her. On the other hand, we didn't discuss any relationship issues. From the outset we never did. The connection that we had was too unique. We could read each other's minds, so the spoken words were of less significance."

Conversely, when Calvin told Betty that he was living with another woman, she pretended to be okay with it, but he knew instantly that she was hurting. Suddenly, she informed him that she was going to be on the island for six months, and straight away he knew that there was going to be some dramatic changes in his life.

That night, he went home before Veron returned from work. The guys were hanging out in front, and they wanted to know where he'd been. He told them that he was at Mount Salem.

Later when Veron came home from work, he went into the house with her. At that point, Delroy suggested to them it was about time they made a baby. This was followed by an echo of laughter from the rest of guys.

As soon as he got into the house, he turned on the television, wanting to avoid too much conversation with Veron, but she was in a good mood, and she began to tell him about her day at work. She'd also brought home cornmeal (polenta) rum pudding, for the both of them, which she bought at the Pelican Grill Restaurant, on the Hip Strip. It was a pudding that the both of them love and they always treated each other with a slice of it occasionally. After some time she noticed Calvin's evasive attitude and asked him what was the matter, but he didn't answer, because he was deep in thought.

"It's time to make or break," he thought, as he calculated how he was going to deal with the complicated situation that he found himself in. On the whole, he knew living with Veron and visiting Betty on a regular basis was going to be a hard task for him. Nonetheless, he was prepared to scheme his way through it by any means necessary. On the other hand, he didn't want to hurt Veron, nor was he prepared to cut Betty out of his life. Both

women were playing a significant role in his life, and he wanted to keep it that way. Finally, he decided to tell Veron half the truth about Betty.

It was hard to tell what feedback you would get from Veron, because at times she was very outspoken and open, yet she was also a "keep it all to myself" type of person. Often she would play the fool to gain knowledge, and she was good at concealing her feelings.

When Calvin told her Betty was back, she kept her response neutral, and he couldn't tell if she was happy or otherwise. Conversely, in the beginning of their relationship, he hadn't told Veron that his relationship with Betty was over, and she never posed the question to him. Ultimately, it was up to him, and he knew that if he handles the situation right, he could come out smelling of roses.

By this the World Cup had started, and Calvin invited Steve at Queen Street to watch one of the matches in his friend's house. Without thinking about Veron's reaction, he bluntly told her that Betty's son was coming around to watch the match; to his delight, she didn't say a word.

When Steve turned up at the yard, she was at home, but she was complaining about not feeling well from the previous day, thus she'd decided to stay in bed.

Calvin decided to cooked ackee and saltfish with dumplings in his mates' house, and when the lunch was ready, he brought some over to Veron and then returned to his mates.

For the rest of the afternoon he stayed in his mates' house, watching the football while bonding with Steve. From that day onwards he and Steve became the best of friends, and they met regularly until Steve returned to England, leaving his mum behind in Jamaica.

*

One Friday morning in early July, the agency contacted Calvin, informing him that there was a possible vacancy at The Native Restaurant. He was very excited when he got the news, and before water could warm, he was on his way to the restaurant.

The restaurant was located about five minutes' walk from the Grandiosa hotel and three minutes' drive from Mobay town.

It was set at a prime location, flanked by the Montego Bay hotel and a small guesthouse, overlooking the expanse of the blue sea below.

On the opposite side of the main road an abundance of big, green trees towered from the hillside.

Inscribed on a piece of board above the front door was the motto of the restaurant, "Before good food waste mek yuh belly burst."

On entering through the front door, there was a small open dining area on the inside, which extended out onto the terrace and around the rectangle swimming pool. There was also a bamboo bar, built at one corner beside the swimming pool.

From the moment you entered through the front door, you were greeted with the most amazing view of the blue sea, below the crest of the hillside. You could see the cruise ships sailing by and watch them dock at the quayside. Towards the left you could also see part of Mobay City. Further out the green mountains stretched from Bogue Hill (one of the rural areas outside of the city) and it continues until it joins with the ridge of the sea. To the right, the sea span for many miles, until it appears as if it touches the hem of the sky.

In the evenings, before sunset, it was the most exquisite sight. For a long time, a sheet of the bright, golden sun would shine across the sea directly onto the swimming pool and the restaurant. Frequently tourists converged around the pool to take photographs in the splendour of the golden sunshine.

The Native Restaurant was owned and operated by Boris Riley and his two sisters. At the time they also had another restaurant, where the two sisters mainly worked, but Boris managed The Native.

That Friday, when Calvin went in for the interview, Boris asked him if it was possible to start working straight away.

Calvin was more than happy to say yes, because he'd been waiting for another chance for far too long. In the end, Boris gave him a chef's jacket and ushered him towards the small kitchen.

There were two other cooks working there at the time, but business was a bit slow.

They had a contract to deliver a number of lunches on one of the local beaches each weekday, but only a few guests came in for lunch most days.

It was much busier at night, and the atmosphere was much better. As for the menu, it was easier than Calvin had anticipated.

All the staff was courteous and respectful, and before the day ended, he'd been accepted as part of the team.

Boris summoned him into the office before he left that night. Initially, Calvin felt a bit apprehensive, but based on his initial performance, he was confident that he'd got the job, because he hadn't put a foot wrong that day.

He knocked on the office door, and Boris, who was on the computer playing solitaire, swivelled around in his chair, smiled broadly, and beckoned him in.

Calvin stood in the small office, waiting eagerly to hear the good news, when Boris exclaimed, "Bwoy," and then paused. Still smiling, he leaned back in the chair, lifted his baseball cap from his head, and scratched his slightly grey hair vigorously. Then he said, "You gave me a big surprise today, in fact, not just me, but all the staff too. I've been looking for a cook like you for a long time. You possess all the qualities that we are looking for in our staff, but I only hope that the first impression will last." His smile stretched from ear to ear.

Calvin was dumbfounded. He wasn't expecting so much praise. It had been a while since anybody commended him, and the little self-belief he'd possessed had long ago melted away. He was only moving with the flow at that point in his life in order to survive.

As he was searching for words, Boris spoke again, and this time the smile was partly wiped from his face. "Normally, we would place all new workers on two weeks' trial, but the job is yours, if you are interested," he announced.

Calvin was delighted! He couldn't believe how the day had finally turned out for him. *"Things are really changing in my life,"* he thought.

"Wah yuh a tink 'bout?" Boris suddenly asked, bringing Calvin back to the present.

"Yah, mon," Calvin replied nervously. "I mean to say tank you for de job. I won't let you down. I promise," he assured Boris, extending his hand.

"Good man." Boris got up and shook his star cook's hand. "Mek sure to be here bright and early in the morning now," he warned, as he ushered Calvin through the door.

"No problem, I will be here," Calvin promised, as he headed towards the front door.

Outside, the rest of the night staff was waiting for him.

"Most nights we usually walk together as a family after work, and then get our taxis to go to our separate destination," Speedy, one of the waiters, told Calvin as they set off down the road.

It was less than fifteen minutes' walk downhill from the restaurant into town, and Calvin couldn't wait to get home and tell Veron about his good fortune. *"Now she'll see that I'm not just a waste of space,"* he thought as he walked along with his newfound co-workers.

It was less than ten minutes' walk to Queen Street from downtown, but he took a taxi and went straight to Betty's house, to tell her the good news. She was genuinely happy for him, and he spent some time with her before he went home to Veron.

Veron was just as pleased to hear the good news, but getting the job didn't solve his problems; it only restores some of his self-confidence.

CHAPTER TWENTY-SEVEN

ACTIONS SPEAK LOUDER THAN WORDS

Calvin reported to work bright and early the next morning as promised. Another cook turned up minutes later, and together they prepared lunch.

After lunch was served, Calvin stayed on and helped cook dinner, although it was very slow that night.

When dinner was completed, the cook who worked on the night shift approached Calvin covertly, wanting to know if he could confide in him. Calvin told him yes, it wasn't a problem.

"Me have somewhere to go tomorrow evening," the cook began, "but I can't get the time off work. De only ting I can do is to call in sick, suh could you cover for me?"

"No problem at all, blood," Calvin, replied. "One day I might need you to do de same ting for me too."

"It's normally slow on a Sunday anyway," the cook reassured him, "so yuh nuh have nothing to worry about."

Unbeknownst to the cook, it was exactly the chance that Calvin wanted, to show off his own abilities.

That Sunday, lunch was unusually busy, and before three o'clock the other cook announced that he had to go.

Calvin suspected that he knew about the other cook's plan, or maybe they both had the same plan, but whatever the circumstances were, he wasn't bothered.

At half past three Boris walked into the kitchen, with a gloomy expression on his face. The young lady working at the salad station asked why he looked so glum. Without responding, he strolled toward the range, where Calvin was busy preparing the dinner, and picked up a piece of carrot and bit into it before walking toward the back door. Suddenly he stopped and turned around. "There's a big problem, guys," he announced, and both Calvin and the young lady stopped abruptly and looked towards him.

"The other cook just rang and told me that he can't come in this evening," Boris explained, directing his attention to Calvin.

"How can he do that?" the young lady asked.

"So is dat de reason why you look so sad, boss?" Calvin put in.

"De man know say yuh just start work, suh me can't understand how him just let me down like that," Boris wailed.

"Nuh watch nutten (nothing), boss," Calvin announced confidently. "I can run de show wid my eyes shut."

By now, a little group had gathered in the kitchen. Speedy, the eldest waiter, boldly came forward and said, "I've been watching how Calvin flex (move) in de kitchen, boss, an' me know him can run de show. Just give him a chance to prove himself."

O'Brien, another waiter, interjected and endorsed Speedy's statement.

For a tense moment, everybody went quiet. The only sounds were coming from the dishwasher, the extractor, and the fridge.

"All right, then," declared Boris, feeling relief. "Let's get the show on the road as usual, guys. Calvin, I'm depending on you. Don't let the waiters down, because they have strong faith in you." And he left the kitchen.

Calvin didn't have any doubts, because his confidence was back on a high, and he wanted to prove to every single one of them that he was "the man".

Unexpectedly, a bus full of tourists turned up for dinner that night, as well as other guests from nearby hotels and guesthouses.

The waiters got very excited when they saw all the guests, because they knew big tips were involved. Still, a few of them were beginning to have second thoughts about the production in the kitchen. Speedy, still trusting in Calvin, told them that everything was going to be all right.

Boris too was excited, because it has been a long time since they had a full dining hall. While everybody was busy running around like headless chickens, Calvin was calmly preparing more vegetables and stocking up the range with the essentials. During the process, Boris sauntered into the kitchen and stood at the door with a big smile covering his face. Calvin pretended not to notice his boss. Calmly he was preparing himself for the rush, when Boris enquired, "Yuh ready fe de show yet, Chef?"

"I'm ready like Freddy," he replied smoothly, without looking up from what he was doing.

"That's exactly what I like to hear," Boris declared, with a tone in his voice that said he had full confidence in his new cook, before he retreated toward the dining hall.

That night, Calvin did not disappoint. The seventy-odd guests were fed on time, and there were no complaints.

As the evening came to a close, each staff member came up and congratulated him. They all agreed that it was the first time they'd beheld someone moving with so much speed and grace on a range. As a result they'd nicknamed him "Chino man".

Over the months that followed, he lived up to his initial performance and served up some amazing dishes.

*

Near the end of July or the beginning of August, Veron got pregnant. It was the best thing to ever happen to them, and they were both very happy – she the more so, because she'd almost given up hopes of having a child. On the contrary, Calvin was happy, because he had proven to her that he could get her pregnant. All his mates around the vicinity were happy for him too, because most of them had a child or two already. In the past, they used to laugh at him and say he couldn't manage Veron, because he couldn't get her pregnant, but when it was revealed to them that she was pregnant, he had the last laugh.

With his head held high, he began to ride on cloud nine with pride. It was also a pivotal moment in his life, and he wanted above all to keep it that way. At that time in his life, the whole meaning of living seemed to have catapulted into a totally different order, and suddenly he was full of joy, pride, achievement, and love. It was the kind of feeling that impelled him to change his lifestyle totally.

Although he was now working, the cost of living was still hard, and like all poor people on the island, he and Veron were struggling to make ends meet. As a result, he eventually decided that he wanted more in his life, much more than the little that was going on around him. Although he had few options, crime was the last thing on his mind. Above all, he was going to be a father, and he wanted to give his child a good start, better than what he'd got, so he was ready to do what was right in order to achieve more.

It was one of his dreams to travel outside Jamaica. He saw it as a life-changing move. His Uncle Roland and many others had done it before, and their lives were completely changed.

He'd got his passport on a whim the previous year. He'd only done it because a few of the guys had theirs. Unlike them, he couldn't foresee the possibility of travelling outside Jamaica. He thought it was hopeless, and he'd almost given up all hope, but one day, while Betty was telling him a story about England, he'd jokingly asked her if she could take him there.

Abruptly she'd told him yes, he could accompany her back. At first he thought she was joking, but when she started to explain to him what was required to travel to England, he suddenly realised that she was dead serious. He got very excited, and all sorts of things started to go through his mind. Before, the possibility of going to England had never entered his mind.

As always, Betty was willing and ready to do whatever she could to support him. He was an essential part of her life, more than he could comprehend, and she would've given the world to him if she could.

"Have you got a passport?" she asked, knocking away the big smile that lingered on his face.

"Yeah, I've got a passport," he replied half-heartedly.

"Then you have nothing to worry about. I'll give you half the money if you can come up with the other half, she concluded.

He was taken aback. He couldn't believe what he was hearing. It felt as if his life was really changing for the better. One of his women was pregnant, and the other was offering him a chance to turn his dreams into reality. How much better could things get?

Still, he went away with little thought of the prospect of travelling to England. He thought it was way out of his league, but Betty thought differently. For her, it was the chance to restart her life all over again with the man that she loved. As a result, she started the ball rolling without his knowledge.

The next time he visited her, she told him that she already done her research and made the necessary arrangements for him to go and see a travel agent. It was the best news he'd heard in all his life, and he didn't know how to react, whether to jump for joy in front of Betty or to run around and tell everybody that he was going to England. In the end he decided to keep the good news from Veron and his friends. On the whole, he'd made a fool of himself many times before, and he was determined to start making amends.

A few days later, he and Betty went to see one of her cousins, who ran a travel agency downtown Mobay.

Initially, he thought the process of going to England was going to take a long time, but he was overwhelmed when the travel agent told him that all he needed was a job letter from his present employer, a recommendation from his previous employer, his passport, a plane ticket, and an invitation letter from a sponsor in England.

Betty didn't have a job in England, so she was unable to invite him into the country. As a result, she asked her son, Steve, to be Calvin's sponsor. Steve didn't hesitate. In less than two weeks he'd sent all the relevant documentation to his mother.

Later that day, after they left the travel agency, Calvin and Betty went shopping in town, and during the shopping spree he mentioned Veron on more than one occasion. Betty wasn't pleased with some of his comments. If he'd been watching, he would've noticed the hurt that he was inflicting on her. Also, if the comments had been critical, it wouldn't have been so bad, but they were actual compliments. To add insult to injury, he convinced Betty to purchase a kerosene lamp for him, which he'd long ago promised to Veron. Betty was even more furious then, but she didn't let on to him how she felt. On the other hand, he saw none of the damage he was causing.

That same afternoon he went to Queen Street on a high. He was over excited on the whole, so that he began to tell his friends that he was planning on going to England, but they were all happy for him.

When he told Veron, she didn't show any emotion. As a result, he couldn't tell if she was happy or not. Still, from the moment he told her that he was interested in the prospect of going to England with Betty, the vibes got somewhat tense between them. He knew that she was hurting, but it was the chance of a lifetime, and he wouldn't have given it up for any reason.

He also tried to reassure her that she had nothing to worry about, but because of the incessant mask that she was wearing over her emotions, he couldn't tell whether he was getting across to her.

Back at the restaurant, his relationships with his employer and fellow co-workers continued to grow, but he kept his plans of going to England a secret.

In early October, Calvin met Robert down town, and out of the blue Robert told him that Sarah had returned to the island, accompanied by her mother and brother, and they were staying at the Ramparts Inn. As for him, he'd long given up on the prospect of getting any money from her, but the sudden news shocked him and stirred up buried anger, which eventually grown into fury. 'After all this time,' he thought to himself, he was finally going to get his money. However, it was a delicate situation, for him to handle. After all, she was a guest at Robert's workplace. In fact, she was a tourist, and she had the law on her side, if she wished to cause any trouble for him. Nonetheless, he decided to confront her about his money once and for all.

On his arrival at the guesthouse he met Robert, who nervously went and told Sarah that Calvin was here.

A few minutes later she appeared with a grin on her face, but he didn't smile. Instead, he got straight to the point and asked her for his share of the money.

She told him that Immigration at the airport, in Canada, suspected her and forced her to pass out the weed. He laughed scornfully and asked her what happened next. "They took half of the weed, and I smoked the rest," Sarah told him, avoiding eye contact. At the same time, Robert was at the bar; pretending to be busy, while listening to the conversation. Calvin glanced at him and realised that his mate was petrified.

Robert caught Calvin's eye in the process and shook his head, Calvin knew instantly that he was begging him to let it go.

"I looked at the girl I had once fallen head over heels for, and although memories of some of the good times we had were still vivid, I felt nothing for her at that point. Eventually I told her that she was a thief, and one day she would get caught, and walked away, and I never look back.

"Years later I learnt that Sarah was in prison in Canada, doing time for a robbery."

Back at Queen Street, one day, while he and Veron were washing their clothes together behind the house, he foolishly decided to discuss Betty with her, telling her that Betty wanted him to have sex with her.

Veron looked at him with a vacant expression and laughed. It was the kind of laugh that had a lot of logic. He knew instantly that he had stepped on forbidden grounds, so he decided to keep quiet and wait for the fallout. He certainly didn't have to wait long, because Veron suddenly stopped laughing and said to him, "If de woman ha guh cyar yuh guh ha England, an' she want a lili fuck, wah yuh nuh want to give it to her? Yuh nuh ha fi let me know. Wah mi nuh know wuon hurt me."

Translation: "If the woman's going to take you to England, and she wants to have sex with you, why don't you want to do it? You don't have to let me know. What I don't know won't hurt me."

He couldn't believe his ears. He sat where he was, looking at Veron in disbelief. He was studying her for any visible signs that could give him a little more insight on what was really going on inside her brain. He looked for signs in her eyes, but she wouldn't look into his.

He knew that she was very smart; therefore he didn't know how to respond to what she had said. As a result he decided to keep quiet instead. However, later he was to find out that his quietness had told her that he was having sex with Betty already. In fact, he didn't know that Veron was only feeding him with bait, and he took that bait like a hungry fish, and Veron had caught him hook, line, and sinker.

After the conversation, he thought everything was okay, but Veron was secretly planning to give him what was good for him.

A week later, he was shocked to see Veron's little sister Judith, who was living at Trelawney, turn up at the house with her luggage. Veron told him that Judith was going to live with them so she could attend college in Mobay.

He didn't have a problem with that, moreover, even if he did had a problem; he couldn't say anything about it, because it wasn't his house in the first place.

Everything went well for the first week. Even though the house was only a studio flat, an additional person didn't matter, because she was family, but it didn't take long before things changed.

One evening he was sitting at the back of the house, chatting with Veron, when she suddenly changed the subject and told him that he couldn't reside at her house anymore, because it was dishonourable for her and him to be sleeping underneath the same roof with her little sister.

He couldn't believe what he was hearing. Veron had taken him completely by surprise, and at that very moment he wondered if her initial aim was to use her sister to squeeze him out of her house.

He wanted to go bananas, but he couldn't, because he knew that he was to be blamed for his own downfall. He also knew that he had failed to play the game right, allowing Veron to outsmart him.

Initially, he didn't have anywhere to lay his head, because he wasn't prepared for the unexpected, and he was also too embarrassed to take up residence at his friends' house, given the fact that they were living in the same yard.

That first night he had to sleep on a lounge chair behind Veron's flat. He didn't want her to know that he had to sleep behind her house, but she knew he was there.

The following morning, before he got the chance to go away, Veron gave him a surprise visit.

He was very embarrassed when she found him sleeping on top of the lounge chair, behind her house, and she on the other hand didn't show any remorse. She was cold as ice towards him. It seemed like she didn't have any feelings left for him at all. He was now like a little stray dog to her.

To begin with, she used her foot to nudge him in his side, and when he woke up, he was surprised and ashamed to see her standing over him.

"A deh suh yuh sleep last night?" she'd asked, but the tone of her voice didn't suggest that she cared.

"What do you expect?" he replied, as he tucked his arms between his legs to keep them warm.

"Mi nuh know. Yuh spread yuh bed hard suh yuh have to lay dung in ha it hard," she replied irately.

Translation: "I don't know. You spread your bed hard so you have to lie down in it hard."

Calvin couldn't believe how cold she was towards him. But even now, he couldn't argue with her, even though he was fuming. On the whole, his love was still strong for her, more than he wanted to admit to himself, but the one you loved didn't always feel the same way about you. And when you hurt someone who loved you that love could turn out to be the deepest hate.

By this Calvin was due to depart to England in six weeks, so he didn't have to go in search of a permanent base. When he told Betty about his mishap, immediately she started to think of ways to help him find a temporary abode. Fortunately for him, Steve's friend Gary had just migrated to America, and Betty, who knew Gary's mum well, decided to ask her to allow Calvin to stay in her son's room for six weeks.

Gary's house was situated on Tate Street, close to where Betty was living. His mother, two sisters, and two brothers occupied the main house, but his room was conveniently separate at the back.

During Calvin's stay at the house, he spoke with Gary's sister Geraldine on a regular basis and later found out that she too was planning to migrate to England. That revelation brought them closer, and they automatically became friends on that basis.

They were both head over heels with the prospect of travelling outside Jamaica, where they thought they could find a better way of living, which also meant to formulate stability for their children, their relatives, and themselves. Most times when they spoke, the conversation was about going to England. The bliss that they felt was exclusively for what travelling to England entailed, in view of a step further out of suffering. In actual fact, every man and woman on the island dreamt of going overseas one day, whether to England, Canada, or the United States of America. Geraldine's and Calvin's time was imminent, but neither of them knew what to expect in England.

CHAPTER TWENTY-EIGHT

Flying without Wings

During the six weeks leading up to Calvin's departure, he had been to hell and back to obtain his half of the money for his plane ticket. Betty on the other hand stuck to her initial promise and paid half the money, and all seemed to be going well, until it was his turn to fulfil his part of the bargain.

The cost of the ticket was only $18,000 Jamaican, equivalent to £225 pounds at the time, but for someone like him to acquire half of that money; it was comparable to digging a well with a penknife. However, he didn't care what he had to do to get the money for the ticket, because the opportunity was worth it, and he wasn't going to let it go without a fight.

He decided to pay his half in three instalments, and he'd managed to come up with the first down payment, but instead of sticking to his initial plans, he headed straight to the gambling house that Friday night with the money, hoping that he could make a bonus on it, but before water could warm it was almost gone.

That night, he left the gambling house late with enough money in his pocket to take him back to work the following day, a bitter taste in his mouth, and a sick feeling in his stomach.

"At that point, I wished I could turn back the clock of my life, because my world seemed to have turned upside down. On the whole, the worst part of my dilemma was the promise I'd made to Veron to give her some money, and I'd also promised Betty to bring the down payment to her.

"Ultimately, because of my own stupidity, I couldn't face either Veron, or Betty, who was waiting up for me all night."Eventually, he had to go into one of his stunt moves (pretending something bad had happened to him, before telling the boldest lies to win someone's compassion).

When he arrived at Tate Street that night he was in a mess, and as he lay wide awake in bed, all kind of things were running through his mind, and he didn't know what to do with himself, because his brain was totally immobilised.

He prayed, but he was convinced that God wasn't going to listen to him, because it was an irresponsible thing that he had done.

Finally, there was only one indisputable thing left for him to do, and that was to lament until he was exhausted, before he eventually fell into an uncomfortable sleep.

The following afternoon he woke up at three o'clock feeling dreary, when he should have been starting his shift at the restaurant.

He lay on his back in bed staring at the ceiling, not knowing what to do. Twenty minutes or so later, he heard a knocking on the door that he could swear he'd heard earlier in the day.

When he opened the door, he saw Betty standing outside with a cup of mint tea in her hand.

"I couldn't believe my eyes, and instantly I wondered if Betty was telepathic, because she always seemed to turn up when I needed her most."

"What happened to you last night?" Betty enquired angrily, as soon as Calvin opened the door. "Why you kept me waiting up all night, and where is the money that you was suppose to bring to me for the ticket?"

When she mentioned the money, if he could've faded away, he certainly would have. However, without answering her questions, he went back in bed and put a distressed look on his face, which would've melted the toughest of hearts. At last, his poignant expression seemed to break the ice.

"What's the matter with you, Calvin?" Betty asked sympathetically.

"I got robbed last night," he replied, his voice heavy with pain. In fact, he had never been robbed in his life. Nevertheless, he was glad the first lie hit the spot, because Betty then seemed to believe every other lie that he told her thereafter.

After he repeatedly filled her head with his polluted stories, his energy returned to him in a flash, but he couldn't let Betty notice it. As a result, he lay where he was and continued to pretend as if his time on earth was coming to an end.

"Have you got any money left for travelling expenses?" Betty asked.

"No. Everything is gone," he replied sadly, and without any delay, Betty headed back to her house to get some money for him.

While she was gone, he went to have a shower, and before long she returned with the money, but his ordeal did not stop there. He had to face Veron, which was going to be more serious.

When he got to Veron's flat she wasn't there, which gave him ample time to regain some money.

That evening he got to work extremely late. He knew he would have to come up with a good story to justify his tardiness and another to get some money from his boss, but he didn't know exactly what he would do or say.

When he arrived at work, he assumed the same distressed look as he had for Betty earlier.

Jerry, one of his close friends who worked there as a waiter, was speaking to Boris in the dining hall when he turned up for work, and as soon as Boris saw him, the penny dropped.

"Blouse and skirt," exclaimed Boris, "ha wah duh yuh, man? How come yuh look suh sad? Ha dead yuh baby dead?" Translation: "What's the matter with you, man? How come you look so sad? Is the baby dead?"

"It worse dan dat, boss," Calvin replied wearily.

"How yuh mean it worse dan dat?" Boris asked. "Come on. Tell mi wahpen (what happened) to yuh."

Boris's invitation was vital to Calvin's plans, so he used it as an opening to tell his stories.

"Veron got sick," he lied, "and I spent all the money I had on the doctor, but I couldn't afford to purchase the medicine that she needed."

Boris smiled. He knew Calvin was pulling a fast one on him, but he didn't mind. After all, Calvin was his best cook, and he wanted him in tip-top shape to produce the finest food that night (it was Saturday, one of the busiest days of the week). Calvin didn't care. He was prepared to lie his way to hell and back or do whatever it took to get some money.

"Nuh worry yuhself 'bout nutten, Chino," Boris told him. "Just put yourself together and gwaan guh run the show. Come check me later, and I'll sort out something for you, cool?" Translation: "Don't worry yourself about nothing, just put yourself together and go and run the show."

Calvin told him thanks, and they went their separate ways.

Although Jerry was busy polishing the cutlery to lay the tables for dinner, Calvin knew he was listening to the conversation. After Boris walked away, Jerry looked at Calvin, laughed and said, "Chino, yuh dangerous yuh nuh. How yuh manage to pull off dat deh one pan de boss suh fast?" Translation: "Chino, you are dangerous you know. How you manage to pull off that one on the boss so fast?"

"De expression on yuh face, have a lot to do wid wah yuh duh or seh, blood," Calvin replied with a laugh.

Translation: "The expression on your face has a lot to do with what you do or say."

"Bwoy, mi have to try dat deh one deh pan de boss one ha dem day yah," Jerry confessed.

Translation: "Boy, I have to try that one on the boss one of these days."

"Yuh done know how it guh, blood. Man ha fe survive by all means necessary," Calvin reassured Jerry as they walked into the kitchen.

Boris was one of those humble, decent black men, and most of the staff was convinced that he and Calvin were related, mainly because they shared the same surname and the relationship that they had. They usually treated each other with respect, and Calvin never stole from him. At times they would also sit down and have a drink and chat as friends or brothers would.

Boris liked to go fishing, and whenever he caught any fish, he would only ask Calvin to cook it for him. Likewise, whenever he wanted something to eat, he would tell Calvin to fix him up, and Calvin would normally choose a meal for him.

One day, while Calvin and the other cooks were preparing for a function, Boris went into the kitchen and told him that he wished to speak to him outside. Calvin wondered what this could be about. Nonetheless, when he got outside, Boris was sitting on a chair smoking a cigarette, and he handed one to him, which Calvin accepted.

"Chino," said Boris, "I want you to do me a big favour." Calvin didn't reply but only puffed on the fag while waiting on Boris to continue. "Yuh see, when the other cooks dem a marinate meat or cooking anything," Boris continued, "I want you to taste the food and add to it and rub your hands in the meat when dem a marinate it."

Calvin was a bit taken aback, and he asked his boss why he wanted him to do those things. Boris laughed and told him that he had flavour in the tips of his fingers, and so he should flavour the other cooks' food when they were preparing them.

Calvin laughed at the time, but later in life he realised how right Boris was.

It was quite the opposite where Boris's eldest sister was concerned. On the whole, she was a nice lady, but very domineering, always trying to change the way things were done at the restaurant whenever she appeared, which made most of the staff nervous. Calvin, though, wasn't scared of her, and he usually ignored her sometime and continued to do things his usual way. As a result, his rebelliousness and her overbearing attitude often clashed, creating a bad vibe between them. Nonetheless, he always showed her love and respect.

By contrast, the younger sister seemed to have an unreadable character, and Calvin couldn't discern her motives. Regardless, they always showed each other love and respect.

That evening, after Calvin lied to his boss, he went into the kitchen and gave them one of his best performances, and at the end of the shift Boris called him to the office and gave him a thousand dollars. The waiters also gave him some of their tips, and eventually he left the restaurant with nearly two thousand dollars. Instead of going home, however, he headed straight to the gambling house, determined to win back some of the money that he'd lost the previous night. He was definitely on a lucky streak that day, because he ended up winning more than he had lost the night before. But history came home to roost a few weeks later, when he was due to pay the last two thousand dollars on the ticket. Fortunately, he had managed to secure the needed sum. Unfortunately, it was burning a hole in his pocket. He decided to try his luck at gambling again, but before water could warm he lost it all.

After losing the two thousand dollars in a Pitta Pat game, he went home and lamented and prayed as he never had before, and he thought his world was coming to an untimely end. He all but convinced himself that somebody had put a spell of obeah on him.

"There was a big poster of an airplane on the wall inside the bedroom. All night long I looked at the poster and prayed and cried, and eventually it felt like the whole world was coming down on my shoulders, because all my life I'd been waiting for a chance to finally make my dreams into reality, and because of gambling I was letting it slip through my fingers. I also thought of a number of places where I could have gone to steal the money, but I was afraid of getting caught, and the mere thought of letting down Veron and Betty, as well as my boss, was enough to discourage me. Eventually, I cried myself to sleep in the early hours of the morning."

A few hours later he was wide awake, and this time he was filled with determination. But he still didn't know where he was going to get the money. Ultimately, he believed God had directed him to his grandparents' house.

At the time, his relationship with them was both bitter and sweet. He was leading the life he had chosen, but his grandparents were not happy with his way of living. Regardless, they always welcomed him into their home.

That day when he arrived at the house, his grandparents were sitting on the veranda. Aunty welcomed him enthusiastically, but Uncle remained calm. Calvin knew Aunty was only pretending all was well between them, but Uncle wasn't the type of person to hide his emotions. Nonetheless, he didn't bother to beat around the bushes, because his chance of a lifetime was on the verge of slipping away from him as the minutes ticked. Therefore, he got straight to the point and told them about his predicament.

Uncle was angry and didn't hold back his feelings. Verbally he began to tear Calvin apart. Aunty, on the other hand, was calm, which was unusual, because normally Uncle was the cool one.

After Uncle was through expressing his discontentment, Aunty went inside her bedroom and returned with a thousand dollars and handed it to Calvin. He was happy for it, but he was still short by one thousand dollars.

He tried to persuade Aunty to lend him the other thousand dollars, but she refused. He sat on the veranda, pondering, now and then pleading with his aunt, until suddenly his survival instinct kicked in. He picked up his grandparents' phone and called Boris at the restaurant.

After he related his problem to Boris, his boss told him to come and get the other thousand dollars. Calvin rang off, thanked his grandparents, and promised to keep in touch while he was away.

As he was about to make his exit through the veranda gate Uncle stopped him. "You've been very lucky throughout your sad life," Uncle said, "but I wish you bad luck on your journey to England."

"Thank you very much, Uncle," Calvin replied sadly, as he gingerly descended the steps with a dismal feeling and a bitter taste in his mouth. "Goodbye, Aunty," he announced with a wave, as he stepped onto the road and closed the gate.

At The Native, unlike his grandparents, Boris told him that he should have come to him as soon as he knew he was struggling to complete the payment. Calvin thanked him and promised that he would repay the money when he returned to work, (after his trip to England). Then off he went to complete his payment .

After he paid the money and collected his ticket, he never felt so relieved and happy in his entire life, and nobody could tell him that he wasn't going to England, because he had a ticket to show.

On Queen Street, he showed his plane ticket to his friends, and they were all happy for him. When he showed Veron the ticket, she looked at it but didn't have much to say.

"I left Queen Street with a mixture of feelings that day, but best of all, I was happy, because I was finally holding the ticket that was going to take me away from my dark world, and into another, where I thought the light always shines. I was about to walk in Uncle Roland's footsteps, so I was confident that my future would be bright, after all that had been said and done.

"I visited Veron, a few days before my departure, and while we were speaking, she began to cry. I wasn't surprised, because I knew how worried she must be – if only because I was leaving her behind pregnant.

"On the whole, Veron did have every reason to be worried, because many Jamaican men left their women behind pregnant, some with many children, and went abroad, leaving them with only promises. Some of those men never returned; some returned in wooden boxes, and some ended up in prison. Others returned with a woman in tow, and some of them never sent a dollar to their families throughout the time they were away.

"I didn't want to fall in any of those groups. I tried to reassure Veron that she and the child were my first priority, but it was best for me not to say anything, because my words weren't having a good effect on her.

"Throughout the six weeks after she'd turned me out, I would regularly visited her and do whatever she asked of me; not a lot of men would have done that under the circumstances, so it was evident that my intentions were true. I also promised her that I would always be good to her if God gave me the chance, but that wasn't enough to stop her from crying. Ultimately, her tears only made me feel even more love for her.

"Through her tears she kept saying that she knew I wasn't coming back, but I should take care of my child when the baby was born. "I reassured her that I was going on a mission for us, but I knew I could not make her believe me on any account.

"Last of all, before the conversation concluded I promised her that I would marry her on my return to Jamaica. This I know was a crazy thing to say. She must have laughed at me under her breath, but in actual fact, I did have a yearning to be with her.

"On the day of my departure, I decided to do my packing at Veron's house. Even though I was no longer living there, I felt as if it was where I belonged.

"When I was leaving, as I said goodbye I kissed her on the lips – a kiss that had a lot of significance."

He and Betty had planned to meet each other at the airport, and when he arrived, Geraldine and the little son of one of her friends, who was also going to England, was standing in the check-in line with Betty.

He knew Betty was surprised to see Geraldine at the airport, because she didn't have a clue that Geraldine was going to England.

Calvin pretended he was also surprised to see Geraldine, because she'd asked him not to let anybody knew that she was going away. Above all, he was on top of the world and he'd felt like he was already in a new world.

"It was the first time in my aimless, reckless life I'd found myself in such a position, and I kept looking to see if there was anybody around that I knew, other than my travelling companions. I'd also convinced myself that most of the passengers were better off than me, one way or the other, but I felt proud to be there too, because I had a ticket just like everybody else, no matter the class or style they were travelling in.

"After we got checked in, Betty suggested that we should sit at the bar in the airport lobby and have a drink, before it was time for our departure.

"While we were there drinking, chatting, and laughing, I took a good look around me and made a silent vow to myself, that I would never forget who I was, where I had been, where I was coming from, and my reason for going to England.

"Ultimately, the time came for us to board the plane, which was going to stop in Kingston to pick up more passengers. But there was a minor accident on the runway; as a result, the flight got delayed. In due course the problem was sorted out, and we all went onboard.

"Inside the plane, I found myself in a different world altogether, a world that I'd always dreamt of entering, and I couldn't believe I was sitting in the seat of a plane finally.

"I was in a window seat, and, as I looked outside and admired the beauty around Mobay, I said a silent goodbye.

"When the plane began to motor along the runway, I braced myself for the take-off. I also felt every single hair on my head begin to grow as the plane engine whistled and the plane kept going faster and faster until it eventually lifted off the runway.

"While the plane was on its way to Kingston, I watched the landscape of Jamaica through the window in amazement.

"It was the first time I'd been to Kingston, and even though I didn't leave the airport, just being there alone was also a massive experience for me too.

"In Kingston, the plane was delayed for another two hours, but after everything got sorted out they finally took off at 10:30 p.m, on the twenty-third of December, 1994.

"I was finally on my way to make my dreams into reality, but there were many bridges to cross, far more than I could ever have imagined."

To be continued . . .

Calvin posing with Geraldine and her friend's son before departure.

Calvin sitting at the bar in the departure lounge observing the rest of passengers

Calvin posing with Betty before departure
and Arnold Harris (Carrot) posing on the
balcony of the house at Cottage Road

CHARACTERS (IN APPROX. ORDER OF APPEARANCE)

Ruby Riley

Percy Riley, Ruby's common-law husband

- Devon, son of Ruby/Percy (her sixth)
- Marika, daughter of Ruby/Percy (her fifth)
- Bungo Pully (who made Marika, age ~14, pregnant)
- Andrew Fletcher (Marika's firstborn, 2 April 1977)
- Budget (Marika's 2nd beau) (Rowan, aka Kaka Waller, his youngest previous son)
- Freddy, son of Ruby/Percy (her seventh) – died in infancy
- Calvin, son of Ruby/Percy (her eighth)
- Uncle Willy (in Bakers Stet), Biran, Papa Beagle, Freddy, and Melvin (in Kingston) – Percy's brothers
- Ivy (in Anchovy) and Sissy (in Bogue Hill, Montego Bay) – Percy's sisters

Mr. James (Ruby's first baby-daddy)

Salomon (Ruby's first baby, first son)

Mr. Beckford (Ruby's second suitor)

Janet (Ruby's second baby, first daughter)

Mr. Bent (Ruby's third suitor)

Van (Ruby's third baby, second son)

Mr. Watson (Ruby's fourth suitor)

- Barbara (Babs) Watson (Ruby's fourth baby, second daughter)
- Winston Angling, aka Twinny Bug (footballer; Babs's husband)

Miss Fan (the children's great grandmother)

Rasta John (construction worker)

Cherry Campbell (neighbour)

Audrey & Maxine (Cherry's sisters)

Aunty Beck & Mass Arthur (Cherry's grandparents)

Mr. Bee (Berres Riley) (one of Percy's older relatives)

Miss Cassie (Mr. Bee's live-in girlfriend)

Pappa Seta (neighbour)

Man-man (one of Percy's cousins)

Mr. Shaw (neighbour)

Sitta & Bauloo (neighbours)

Precious, Dimples, Paul Rose, & Carl Scott (Sitta's & Bauloo's grandchildren)
Mother Mira (local bush doctor)
Money Man (another of Percy's relatives) & wife Miss Jeneita
Miss Ivy (Money Man's mother-in-law) & husband Bad Son
Mass Johnny (another of Percy's relatives)
Miss Dinie (neighbour)
Miss Maude, Aunt Maude (another of Percy's relatives)
Mr. Smith and Miss Heffy (an elderly white couple)
Miss G-G (a nearby relative) [OR Gigi]
Miss Winter (elderly member of the community who conducted school in her house)
Cleveland Shaw (aka Monkey) (Mr. Shaw's grandson, Calvin's friend in school)
Carl Scott (Calvin's friend in school)
Lawyer Stenit
Rema (Audrey's common-law husband)
Grand-Uncle Roland [or Great-Uncle], Uncle Roland (in Mount Salem) (Percy's mother's brother or brother-in-law)
Aunty Millie (with Uncle Roland) (called Millward at times by Roland)
Bee, a sister of Roland
DC Brown
Paul Boggle (resident at Uncle Roland's)
Michael Manley, PM in January 1980
Edward Seaga, Jamaica Labour Party (JLP) leader; prime minister after Manley
David Coore and Vivian Blake, PNP senior members
Eric Bell, Finance Minister
Roy McGann, the PNP's candidate for East Rural St. Andrew
Acting Corporal Errol White (McGann's bodyguard)
Lambert Brown, of Workers Party of Jamaica
Ulises Estrada, Cuban ambassador to Jamaica until late 1980
Mr. Street and his wife, Miss Liddy, who had 8 children
Mother Mira (and son Dooba) – obeah woman and Poco Church leader
Mr. Spence, supervisor at the hardware store
Martin, worker at the hardware store
Miss Eve (white lady, owns land neighbouring Lawyer Stenit's property)
Barber Shaw ("Manity") – Monkey's grandfather
Buchanan (Mr. Buck) from Trelawny
Osburne and his younger brother Melvin, Mr. and Mrs. Tinglin's two sons
Austin, a grandson of Aunty Beck

Mr. Boswell, father of Osburne's girlfriend
Susie Boswell, Calvin's first love
Papa Seeta (another painter/ decorator who lived nearby the home place)
Sarge (brother to Austin) (member of Popsy gang)
Constable James (aka Horse Mouth)
Base, a wannabe bad man
Lee and Victor (two of Money Man's sons)
Clarkie (Lee's brother-in-law, married to his sister Grace)
Doctor Airance
Miss Molly (the widowed Doctor Airance's mixed-race secretary & live-in companion)
Asley (aka Bad Man)
Detective Minto
Detective Barns
Goodall
Wade
Debby (rookie police officer)
Ann Marie, a little girl from St. Elizabeth living with Roland & Millie
Mass Vick and Miss Delta (renters at 10 Crichton's Drive)
Dawn (girlfriend of Devon)
Dawn (girlfriend of Calvin) and their son, Kenique Brown
Melissa (friend of Devon's Dawn)
Chuck (brother of Mass Vick)
Patrick (Calvin's fellow new recruit security officer at City Centre Mall)
Ian (a fellow security guard)
Sister Clymis (from Calvin's church)
Mr. and Mrs. Williams ("Mummy and Daddy", owners of a cook shop at Freeport) (oldest son Donovan; Natalie, 13; and Butty, 7)
Peter and Paul (criminal friends of Donovan)
Mr. Jump (Aunty's friend who offered Calvin a hotel job)
Anne Palmer, the White Witch of Rose Hall
Bennett, the breakfast supervisor at Wyndham
Spanky, the lifeguard at Wyndham
Junior Reid, another cook at Wyndham
Arnold Harris (aka Carrot; co-worker at Wyndham)
Betty (Carrot's cousin)
Margo (leased restaurant, bar, & bedrooms from Carrot's aunt)
Skiers (Margo's live-in caretaker)
Akroman (range cook & best friend at Wyndham Hotel)
Bwoysie (butcher & best friend at Wyndham)
Eric (aka Chino)
Winston Angling, aka Twinny Bug (footballer; married to Babs)
Slowly, Chino, Author, and Shippy (new breakfast crew)
Shippy's brother Banton and Author's cousin Renroy ("crewmates" living in Queen Street with Calvin & breakfast crew)

Delroy, Tilly, and Rupie (young neighbours on Queen Street)
Reverend Doctor Leo Robinson (Uncle's and Aunty's pastor)
Veron Brown (new lady friend)
Lisa (leader of smuggler group)
Pauline (a waitress at Grandiosa)
Henry (handyman at Grandiosa)
Trudy and Johnny (older American stoner couple, guests)
Sarah (Canadian woman)
Caroline (Sarah's mother)
Ivadnie (laundry worker & hairdresser)
Valda (a receptionist at Grandiosa)
Big Al
Robert, Sixteen, and Dundee (Robert tends bar at Ramparts Inn)
Knish (works at Margaritaville on Gloucester)
Steve (Betty's son from England)
Boris Riley (owns/operates The Native Restaurant with his 2 sisters)
Speedy (waiter at The Native)
Judith (Veron's little sister)

PLACES

Anchovy (near Mobay)
Appleton, district of St. Elizabeth (80 miles from Mobay)
Bakers Stet
14 Barnett Street Police Station (Mobay)
Bogue Hill
Burchell Memorial Baptist Church
Cambridge (district ~7 miles from Mount Carey)
Canterbury (a ghetto near Mobay, allied with Cyril Gully)
Capture Lands (one of the ghettos closest to Mount Salem)
Carey Village
St. Catherine District Prison
Church Street
City Centre Shopping Mall (Mobay)
Colombia (origin of cocaine)
Cottage Road
Crichton Brother's Hardware Store (downtown Mobay)
10 Crichton's Drive (Uncle Roland's address)
Cornwall Regional Hospital, Cornwall Hospital
Cotton Tree (neighbourhood 1-1/2 miles from home place)
Cyril Gully (a ghetto near Mobay, allied with Canterbury)
Dead-End (a free beach on Gloucester Avenue)
Doctor's Cave Beach Hotel
Donald Songster International Airport (Mobay)
Dunn's River Falls
East Rural St. Andrew

St. Elizabeth (80 miles from Mobay)
Farm Heights (ghetto near Mobay)
Flanker (ghetto near Mobay)
Freeport, near the Montego Bay wharf
Gloucester Avenue (the Hip Strip)
Gold Street Massacre, in central Kingston (April 1980)
Gordon Town
Grandiosa Hotel,
Granville (rural area outside Mobay)
Green Pond (rural area near Mobay)
Half Moon Resort Hotel
Hannah Town Police Station, in west Kingston (April 1980)
Harbour Street
Hart Street (war zone in Mobay ghetto)
Hendon, Paradise, and Clendevon (allied ghettos near Mobay)
Hometown Supermarket (downtown Mobay)
Jamaica Credit Union Bank
Jarrett Park (Montego Bay's number-one football stadium)
Lethe (community adjoining Anchovy)
Lucea, Hanover (close to Negril Bay)
Madden's Funeral Parlour (Montego Bay)
Margaritaville (club on Gloucester)
Margony Basic School
May Pen
Montego Bay, Jamaica (Mobay)
Montego Bay High School
Mount Carey
Mount Carey Baptist Church
Mount Salem
Mount Salem All Age School
The Native Restaurant
Negril Bay
Norwood (ghetto near Mobay)
Pan Bottom Hill
Queen Street (quieter ghetto in Mobay)
Railway Lane (dilapidated, war-zone ghetto area in Mobay, where Janet work)
Ramparts Inn Guesthouse (next-door rival to Grandiosa Hotel)
Revivalist Zionist or Poco Church
Rocklands Bird Sanctuary
Rose Hall
Salt Spring (ghetto near Mobay)
Sam Sharpe Square (Mobay)
Sir Winston nightclub
Spanish Town District Prison
Strand Theatre
Tate Street (Mobay)
Top Hill, St. Elizabeth
Trelawny
Westmoreland (district 30 miles from home place)
Wyndham Rose Hall Resort Hotel and Country Club (12 miles from Mobay)
York Bush, Eden, Flower Hill, Margony, Mount Pelier, Ruhamton, Lethe, Catherine Mount, Comfort Hall – surrounding districts

WORDS & PHRASES

Ackee (*Blighia sapida*)
affix brakes (*affix* is a brand name that's LC online; I'll allow it ☺)
after-effect
babysit, babysitter, babysitting
back door
back seat
backyard
banknote
bath towel
batty bwoy (dialect for "homosexual")
bloodclaat (dialect insult)
breadfruit (*Artocarpus altilis*)
breadline
broken-hearted
bumboclaat (a profanity)
bwoy (dialect for "boy")
cho, cho, cho-cho leaf
cling film, what Americans call plastic wrap
clothes line
cloud nine, on cloud nine (no quote marks necessary)
Coca-Cola
coco bread (folding bread)
coconut toto (a Jamaican cake)
coconut grater cake
coco plum (otaheiti apple)
Cooncan, a card game
co-worker
custard apple
Desnoes & Geddes (D&G, makers of Red Stripe beer)
diarrhoea
dominoes
dreadlocks
drug dealer
"Dulcemina, Her Life in Town" (radio drama)
enquire (instead of *inquire*)
enrol
escovitch (fish)
"fuckries" (nonsense or worse)
ganja
Garnet Silk (a Jamaican reggae singer)
genep – a fruit
ghettos
goodbye
grand-uncle [or great-uncle]
Green Bay Massacre
guest room
haemorrhage
half-hearted
heartbroken
holdall bag, holdall
home town
homey (like home)
hopping dick bird
hung-over
incorrupt
Jamaica Labour Party (JLP)
jerk chicken, jerk pork
jolly bus (passenger bus)
joyride
khaki
Lams Bread weed
Leonardo da Vinci
logwood tree
lumberyard

lunch box
manity
midafternoon
minibus
miniskirt
National Heroes Day
nessberry
nettle bush (scratch bush)
obeah (witchcraft in Haiti)
oftentimes
omelette
otaheiti apple (coco plum)
passerby, passersby
Peenie-wallie (a nocturnal flying insect)
People's National Party (PNP)
per cent
pickpocket, pickpocketing
Pitta Pat, a card game
Poco Church
polenta (cornmeal)
Popsy gang (Mobay)
precolonial
pretence
price tag
Proof (a Bible game)
pushbike (= bicycle)
put-down (noun; verb = 2 words)
raas (swear word)
Rastafarian, Rasta
red-handed
renta yam (white yam)
rum bar
sceptic, sceptical, sceptically
schoolchild, schoolchildren
scratch bush (nettle bush)
sell-out (noun; verb = 2 words)
shamefaced
shoeblack flowers (Chinese hibiscus)
shoot-out (noun; *shoot it out* = verb)
short-lived
single-handed
sinsemilla (seedless)
skilful, skilfully
skin-tight
sky juice (not coconut water & gin, but shaved ice with syrup)
sleepover (noun; verb = 2 words)
soft-hearted
soursop – a fruit
star apple (otaheiti)
straight away (adv. – at once)
sweetsop – a fruit
take-off (noun; verb = 2 words)
theatre
ting – a Jamaican grapefruit drink (or soda)
tip-top
turn cornmeal
vendor
washbasin
well-being
white yam (renta yam)
wholehearted, wholeheartedly
wildfire (like wildfire *OR* like a wildfire)
willpower
Workers Party of Jamaica, including Lambert Brown